Power from Powerlessness

TRIBAL GOVERNMENTS, INSTITUTIONAL NICHES,
AND AMERICAN FEDERALISM

Laura E. Evans

OXFORD
UNIVERSITY PRESS

OXFORD
UNIVERSITY PRESS

Oxford   University Press, Inc., publishes works that further
Oxford University's objective of excellence
in research, scholarship, and education.

Oxford New York
Auckland   Cape Town   Dar es Salaam   Hong Kong   Karachi
Kuala Lumpur   Madrid   Melbourne   Mexico City   Nairobi
New Delhi   Shanghai   Taipei   Toronto

With offices in
Argentina   Austria   Brazil   Chile   Czech Republic   France   Greece
Guatemala   Hungary   Italy   Japan   Poland   Portugal   Singapore
South Korea   Switzerland   Thailand   Turkey   Ukraine   Vietnam

Published by Oxford University Press, Inc.
198 Madison Avenue, New York, NY 10016

www.oup.com

Oxford is a registered trademark of Oxford University Press

Library of Congress Cataloging-in-Publication Data

Evans, Laura E. (Laura Elizabeth), 1972–
   Power from powerlessness : tribal governments, institutional niches,
and American federalism / Laura E. Evans.
        p.   cm.
   Includes bibliographical references.
   ISBN 978-0-19-974274-5 (acid-free paper)
   1.   Indians of North America—Politics and government.   2.   Tribal government—United States.
3. Indians of North America—Government relations.   4.   Intergovernmental cooperations—United
States. 5.   Federal government—United States.   I. Title.
   E98 . T77E83   2011
   323 . 1197'073—dc22   2010027666

Printed in the United States of America
on acid-free paper

For my husband Mark.

Contents

Acknowledgments ix

1. *American Indian Tribal Governments' Fight for Change inside Institutions* 3

2. *The Historical Evolution of American Indian Political Strategies and Background* 24

3. *Quiet, Yet Ever-Constant Advocacy: How American Indian Tribal Governments Have Confronted and Changed Federal Indian Policy* 54

4. *Expertise-Centered Behaviors: How Knowledge Changes Organizations and How to Know When It's There* 98

5. *Expertise and "Soft" Disempowerment: Race, Land, and Local Power in American Indian Politics* 125

6. *Channels of Access, Frames for Persuasion: The Influence of Tribal Governments in State Politics* 167

7. *Forging the Future* 201

NOTES 211
REFERENCES 223
INDEX 235

Acknowledgments

Many people have helped and supported me throughout this project. All errors are my own in spite of their many efforts to steer me in the right direction.

Primary funding for this line of research came from the National Science Foundation Doctoral Dissertation Research Grant SES-0212421, the Gerald R. Ford Research Fund of the University of Michigan's Department of Political Science, the University of Washington's Research Royalty Fund, and faculty research grants from the University of Washington's Evans School of Public Affairs. I received additional support from the Institute for Ethnic Studies in the United States at the University of Washington, from the Nonprofit and Public Management Center at the University of Michigan, and from the American Political Science Association's Paul A. Volcker Junior Scholar Research Grant.

This project has benefited from access to documents through the Arizona State University's Labriola National American Indian Data Center, the National Archives and Records Administration, and the American Indian Records Repository. Collections maintained by tribal libraries, tribal clerks, state libraries, state archives, and county clerks across the regions in the sample were vital resources. I am also extremely grateful for the guidance that a number of tribal officials have provided.

My education about tribal government began with two internships with the Navajo Nation Division of Economic Development. There were many people in and around Window Rock who gave their time to educate, explain, and mentor. I am indebted to all of them for their generosity and patience.

A number of research institutions have given me a home while this project has unfurled. At the University of Michigan's Political Science Department, both faculty and fellow graduate students helped me develop intellectual rigor and gave me vital encouragement. At the Brookings Institution, the Brookings Research Fellowship gave me space to finish writing my dissertation. The University of Washington's Evans School of Public Affairs has provided a supportive and stimulating environment as I engaged in additional data collection and analysis. Most recently, I finished a stay with the Robert Wood Johnson Scholars in Health Policy Research Program at Harvard University, where I benefited from a generous and collegial community.

I was privileged to work with remarkable mentors while I was a graduate student at the University of Michigan. Nancy Burns was an amazing adviser, offering time, careful readings, and stimulating and insightful comments. Her enthusiasm for this project helped sustain me; her guidance has been ongoing and invaluable. Rick Hall has also provided fantastic ongoing advice, including his recent, much-needed help with the book's title. Jenna Bednar, Phil Deloria, and Don Kinder gave feedback that allowed me to see this project in new, better ways. Along the way, Jeremy Hall, Lauren Morris MacLean, Lynn Sanders, and Gary Segura offered helpful feedback on early versions of chapters. The two anonymous reviewers provided great feedback.

A number of research assistants have pitched in. Nicole Caven produced remarkable analysis of several tribes' newspapers. Ryan Schoen collected data on state legislation. Additionally, I am grateful for the work of Mark Arduini, Dustan Bott, Malia Langworthy, and Chuck Tanner.

At Oxford University Press, I was incredibly fortunate to be in the hands of David McBride, Marc Schneider, and their teams.

I owe my greatest thanks to my family. All have tolerated more weekends and evenings at the office, and holidays behind a laptop, than anyone has the right to ask. Their love and support provide an essential foundation for all that I do. My parents, Al and Carolyn Evans, and my sister, Kathie Evans, guided me toward intellectual curiosity, the pursuit of justice in the world, and confidence that I could accomplish the things I imagined. Thank you! My children, Theo and Vivian Long, both arrived while I was writing this book. They give me much-needed laughter, perspective, and inspiration. My husband, Mark Long, has gifted me with motivation, encouragement, and incredible patience. As a fellow scholar, he has shared enriching discussions of research design, analysis, and the big unanswered questions about political life. He also provided very cogent feedback on drafts. On top of all that, he has given me remarkable amounts of space and time needed to advance this work. I dedicate this book to him.

POWER FROM POWERLESSNESS

1 American Indian Tribal Governments' Fight for Change inside Institutions

I. Introduction

A. THE QUESTION

The president of the Navajo Nation spends a lot of time on the road. Not surprisingly, he devotes a great deal of time to traveling the expansive Navajo reservation. He frequently visits Washington, D.C., to meet with policymakers in charge of federal agencies delivering services to Native Americans. In addition, the president also spends a good amount of time in nearby state capitals, county seats, and city halls. For instance, in 1999 and 2000, the Nation persuaded the state of Arizona to allocate funds for the Navajo Nation's community college, welfare-to-work program, tourist facilities, corrections center, highway improvements, and elementary school construction. Furthermore, the Navajo Nation entered partnerships with neighboring localities to jointly promote area tourism and to jointly deliver behavioral health services.[1]

The Navajo Nation is not alone among American Indian tribal governments in its frequent interactions with states and localities. Tribal governments across the nation have hammered out arrangements where states and localities have signed off on the creation of tribal casinos. Some tribes have successfully challenged state and local fisheries and waterways management. There are also the lower-profile agreements that don't capture much attention but do allow for more efficient administration—such as when tribes and counties create a host of cooperative programs, providing for the joint provision of basic services like trash collection and the cross-deputization of area police.[2]

Both this degree of participation and of successful influence in regional affairs is surprising: Native Americans' history and contemporary circumstances heavily stack the odds against them in politics. The fact that tribal governments summon up the wherewithal to even participate in regional affairs is impressive. Native communities are plagued by deep poverty, low levels of education, and the legacy of centuries of extreme social and political marginalization. In Census 2000, per capita income for reservation Indians was $7,958, as compared to a U.S. average of $21,587. The reservation poverty rate was at 39% (versus 12% nationwide). Nearly a third of reservation households lacked telephones, in a nation where 98% of households have phones. Only 6% of American Indians on reservations were college graduates, in a country where one-quarter of the population has earned a college degree. While much public attention in the past decade has focused on tribal casinos, the reality is that casinos have transformed the fate of only a fairly small number of Indian communities. As of 2002, 198 of the 562 federally recognized tribal governments had casinos. By 2010, 240 tribes had casinos. Ultimately, highly profitable gaming depends on a circumstance that most tribes lack: an advantageous geographic location that provides easy access to a large customer base. Consequently, various studies calculate that the median casino tribe sees relatively modest earnings from gaming, with about one-sixth of tribal casinos generating well above two-thirds of all tribal casino revenue (Henson et al., 2002, 106–115, National Indian Gaming Commission 2006, 2009, 2010). Finally, to cap off this list of disadvantages, it is important to note that as American Indians are less than 2% of the national population, they hardly constitute a large electoral bloc.

In short, with a few notable exceptions as of late, tribal officials often plan and execute their political strategies from dilapidated office buildings, on meager budgets, amidst populations that struggle against the ravages of shockingly low incomes, inadequate housing, and poor health. If native nations were simply overwhelmed or incapacitated by these challenges, it would be hard to be surprised by that outcome. And yet, we find examples of tribal governments advocating for and winning new courses of action by nearby governments. In light of these harsh realities and stark disparities, how is it that some tribes manage to achieve influence?

This analysis explores the avenues through which tribal governments can succeed in American politics; more broadly, it speaks to how marginalized groups sometimes win political victories. The American Indian experience offers valuable lessons—lessons that are portable to a variety of other political settings—about how political underdogs can challenge obstacles. Existing literature leaves us without a very clear understanding of the circumstances that result in victories for marginalized interests. Existing work on local politics probably captures the most common outcome, of the powerful becoming powerful. All the same, there are reasons why we would want to better understand exceptions. Most notably, if scholars are troubled by the finding that social disadvantage often translates into political disadvantage, then we should be equally concerned with clarifying the ways in which the patterns get broken.

Many thinkers about local politics give us good reason to be concerned about the place of disadvantaged groups in local decision-making. We can date these ideas in their earliest form to James Madison's writings in *The Federalist Papers*. To paraphrase Madison, the smaller the sphere, the easier it is for the more powerful faction to dominate government. In short, we would expect small, often impoverished American Indian populations—and other groups with comparable disadvantages—simply to be left out of local politics. Political science has long been concerned with the ways that social disadvantage translates into political marginalization in local government—finding that, usually, strong voices are amplified and weak voices are diminished in local politics (McConnell 1966, Minow 1990, Schattschneider 1960). Along similar lines, Peterson (1981) and Elkin (1987) argued that business influence will predominate in local politics.[3] Scholars have been equally interested in the ways that institutions and federal interventions structure local politics, and have often documented how these arrangements can exacerbate social disadvantage in a region.[4]

Yet this is not the whole story. Certain strategies—heretofore underappreciated—can help groups challenge these obstacles. With time and sustained effort, resource-constrained political entrepreneurs cultivate unique pathways of change. Groups can achieve influence by working carefully at growing their political and policy expertise. To reach those ends, groups can make use of particular kinds of outside support, what I call *institutional niches*, that can provide key subsidies for the cultivation of expertise. In variegated institutions, marginalized political entrepreneurs can find actors and organizations that provide subtle forms of assistance with building expertise. Some tribal advocates, under certain circumstances, have made use of opportunities for federal support of expertise cultivation. Thus, tribes' effectiveness in multiple arenas results from generalizable skills that are developed in niches in the political process.

Institutional niches help marginalized groups to alter their underlying capacities, with far-flung consequences throughout the political system. Disadvantaged groups do not suddenly begin winning high-profile victories. Instead, the effects are indirect and of low visibility. In isolation, each new success seems unremarkable; cumulatively, the effects are impressive.

B. INSTITUTIONAL NICHES

There are two key questions about an institutional niche. First, why is minor assistance ever really useful? The answer is that incremental aid with cultivating expertise can open important opportunities for a marginalized group. But with this answer, a second question emerges. Since the impact of minor assistance hinges to large degree on the accretion of support over time, how is the institutional niche maintained? Why doesn't the institutional niche just dry up? The answer is that certain strategies enable marginalized advocates to slowly reinforce and stabilize niches of support.

Step 1: Building Expertise

We begin with the puzzle of why the seemingly minor aid that is delivered through an institutional niche is useful. An institutional niche is a source of outside support that can provide small but meaningful subsidies for the cultivation of expertise. Other agents can aid groups in developing technical policy expertise, provide opportunities to get to know the external environment, and offer exposure to a variety of strategies and organizational forms.[5] More specifically, technical policy expertise can include detailed knowledge of specific problems and policies, and of tools of evaluation and remediation. Opportunities to get to know external environments support abilities to build networks, understand outside interests, and develop demonstration or pilot projects that can be persuasive to potential outside supporters. Exposure to strategies and organizational forms provides access to new organizational repertoires. Consequently, it provides access to new tools of program management, planning, and of envisioning frameworks. The three domains of expertise that are accessed via institutional niches—technical information, external environments, and organizational forms—all ultimately support the program infrastructure of an expert organization that can generate, sustain, apply, and reproduce expertise. The right program infrastructure creates a space where knowledgeable people can operate effectively: thus, the opportunities afforded by institutional niches lay groundwork for greater and broader accomplishments.

Tribes rarely receive help in one instance that transforms their capacities. Rather, they pursue an incremental approach. Small amounts of aid over time allow for important changes in knowledge. Another part of the recipe is the pursuit of segmented, lump-sum aid. Tribes use aid to address discrete steps in building program infrastructure. By doing so, advocates acquire assistance that produces benefits that will endure even if further outside support fluctuates or is delayed. Knowledge is an important asset in part because it is an enduring, flexible resource.

Step 2: Buttress Opportunities

Ultimately, making the fullest use of an institutional niche hinges on the long-term, sequential delivery of small amounts of help. The next puzzle is how tribes maintain this assistance over time. After all, sources of outside support might naturally emerge and then fade. To forestall such an outcome, tribes buttress an opportunity by pushing for gradual adjustments in programs that can make the institutional niche even more receptive over time. There are three elements to this tactic: tribes seek modest yet serial adjustments in their access to federal officials, in overall policy frameworks, and in specific procedures. These three elements offer important advantages. With access, tribal officials can gain information about federal officials' sympathies and susceptibilities and about obstacles that lie ahead. Access also enables tribes to transmit information to the feds about their own preferences and powers, and about programs' effectiveness. Second, by nudging frameworks, tribes slowly alter the rules of the game. They can redefine their federal relationship in ways that acknowledge tribes' importance and endorse collaboration and consultation. Third, adjusted procedures mean that tribes gradually win more favorable, flexible, simple, and stable policies.

The changes don't seem particularly noteworthy, especially when viewed over the short run. They might push programs toward a bit more clarification or discretion; toward slightly relaxed regulations; toward modest redefinition of a program's responsibilities and beneficiaries. They might nudge toward seemingly dry restructuring of functions that, at first, just looks like shifting around a few cells on an organizational chart. In its boldest form, they might want some steps toward transferring power: having a say in oversight and regulation. Over time, the adjustments add up with greater significance. The pursuit of long-term program adjustments requires low-visibility, gradual nudging. To this end, tribal advocates seek repeated, long-running interactions. In short, they invest in relationships with a small circle of officials.

In sum, tribes do two things with Steps 1 and 2. First, they extract help for expert organizations. Second, they gradually push niches so that they can provide more desirable and reliable aid in the future. In short, they pay attention to the tools needed to build their own skills, and also to the structures and adjustments needed to secure access to that aid. Ultimately, tribal officials have been attentive to a wide range of ways to adjust relations within institutional niches. They are certainly glad to act upon opportunities, when they emerge, for big or quick changes in federal funding and programs. But they still have a strategy for when big changes aren't on the table, which, alas, is most of the time. They have a backup plan built around the recognition that simple yet cumulative changes can make a difference.

II. Strategies within Federalism

The existing literature on external involvement has often looked too hard for big, blunt actions and consequently has overlooked the myriad of more nuanced roles that government can play in complex environments. Common thinking treats separation of powers as a system that provides lots of opportunities to hold other actors in check[6]. Yet if we turn around that conventional perspective, we have before us a system where many different actors can take small actions promoting a spectrum of goals.

It is prohibitively difficult for any one actor, no matter how powerful, to monitor or control all domains or to foresee all outcomes. As Madison argued at the founding of the republic, arrangements such as federalism and other separations of power create a variety of settings in government, each with its own bit of control. As we delve further into analyses of how institutions really work—and in particular the institutions of federalism and separation of powers—we find structures rife with stickiness, overlapping goals, path dependency, and unforeseen outcomes. Large, multifaceted institutions like the federal government house multiple, conflicting, and changing interests. Power struggles get filtered through institutional arrangements that weren't devised by either side in a particular political contest. Institutions can restructure power and thus produce outcomes that are unintended by the actors who set those forms into motion.[7] Furthermore, actions, once underway, are not always undone so easily by powerbrokers, because of the host of changes they provoke (March and Olsen 1984). Limited information means that not all consequences of institutions are foreseeable, and increasing returns mean that actors cannot necessarily afford to reverse institutional changes that run counter to their interests (Pierson 2004).

Standard models of institutional development then explain what advocates do once they discover a small setting that is receptive to their interests. Political entrepreneurs—in this instance, tribal entrepreneurs—adapt their behavior to maximize what they can achieve from these opportunities and they work to pro-voke incremental changes in institutions that will further serve their interests (North 1990). When American Indian tribal governments and other disadvan-taged actors succeed at this task, sympathetic outside actors then subsidize their efforts to acquire specialized knowledge and to learn about various environ-ments and strategies. As a result, tribes escape the notice and control of primary players.

A. CONSEQUENCES FOR INSTITUTIONAL THEORY

Our understanding of advocacy groups can be expanded by thinking carefully about institutions. At the same time, our understanding of institutions is enhanced by considering in greater detail the features of advocacy groups. Theories of histor-ical institutionalism, path dependence, and bounded rationality have done much to advance our insights into institutions. Yet much thinking about the causes and consequences of institutional change focuses on broad differences between "win-ners" and "losers"; scholars have begun pushing forward in thinking about the ways that different features of "losers" might matter for institutional paths. For example, Mahoney and Thelen (2009) explored how some "losers" in one domain may actually be powerful actors in other domains who can transport power across venues. Hall (2009) considered how coalitions among less powerful groups can produce institutional change.

We can go further. Losers vary tremendously by their circumstances and resources. When we consider the particular traits of marginalized groups, our expectations of the place of "losers" in institutional development changes funda-mentally. Highly marginalized interests push institutions along unique paths of change. When I speak of marginalized groups, I am referring to groups that pos-sess quite low levels of resources—money, members, organizational development, opportunities for coalition formation, and the like. Often, these disadvantages are exacerbated by the marginalization and trivialization of a community's concerns in the wider public imagination. In the case of American Indians, there is an exten-sive literature on the stereotyping and misrepresentation of American Indian political objectives in the popular press.[8]

A common, implicit assumption may be that if a group loses a political battle in one time period, it will either change or wither away in subsequent time periods. It seems like such a simple, obvious expectation: if your approach isn't working, then you need to do something differently. And yet, for some political actors, that prescription may be entirely wrong. While constancy in the face of defeat appears foolish in the short run, it may be an optimal approach for resource-constrained

groups in the long run. First, it is questionable to assume change is innately beneficial. Second, it is even more doubtful that change is the right pick for marginalized groups.

Indeed, there is no reason to assume that new tactics are the right response for
any actor. Even the most successful political strategies have yield rates of less
than 100%, which means that even the most optimal approach will fail from time
to time. Furthermore, no group is completely nimble; all face constraints based
on their resources, internal structures, norms, members, needs for some consistency with past positions, and solutions to the collective action problem. In other
words, groups are unable to pursue every imaginable strategy. Even fewer strategies are available in the immediate run, as some strategies might require internal
adjustments that take time to implement. Jones and Baumgartner (2005) and
Jones, Sulkin, and Larsen (2003) described four forces of friction that can impede
change—decision costs, transaction costs, information costs, and cognitive costs—
and leave open the question of how and when those costs vary.

This basic caution against new strategies holds true even in the face of institutional change. A new institutional environment will alter the payoffs of different
strategies. All the same, the strategy that was most optimal before institutional
change does not necessarily lose its relative ranking. In fact, new tactics for the
sake of newness could leave anyone worse off. Advocates who jump from strategy
to strategy are overlooking the importance of expertise in politics. Adjustment
will always entail costs of searching, implementation, and evaluation. In complex,
uncertain, and changing environments, it can be difficult to assess the possible
returns for any approach. Actors have more information about the strengths and
weaknesses of their current tactics than about the features of untried tactics
(Williamson 1981). It would seem quite reasonable to hesitate about shifting to a
new approach that appears promising but has never been road-tested. Pierson
(2004) visited the constraints that arise from a group's "asset specificity." He noted
that circumstances can lead groups to make radically different investments in
asset development. Pierson went on to remark, "What has been missed is the cru-
cial implication that the investments will alter actors' assessments of the benefits
of institutional change." (149)

For new strategies to result, groups need to be both properly motivated *and* ade-
quately endowed. Absent either force, the best bet may be to stick with the status
quo. For very well-endowed groups that lose political battles only occasionally, the
incentives to adapt are relatively small, but the capacity to implement adaptations
are relatively high. For highly marginalized groups that lose frequently and profoundly, the incentives to find new strategies are intense, but the means to implement new approaches are often lacking severely. Marginalized groups face even

tighter constraints on strategic adaptation, and therefore they may be more likely to stick with a seemingly "losing" strategy. And yet paradoxically, in the long run, the losing approach may still pay off.

It is worthwhile to explore further the unique constraints faced by marginalized groups. First, their limited tangible resources mean they simply can't adapt on a dime; they have far fewer resources to implement and evaluate tactical experiments. Gathering information about options may take more time, and so any change may emerge more slowly. Resource limitations also impose a strict budget constraint—more options are ruled out because they prohibitively costly. Social marginalization poses other limits on agility, by creating tight constraints on the appeals and coalitions that are possible. As a consequence, the universe of available strategies shrinks for the marginalized and they may be forced to maintain approaches with rather unimpressive yield rates. As my findings will illustrate, marginalized groups can address this limitation by developing strategies slowly over time and then sticking with them. When groups face severe limitations, any experiment in tactics poses relatively high costs, and so adjustments are often made across a long time frame.

Thus, the most feasible tactic may be a slow, long-term approach that requires fewer resources in a given year in order to realize a gain at a later date. Such "layaway" politics only reward the persistent. Indeed, in the short term, it can be hard to see what benefits these approaches bring; but in the long-term view, their rewards are much clearer. In a similar vein, Thelen's (2004, xii) analysis of institutional change in worker training regimes noted the power of "the subtle incremental changes that, over time, had turned the system, in political and especially power-distributional terms, on its head."

Also, I find that many of these long-term strategies are key to capacity-building efforts. In short, marginalized groups are not just seeking policy victories; they also seek help with building the expertise that they need to succeed in politics. Because these long-term approaches often fuel the knowledge needed for success in many domains, they are often the most vital strategy of all, although they are certainly not the most flashy political outcome. If support for the cultivation of expertise falters, then all other activities will suffer. Once again, an approach that may seem to yield little in the short term may have tremendous long-term implications.

Many analysts have rightly noted that marginalized groups can possess unique opportunities for remarkable tactical innovation, without speaking specifically to the frequency of such events. Given my analysis above, and my findings that follow, the logical implication is that those innovations should be powerful but rare. Many scholars have noted the great tactical innovations made in the civil rights movement (McAdam 1996, Payne 1995). Along similar lines, Ganz (2000) described how the United Farm Workers, with little organizational history to confine them and little to lose anyhow, landed on remarkable new approaches that more established groups could not achieve. Clemens (1997) has given us a theoretical framework for understanding such bounding innovations: in her analysis, innovations draw on a reordering of a community's organizational repertoire. Groups outside of the mainstream are immersed in a different repertoire, so they have more opportunities to land upon truly creative recombinations.

Clemens and others make a compelling case for why marginalized interests have unique potential for revolutionary reassemblies of tactics. Nonetheless, marginalized groups have especially limited means to design, implement, and evaluate fundamentally new approaches. Thus, we should expect that they possess knowledge that can allow more dramatic innovations but with much lower frequency than more mainstream interests. Indeed, alongside the many tales of creative, explosive innovation, we should notice the stability as well. I find that American Indian tribal governments landed upon some important tactical innovations in the late 19th century, and they have maintained many of those same approaches into the present day.

If strategic consistency is far more common than typically expected—and certain advocates are more likely to pursue strategic consistency—then there are important consequences for institutional theory. At the broadest level, it means that *who's* involved matters for *how* institutional change happens. Furthermore, although it seems paradoxical, important institutional change over time may sometimes flow from largely stable behavior by actors. Finally, when marginalized groups bring about institutional change, they do so along unique pathways: through constant nudging in stable but complex environments.

There is a vigorous scholarly debate on the importance of incremental change versus punctuated equilibrium. Clearly, both incremental and dramatic change occur; the debate comes down to the frequency and ultimate impact (both for policy and politics) of each force. It is an open question as to whether those frequencies and impacts vary by contextual dynamics—such as by features of the advocates involved. Certainly, we know full well by now that the preferences and efforts of actors do not wholly determine institutional paths. All the same, institutional change does not come from the ether; it depends on someone expending some sort of effort. Actors choose whether to set their sights on incremental or dramatic improvements. To the extent that groups vary systematically by the efforts that they take and the costs they can bear, we can further specify the kinds of institutional change to expect.

There are three particular implications. First, marginalized groups chip away at existing arrangements. They can rarely subsidize the costs of dramatic, immediate change. On a certain level, marginalized groups may not want to initiate big change—they're less capable of managing rapid change as it starts to unfold. As a result, they are at greater risk of starting a process that gets away from them and then gets co-opted by others. The implication for scholars is that the study of marginalized politics in institutional change requires a very longtime view. Strategies change slowly and endure over long periods. Models of institutional development that rely on groups countermobilizing in response to the most recent institutional changes may be an especially poor fit. Furthermore, the consequences of marginalized strategies may be very hard to spot in the short run. Indeed, their tactics can first appear to be unprofitable lumbering. Marginalized groups may be able to engineer bigger kinds of punctuated change, but they will do so less frequently than other groups.

Second, marginalized groups will play more of a role in institutional change within complex systems and they are more likely to limit their efforts to particular nodes of the system. In complex environments, groups can hunker down into a particular domain and build gradually a focused set of knowledge and skills. They are saved the costs of mastering and assessing the entire environment because they can cleave off small spaces where they will work for change. Better-endowed losers respond to complex environments by venue-shopping: searching for new domains that are sympathetic to their demands. Baumgartner and Jones (1993) described advocates' efforts to find policy subsystems—"niches within the governmental system" (6)—where they can build a policy monopoly. In their model, policy subsystems proliferate within federalism, thus creating even stronger incentives to search for hospitable coves. I offer an account where venue-shopping becomes less feasible and actors instead work to change the venues where they are already located. Highly marginalized groups have fewer means to bear the high search costs of venue shopping; as a result, hunkering down in a known, defined venue can be more profitable.

Thirdly, and perhaps most paradoxically, marginalized groups do best at achieving institutional change within more stable domains. Naturally, one's first instinct is to interpret statis within an institutional node as evidence that new power arrangements are unlikely in that venue, most especially at the impetus of weak actors. Yet in fact, marginalized groups are most disadvantaged in settings of rapid change. This consequence comes into view when we center our thinking around the importance of expertise. Better-endowed losers can deploy quickly the resources to relearn, experiment, and adapt to a changed environment. Marginalized groups are forced to climb the learning curve more slowly; they need far longer to reconstruct relevant knowledge and suitable approaches. In settings of rapid institutional change, there is greater disadvantage to groups that rely on long-term strategies. Where marginalized groups are concerned, institutional stability can provide better opportunities to identify and act upon institutional vulnerability.[9]

In sum, differing actors can bring pressure to bear in differing settings. As a general point, it is true that losers matter a great deal for future institutional change. But the ways that they matter can vary dramatically, as their resources and strategies can unfold in vastly different ways. Marginalized actors can drive institutional change, but their greatest successes emerge in complex yet stable institutions. The greatest pitfall in analyzing political entrepreneurs may be dual assumptions that institutions are sticky, but that the actors who shape them are nimble—and that the actors who lack agility will fade away. Much of institutional theory has tried to move away from what Pierson (2004) described as "actor-centered functionalism"—in other words, beyond the idea that institutions merely reflect the preferences and traits of the actors that they affect. This is a powerful insight. There is an equal danger of departing too far from considering how exactly actors matter in institutions.[10] We can build models that are actor-centered without being functionalist. "Actor-centered institutionalism" is not the oxymoron that it may first appear to be.

B. CONSEQUENCES FOR THEORIES OF ADVOCACY MOVEMENTS

Thinking about advocates changes our understanding of institutions. At the same time, thinking about institutions—and both the incentives and opportunities that they create—changes our understanding of advocates. Much prior scholarship has described how advocates seek outside help—resources from the federal government most particularly—and that policy learning has helped many groups. But theories at hand do not offer a full set of tools for describing differences in strategy across types of marginalization and context. In short, I separate the occasional losers in politics from those who lose repeatedly and profoundly.

In particular, most scholarship to date focuses on one or more of the following three circumstances. First, the work concentrates on activists who use the knowledge and capacity that they gain from outside relations to position themselves for impressive accomplishments at the national level. In contrast, I describe what happens when outside help doesn't appear to yield much and when agency capture is nowhere near being a possibility. Tribes extract federal help with internal capacity building but not much else (Goss 2006, Morris 1984).[11]

Second, existing studies concentrate on successes by activists with more or less straightforward means to compel federal support—such as control of a key electorate, other clear means to facilitate the needs of bureaucrats or legislators, or ways to capitalize on moments of political upheaval. The existing literature lacks clear theoretical tools for explaining why federal officials would accommodate, even in small ways, tribal activists who have so very little to offer in return, and why political stasis can be a hospitable environment for such changes (Manna 2006, Miller 2008).[12]

Third, much work on interest groups either concentrates on interactions within a single level of government or narrowly conceptualizes federalism's consequences. As a result, it tells only part of the story. When scholars do think about the consequences of federal policy for state and local politics, typically they approach the subject with a particular model: the feds provide a regulatory structure or financial incentives that change behavior at the state and local level. I argue that federal policy has softer consequences as well: it can change the resources of advocacy groups, with consequences that unfold at the state and local level. This is a new, important point for our understanding of federalism. What appear to be minor successes at the national level have a very different cast once we consider their effects throughout the federalist system.[13]

In short, consequences ripple across institutions. Mine is a federalist story because the measure of political success does not come solely from accomplishments and failures on the national stage. Indeed, tribes' primary objective is not to win federal support; it is to build their internal capacity and gain the flexible, fungible advantages that ensue. By carefully managing relations with players beyond their own community, tribal leaders change their organizations.

In sum, the benefits from political strategies depend on features of both the policy environment and an advocacy group's own resources. As conditions vary, stable strategies in stable contexts become promising opportunities. In the right circumstances, stability offers opportunities for slow, unobtrusive, and steady process; it is not as fruitless as we might fear.

III. Access and Expertise
C. ROLE OF EXPERTISE

The approach that I describe centers on the idea that amassing political and policy expertise is critical for success. Organizations with better information, and better opportunities to learn, have greater possibilities for political success. Expertise stands in contrast to the many political resources that are more or less fixed. Exogenous forces that are beyond a group's control often determine funds, group cohesion, the intensity of group preferences, and the size of the population that the group represents. In contrast, groups can *learn*: they can learn more about how to approach other players, about the problems that the group faces, what resources they have or need to get, and how to organize their efforts (see Moe 1980 for more about pertinent knowledge). Furthermore, the benefits from more expert organizations can weather changing winds. Funds from outside supporters may evaporate but knowledge persists. Additionally, some expertise—such as knowledge about organizational forms and strategies—can contribute to a range of initiatives, generating consequences throughout the political system.

Of course, the importance of information in problem-solving is not a new idea. Stinchcombe (1990), for one, places issues of information at the center of his analysis of organizational design. Specifically, the more an organization builds links with outside actors who can provide information, the greater the likelihood that the organization will be able to innovate and thus improve its performance. Many studies of bureaucratic politics center on the importance of expertise. Heclo (1974, 305) took up the theme that learning and uncertainty are critical factors in politics, musing in his classic remark, "Governments not only 'power' (or whatever the verb form of that approach might be); they also puzzle." In Heclo's model, influence can result from both power and knowledge.[14] Finally, even standard models of individual-level political learning are relevant (see, most notably, Verba, Schlozman, and Brady 1995). Just as individuals must learn how to participate in politics, so too must groups. Furthermore, there is compelling empirical evidence of the importance of information and of networks for acquiring information. Clemens (1997) offered powerful examples of how networks and knowledge acquisition altered organizational innovation. Carpenter (2001) also illustrated how expertise contributed to effectiveness and thus to influence. Esterling (2004) and Sonenshein (2004) provide examples from contemporary politics of how policy knowledge provides influence over political outcomes.

My analysis brings these familiar arguments into settings where they haven't always received regular treatment. Ideas about information have applicability to understanding advocacy by underresourced groups, where expertise is built around scant other resources. Learning more about politics and policy opens new political opportunities even in marginal circumstances. How do such groups overcome the information challenge? By identifying and building upon their capacities but also by making use of outside help. Other agents can aid marginalized organizations in developing technical policy expertise, provide opportunities to get to know the external environment, and offer exposure to a variety of strategies and organizational forms.

D. ROLE OF OUTSIDE AID

My framework of relations between marginalized groups and outside actors— where external sources provide small but meaningful assistance for expertise cultivation—is absent in much of the existing literature. Some of the closest discussion lies in the debates within the social movement literature, which concerns itself with fundamental questions about marginalization and attempts to overcome it. McCarthy and Zald (1977, 1217–1218) adopted one of the broader definitions, arguing "[a] *social movement* is a set of opinions and beliefs in a population which represents preferences for changing some elements of the social structure and/or reward distribution of a society," and then added that "we are concerned with the margins of the political system rather than with existing party structures." When the social movement literature speaks to the role of external support in political endeavors, it offers models that conflict with the outcomes we observe in tribal politics. I contend that the current literature is missing a needed in-between model, where a group's own resources matter, but external assistance (not control or dependence) is important as well.

Proponents of resource mobilization theories of social movements (McCarthy and Zald 1977, Zald and McCarthy 1979)[15] see relationships with outside actors as, really, a sort of politics by proxy. In brief, outside actors help by doing some of the necessary, hard political work for disadvantaged groups. This account is then critiqued in indigenous processes models of social movements.[16] Proponents of indigenous processes argue resources really ought to be developed internally, to safeguard against relationships that lead to cooptation or dependency (Morris 1984, McAdam 1982). Others (Tarrow 1994, Gaventa 1980, and Piven and Cloward 1977) express concern that outside aid will be fickle or fleeting.

At one extreme, relationships with outsiders could lead to cooptation or dependency; at the other extreme, to trivial or purely symbolic assistance that fails to change outcomes. Yet some tribal governments have found a way between destructive and dissatisfying relationships. My findings suggest that relations between actors with unequal power can be bilateral in some ways, in some contexts. Tribal governments use outside assistance—this analysis concentrates on federal government assistance in particular—to develop their own internal capacities. Theirs is a rocky, sometimes tenuous, yet ultimately sustainable path.

Hints of such a model can be found in a number of existing accounts of advocacy. Walker (1983) offered a classic account of interest group "patronage" from the federal government. Walker and others conceived of this process as "political mobilization from the top down" (403). In contrast, I find that federal support can have very different, bottom-up consequences. Furthermore, much other work has noted instances where more nuanced federal subsidies can be observed. Examples have included aid with information-gathering, guidance and aid for organizational development, and outside aid that marginalized groups slowly reshaped over time.[17] I submit a theoretical frame for interpreting such events, one that values their contribution to advocates' aims and the delicate yet effective tasks that group leaders must accomplish in these contexts. Suggestions of this strategy are all around us; we just have not yet fully appreciated the nature and significance of this repeating motif. Katzenstein (1998) took up a comparable cause in her exploration of "protest within institutions." She noted the "unobtrusive" mobilizing structures that feminists can find within broader institutions, nestled in "protective spaces" or "habitats." I join Katzenstein in inviting scholars to see political mobilization differently—to search for subtle assistance that can contribute to larger, longer-term endeavors.

IV. How to Know an Institutional Niche When You See One?

An institutional niche is a source of outside support that can provide small but meaningful subsidies for the cultivation of expertise. This improved knowledge can contribute to initiatives in many different settings. My analysis focuses on institutional niches in the federal government, since federal institutions are particularly favorable to the appearance and endurance of niches, but institutional niches can emerge elsewhere as well.

Institutional niches of federal support did not just result from some remarkable combination within the federal bureaucracy of magnanimity and acute perception of Indian interests. Tribal advocates were very present in shaping these relationships. Tribes kept a sharp eye on overall structure and on possible footholds. They appreciated the potential of each place in the process and each moment of access. Outside actors may be amenable to this role because they are sympathetic to a disadvantaged group's agenda, because a group's communication can improve their program performance, and because a group's approval can improve their relationship with other actors. All the same, absent a strong role by a disadvantaged group's own advocates, there is great danger that the relationship will drift toward co-optation or toward assistance that really is not very useful.

As a consequence, there are some critical ingredients to successful, enduring institutional niches. Ultimately, a disadvantaged group must find a potential niche with the following components. First, the institutional niche must be located in an organizational subunit that houses actors sympathetic to the disadvantaged group's goals and with enough separation and autonomy to alter its agenda in subtle ways. Second, the marginalized advocate has the opportunity for regular, long-term interactions within the subunit that is not too costly or burdensome. In other words, frequent contact is something that the disadvantaged group can sustain. Third, the environment makes it possible for marginalized advocates to challenge actions within the subunit while only moderately expanding the scope of conflict. In short, those who provide oversight or otherwise keep the subunit in check also are somewhat sheltered. Their incentives need to be close enough to the subunit's so that they possess some of the underlying sympathy to the marginalized group's goals but different enough to occasionally respond to different incentives, reach different conclusions, and demand different actions.

Potential niches can lie unused by disadvantaged actors. Managing relationships requires time and energy, and there is only so much of each to go around. Since niches offer a long-term benefit, they may be less attractive in times when organizational instability or crisis demands short-term solutions. Finally, basic awareness of a potential niche, and a clear understanding of what it can and cannot offer, are precursors to cultivating a relationship.

What do institutional niches mean for what tribes don't do? For one, they don't pour all their efforts into the pursuit of high-profile changes in federal policy or big increases in federal dollars or programs in Indian Country. This is not to say that tribes avoid these approaches: they are certainly interested in opportunities for major changes, but they diversify their efforts. They invest a lot in far less ambitious goals.

Also, they don't focus exclusively on direct service delivery for ongoing needs from other governments: in other words, they don't ask the feds to do the job for them, even if the feds have more means and experience for carrying out the job. Furthermore, when they pursue technical assistance, they are not asking someone else to insert their knowledge (which could then be easily withdrawn at another date), even though that could be the quickest way to achieve an immediate objective. Rather, tribes seek technical assistance that is collaborative and functions as form of training. Or they seek technical assistance for one-time tasks and not for continuing activities. Along similar lines, the support for physical infrastructure is a secondary priority. Physical plant complements, but doesn't replace, intellectual framework for programs.

Also, tribes in this study don't flit among federal programs or agencies. They don't even maintain a terribly wide range of relationships in the federal government. As they seek to gain influence, they don't conduct quick in-and-out strikes or pushes on multiple fronts. They don't invest solely in efforts with immediate impacts. Over time, they focus on the same agencies, the same programs, and the same objectives within those agencies. Tribes work on long-term gains, not just short-term victories.

I offer an account of how to build new opportunities; but clearly, groups are almost always better off if they have a panoply of resources at their disposal. This new lens should not blur our awareness of political inequality and its very real consequences: opportunities to partially offset disadvantage do not mean disad-

vantage is erased. However, scholars who are deeply troubled by political disparities do few favors if they despair at political obstacles and stop their analyses
there. For students and for scholars who have lived these inequalities, and for
community leaders who face these disparities in their work each day, there is
hardly any revelation contained in pointing out that differing political opportunities exist. Concern about troubling realities in political life can and should translate into attention toward avenues of change. Acknowledgement of accomplishments
should in no way detract from recognition of the daunting challenges that persist.
Rather, investigations into the sources of success feed directly into the agenda of
confronting the problems not yet conquered.

V. Generalizability

Before proceeding further, it is worthwhile to address the unique and generalizable characteristics of studying American Indian tribal governments' participation
in politics. There are features of tribal politics that are quite context-specific, but
there are also some portable concepts generated in the study of American Indian
tribal affairs. This book seeks both to understand American Indian politics in its
own right and to expand our understanding of broader political forces through the
study of the American Indian experience.

To be sure, tribal governments are very unique entities. At the same time, American
Indian communities share much in common with other groups that have experienced
economic, political, and social marginalization. Tribal governments serve populations in desperate circumstances, seeking to improve their lot but without much
funding, many votes, or other wherewithal to provoke change. On multiple
dimensions, American Indian politics is about isolation from centers of power.

Some elaboration on the unique features of American Indian tribal governments
is necessary. Note that chapter 2 provides a great deal more detail on this topic;
here, I present a basic overview. First, tribal governments are long-standing,
legally recognized sovereign powers with land bases that they govern. Tribal members are citizens of their tribal nations, the United States, and the states where
they reside; they are entitled to participate in the political life of all three sovereigns. These legal structures endow a permanence and structure that other organizations may often lack. Of course, a long-standing organization offers both
advantages and dangers: it can translate into a lack of flexibility. Indeed, tribal
governments often face a clouded history, with some important features that were
imposed by outside forces and that fit poorly with their communities' needs and
values (Cornell and Kalt 1992, Biolsi 1992, Alfred 1999).

Furthermore, tribal governments have a particular, enduring relationship with the federal government, rooted in the history of this country. As Indian peoples sought to improve their lives in earlier generations, their first challenge was confronting federal policies hostile to tribal powers and indigenous ways of life. In many ways, centuries of Indian activists have been forced to become experts on managing the federal government. This is a political task that, in certain respects, won't change over time: in a federalist system, other governments continually face a certain temptation to encroach, which means that advocates of tribal sovereignty must remain forever attentive. Of course, one tool that tribal advocates have always had at hand is a legal status that recognizes native nations' powers as governments. Yet centuries of realpolitik have shown that legal documents are not enough; tribal advocates have had to build on-the-ground political power in order to protect their communities' interests.

I do not expect other organized groups to replicate precisely the organizational forms of tribal government or the tribal-federal relationship as it exists today. But it would be a mistake to let these distinctions eclipse the powerful commonalities that exist between tribes and other groups. While a variety of mechanisms have been used to enforce the marginalization of different communities, the final consequences of those processes remain fundamentally similar, and a common strategic challenge results. American Indian communities are certainly not the only ones that have faced a grim history of federal institutional racism and its enduring, devastating legacies. Other groups may have their own, path-dependent points of interaction with outside actors, and they may be able to achieve the kind of relative organizational stability (with all its pros and cons) that tribal governments experience. Furthermore, the problems that Indian nations face are just as extreme, and oftentimes far worse, than the obstacles that many other disadvantaged groups face.

As Vine Deloria, Jr.—who laid much of the foundation for the contemporary study of American Indian law and politics—put it, while we should not overlook important distinctions, many minority communities face a core challenge. They all must establish local autonomy for their communities, exercise meaningful power through existing governments, and protect what he explicitly terms their "sovereignty" (1970, see pages 100–137 in particular). Furthermore, he argues that the backlash by power structures against such claims is parallel across group contexts. Many powerholders seek to atomize marginalized communities and define their problems as individual and behavioral. In Deloria's framework, the key battle for all marginalized communities is the meaningful, unapologetic defense of group identity and real-world self-determination.

Furthermore, as Lawrence Bobo and Mia Tuan (2006) have shown, and a bevy of scholars of American Indian studies have also demonstrated, white attitudes about American Indians contain features in common with attitudes about other racial groups. Many whites tend to see American Indians as seeking special rights and special treatment, as undermining values of equality and hard work, and as showing insufficient individual initiative and personal responsibility (see also Dudas 2008).

The real test is on the ground. Can other advocacy groups learn from tribes? The answer is yes. Indeed, scholars and activists have documented tribal activists that engaged in collaborative strategy sessions in the 1960s and 1970s with the leaders of other minority organization and of the Industrial Areas Foundation, a community organizing group (Nagel 1996, 182; Beck 2005, 162; Pleasant 2009). Furthermore, the experiences of other marginalized groups, and the on-the-ground strategies that community organizers advocate, point to similar patterns of interactions (see, for example, Cortes 1993 and Kretzmann and McKnight 1996). There are strikingly similar approaches that focus on building on existing capacities and existing outside relationships. Finding supportive outside actors, and cultivating the right relationships with them, is an important component to much activism. In short, all groups come into contact with a variety of outside actors, and all those interactions offer the potential discovery of latent institutional niches. The institutional complexity of the federal government makes it easier for niches to emerge and endure there; however, such spaces can exist in a multitude of other institutional settings, as long as a niche is sheltered through institutional separation.

The frames through which we view tribal governments also matter for generalizability. Drawing on others' work (see Wilkins 2002 and Boehmke and Witmer 2002), I treat American Indian tribes as both governments and pressure groups for the purpose of my analysis. More precisely, they are governments that sometimes choose to function as pressure groups do. I argue that all governments should be seen through this lens: each has spheres where it decides and spheres where it wishes to influence others' decisions. Behaving as a pressure group does not contradict status as a government. When local governments ask neighbors to change behaviors that have negative externalities for them, when states lobby the federal government for more aid or beneficial programs, and when the U.S. government seeks to influence decisions of foreign powers or international organizations, all these governments are acting very much like ordinary pressure groups act. Likewise, there are spheres where Indian nations have decision-making authority and spheres where they seek to sway decisions made by others. Indeed, much of our thinking about relations between governments could benefit from drawing on the theoretical tools that the studies of interest groups can offer.

Finally, the study of American Indian politics addresses the dilemma of harnessing the potential of a vulnerable government. Tribal governments face a precarious status: on the one hand, they are sovereign authorities and as a result have a privileged legal status. On the other hand, in light of stark power differences that have driven much federal policy and the doctrine of plenary power that has resulted, the federal government has been able to assert and exercise control over the existence, regulation, and termination of tribal governments, essentially rendering them "creatures of the state" at will.[18] What happens to governments when they are surrounded by actors holding greater social and economic power, when they sometimes face discourse treating them as implicitly illegitimate or inferior, and when they must tend to the unhealed injuries of brutalities? We can't understand the nearly 600 American Indian tribal governments without engaging that question. Indeed, in a federalist system with 51 other sovereigns and upward of 89,000 total governments (U.S. Census Bureau 2008), there are many more governments that we can't really understand without engaging that question.

2 The Historical Evolution of American Indian Political Strategies

THIS CHAPTER SEEKS to accomplish three things. First, it provides an overview of the legal status and history of American Indian tribal governments. Second, it examines the historical evolution of American Indian political strategies. Finally, it details the research design and case selection used in the chapters that follow.

I. Basics of Tribal Government

A. WHAT'S A TRIBAL GOVERNMENT?

First, some basics of tribal government. As of 2002, there were 562 federally recognized American Indian tribal governments in the United States (USCCR 2003), which varied tremendously in their land base, population size, cultural heritage, and economic circumstances. 33 states have at least one federally recognized Indian reservation within their borders (Tiller 1996).[1] The number of federally recognized tribes has grown slowly over time; there were 565 such tribes in 2010 (Bureau of Indian Affairs). In Census 2000, 4.1 million Americans, or 1.5% of the population, identified themselves as American Indian; 2.5 million Americans identified their race only as American Indian; and 1.6 million Americans self-identified as American Indian and some other group (Ogunwole 2002). Nearly half (43%) of the American

Indian population in 2000 lived in Western states; 31% lived in the South, 17% in the Midwest, and 9% in the Northeast. The 1990 Census indicated that about 38% of American Indians lived on tribally controlled lands and 62% did not. Another way of evaluating the size of the American Indian population with reservation ties is by looking at the number of American Indians using the programs of the federal Indian Health Services, which operates on and near Indian reservation lands. According to data presented by the Indian Health Services in 2001, 1.5 million American Indians made use of their services. Of that population, 36% resides off Indian lands but close by, and 64% resides on Indian lands (Indian Health Service 2001, 20 & 93). In other words, a notable portion of American Indians living off reservations have chosen to stay very near reservations.

In their simplest form, tribal governments are the governing bodies with authority on Native American reservations. From a perspective of sheer political power, the whims of the federal government determine whether tribal governments have actual power. Throughout most of American history, the federal government has pursued the political subjugation and cultural oppression of Native Americans; since the 1930s, the federal government has opted at times to grant reservations greater independence in decision-making. In a society where principles matter, however, there are other frames through which to view tribal governments. Tribal governments are sovereign nations that have existed from time immemorial. These entities made certain concessions to the United States government but never surrendered their sovereign powers and they still exercise the right to govern their nations. In this light, American Indian tribal governments occupy a particular legal space, whereby the federal government does exercise some authority in their affairs, but tribes still retain independence and sovereignty over designated land bases.

Felix Cohen (1988, 122), in his landmark text on federal Indian law, summarized this legal principle of enduring tribal sovereignty when he noted:

Indian self-government, the decided cases hold, includes the power of an Indian tribe to adopt and operate under a form of government of the Indians' choosing, to define conditions of tribal membership, to regulate domestic relations of members, to prescribe rules of inheritance, to levy taxes, to regulate property within the jurisdiction of the tribe, to control the conduct of members by municipal legislation, and to administer justice.

Perhaps the most basic principle of all Indian law, supported by a host of decisions hereinafter analyzed, is the principle that *those powers which are lawfully vested in an Indian tribe are not, in general, delegated powers granted by express acts of Congress but rather inherent powers of a limited sovereignty which has never been extinguished.* Each Indian tribe begins its relationship with the Federal Government as a sovereign power, recognized as such in treaty and legislation. The powers of sovereignty have been limited from time to time by special treaties and laws designed to take from the Indian tribes control of matters which, in the judgment of Congress, these tribes could no longer be safely permitted to handle.

Much of the legal foundation behind these concepts was articulated in a trio of decisions known as the Cherokee Cases (*Johnson v. McIntosh* in 1823, *Cherokee Nation v. Georgia* in 1831, and *Worcester v. Georgia* in 1832), all authored by Chief Justice John Marshall. The decisions established the principle of a limited but unalienable tribal sovereignty (see Harring 1994, 32–33). Contained in these decisions were the discovery doctrine and the trust doctrine. In *Johnson v. McIntosh* (1823), the court held that the established legal practices of European discoverers extinguished the territorial rights of tribes. Marshall wrote of the legal concept behind European colonization:

However extravagant the pretension of converting the discovery of an inhabited country into conquest may appear; if the principle has been asserted in the first instance, and afterwards sustained; if a country has been acquired and held under it; if the property of the great mass of the community originates in it, it becomes the law of the land, and cannot be questioned.

In *Cherokee Nation v. Georgia* (1831), the court affirmed tribes' status as governments. Indeed, the act of making treaties with tribes had acknowledged that they were governments. But Marshall qualified his definition; he described American Indian tribal governments as "domestic, dependent nations." In that status, tribal governments are sovereigns that exist under guardianship of the U.S. government. The U.S. government's resulting trust obligations are to provide protections that tribes themselves can no longer provide because of treaty concessions. Of course, history has confirmed a natural suspicion: trusteeships can be advantageous at times but risk the great abuse of power. The trust doctrine gives tribal governments a point of entrée for demanding support from the federal government. All the same, it leaves tribes vulnerable to federal discretion about what policies serve Indian interests.

Marshall's framework reflected a long history of interactions with Indian nations, by European powers as well as by the fledgling United States. The Commerce Clause of the U.S. Constitution, which remains the constitutional basis for most Indian-federal relations, gave Congress the power to "regulate commerce with foreign nations, and among the several states, and with the Indian tribes." The Constitution made relations with Indians a federal matter and a foreign relations issue, an approach deeply rooted in colonial practices. In *Federalist* 3, John Jay made the case for why the federal government would be a more prudent arbiter of relations with foreign powers, and he included Indian nations in this discussion. Leaders of this new nation faced the challenge of managing a long, precarious frontier. In that light, they saw relations with Indian tribes as a sensitive and serious component of international diplomacy.

In practice, the implementation of the idea of tribal sovereignty would vary over time. Political contexts altered how Congress approached its discretion to expropriate powers that, in Cohen's words, "tribes could no longer be safely permitted to handle." Tribes' actual political power mattered tremendously for the decisions that the federal government felt free to make. The actual exercise of sovereignty eroded steadily over the course of the 19th century, as the United States became more powerful and native nations less so (Wilkins and Lomawaima 2001).

Deloria and Wilkins (1999, 27–29) took up this same theme (see also Harring 1994 for a similar discussion), declaring, "The course of American history has demonstrated that where Indian tribes have no resources within the American political system, new laws and new theories of the relationship between the United States and Indians are allowed to go unchallenged and—whether in fact constitutional or not, and whether in fact just or not—become part of the law of the land." A key example is the Supreme Court's decision in *Lone Wolf v. Hitchcock* in 1903, which offered an expanded interpretation of congressional authority in Indian affairs, by extending plenary power. The court ruled that federal legislation could unilaterally restrict tribal autonomy for a broad range of activities; renegotiated treaties were not needed. The *Lone Wolf* decision was among several key Supreme Court decisions of the late 19th and early 20th centuries that asserted greater federal authority to supervise Indian affairs.

B. HISTORICAL BACKGROUND ON TRIBAL-FEDERAL RELATIONS:
    ASSIMILATION

Through most of the 19th century, the federal government sought to remove territory from Indian hands to satisfy settler demands, by force as necessary, while also striving to minimize the costs in dollars and in the lives of U.S. soldiers associated with that effort.[2] In the late 19th century, federal Indian policy shifted. With land removal and military domination largely accomplished, cultural assimilation of Native Americans moved to the forefront. Proponents viewed these policies as promoting Indians' well-being. Needless to say, these endeavors met resistance in Indian communities. The imposition of assimilation policies required the use of force and came at great cost to those who defended their ways of life.

Under assimilation policies, American Indian life was shaped by the potent combination of intense federal intrusion into daily personal affairs and the wide-scale destruction of traditional indigenous economies. Federal agents regulated religious ceremonies, marital practices, access to food and money, and the ways that adults and children spent their days. Indian children were routinely forced to attend boarding schools far from home where they were not permitted to wear traditional dress or to speak their native languages. Felix Cohen (1942, 174–5), described this era as "perhaps the greatest concentration of administrative abso-lutism in our governmental structure."

When federal officials weren't regulating the minutiae of personal conduct, they were upending the basic structure of reservations. With the General Allotment Act of 1887, the federal government carved many reservations up into individual homesteads, selling to white settlers the "surplus" lands that remained after home-steads were allotted. Furthermore, Indian peoples who were unfamiliar with private property ownership often lost their land holdings when they became indebted to creditors, fell behind on property taxes, or fell prey to unscrupulous speculators. Before the General Allotment Act, there were 104.3 million acres of tribal lands in the United States; afterward, land holdings decreased to 52.7 million acres by 1933 (Wilkinson et al. 2004, Rusco 1976, 55–56).

Yet in spite of these repressive practices, Native Americans found subtle tools to eke out small changes in federal policy. Cornell (1988, 61) noted the myriad strat-egies across reservations:

[E]fforts by often shrewd, determined, but politically handicapped tribal leaders to maintain their own sense of authority in the face of official usur-pation or to follow their own sense of their peoples' needs and interests against the obstructionism and disapproval of reservation agents, superin-tendents, and the BIA. They include struggles over everything from the size of allotments and annuities to the suppression of ceremonial activities, from compulsory schooling to demands for further land cessions.

As Biolsi (1992) noted in his discussion of the Pine Ridge and Rosebud Sioux reser-vations, the Lakota used basic tools of dissimulation to deflect federal intrusion to a small degree. For example, when federal officials in 1881 conducted the census that would be used to determine food rations on the Pine Ridge reservation, many Lakota registered more than once or sent children to be enumerated in multiple families. This tactic probably inflated population figures by 70% (1992, 21) and thus stretched out the meager federal food rations, at least until the next census when federal officials caught on to the trick.

Biolsi also describes the savvy use of federal bureaucratic procedures. American Indians had no real power over federal policy, but they found creative mechanisms to keep federal bureaucrats in check to some degree:

> The Lakota understood clearly that the agencies were expected to manage blindly and humanely Indian affairs in the interests of Indians (as, of course, those interests were defined by the OIA [Office of Indian Affairs])....Even unfounded allegations of malfeasance from Indian people, if directed to the right place, could bring on scrutiny. (1992, 22)

Thus, on both reservations, tribal members were sure to take advantage of the visits of federal inspectors. They used these occasions to raise concerns and to stimulate investigations that would make local federal agents somewhat more cautious in their future actions. There were, of course, multiple arenas where the Lakota had no choice but to comply with federal directives. But still, tribal members noticed and acted upon small windows to change the content or impact of federal policy.

Across the Plains, many Indian communities worked to protect cultural practices. When federal agents banned traditional dances and ceremonies, Native Americans responded in multiple ways (Holm 2005). Strategies included removing from public events those practices that most offended Christian sensibilities, yet continuing those practices in private settings. In some cases, these changes involved minor alterations. In one instance, changing the name of an event was enough to convince federal agents that the gathering would no longer have religious content. A cycle typically ensued: federal agents would ban an event, and tribal members would propose a particular modification that would either soothe or confuse federal officials. In a few years, another ban would be proposed, and Indian leaders would offer another modification there. Thus, tribes fought to maintain key social elements to religious practices by creating a more amenable public face of dance, yet continued some traditional practices in secret. In the case of the Northern Cheyenne reservation, the cycle of negotiations ended when federal agents permanently banned religious dances in the 1910s, at which point the Cheyenne continued the dances surreptitiously. Still, a process of negotiation had succeeded at preserving valued public events over precarious decades.

Hoxie's studies of Crow Indians pointed to similar patterns. Indian political resistance continued as an important, yet often unobserved force:

In 1930 an outside observer traveling through the American West in a railroad car would have had to conclude that the oppression of the early reservation era had succeeded in destroying the political power of nineteenth-century tribes....

From the perspective of local native communities, the reservation system had not achieved its objectives. While outsiders had succeeded in altering Indians' dress, economic life, and religious practices, the oppressive reservation regimes had not succeeded in "dissolving the bonds of tribalism" as so many nineteenth-century reformers had hoped they would. Most residents of areas whose majority traced their descent from aboriginal populations continued to think of themselves as members of a distinctive group. As distinct social entities, these ethnic enclaves continued to recognize their own leaders and to pursue a unique, community agenda. (1992, 39–40)

In the first few years of the 20th century, the Crow fought successfully against federal agents' plans for further land cessions and against more extensive leasing of Crow lands to white farmers. By the 1910s, the Crow Nation pushed federal agents to allow for an elected tribal council. The council had few real powers, but it served as an important public forum. In the following decades, the tribal council was a key actor in the fight for greater Crow control over Crow lands (Hoxie and Bernardis 2001, Hoxie 1992).

Similar patterns of small pushes for federal policy change occurred on the Menominee reservation in Wisconsin (Hoxie 2001 and Hosmer 1991), the Fort Yuma reservation in Arizona (Hoxie 2001 and Bee 1981), and among the Arapahos in Wyoming (Fowler 1982). No one would say that tribal leaders won great concessions in any of these places. But in light of the formidable political obstacles that tribes faced, the fact that they won *any* federal concessions is astounding.

C. THE INDIAN REORGANIZATION ACT

In the 1920s and '30s, new trends in federal Indian policy began emerging. Among artistic and academic circles, concern was growing about traditional Native American practices and the loss of cultural heritage that would result from assimilation (Cornell 1988, 89). Furthermore, new studies revealed that assimilation had failed to live up to its claim of improving Indians' material well-being; instead, Indian reservations were marked by deplorable living conditions. New Department of Interior leadership in Franklin Roosevelt's administration—and in particular, Commissioner of Indian Affairs John Collier—promoted the end of allotment, reductions in federal interferences, and return of self-government powers to tribes. Collier's efforts succeeded in the passage of the Indian Reorganization Act (IRA) in 1934. The law reversed core elements of assimilation policy and allowed for certain powers of self-governance for formally recognized tribal governments on reservations.

A number of tribal governments had laid the foundations for these reforms by maintaining their traditional governments or documenting new official governments in the 19th and early 20th centuries (Deloria and Lytle 1984, Rusco 1976). Some of these governments were shells created by Bureau of Indian Affairs (BIA) agents, but some were more genuine. Tribal governments often had very little real power, but they provided an underlying structure for organizing communities. The governments could also communicate tribes' preference to BIA officials. Some BIA officials saw these governments as an easy mechanism for communicating their requirements back to Indian nations; but in doing so, they were recognizing governments as official and authentic leadership. Once Indian affairs were framed in that way, it would be hard to move backward. From the 1880s through 1910s, to take one slice of time, BIA agents reported back to Washington that tribe-initiated governments functioned in places as diverse as Grand Ronde Agency in Oregon, Sisseton Agency and Cheyenne River Agency in Dakota Territory, Union Agency in Indian Territory (soon to become part of Oklahoma), Cheyenne and Arapahoe Agency in Oklahoma, and Southern Pueblos Agency and Northern Pueblos Agency in New Mexico Territory (Wilkins 2009).

While the final IRA legislation that Congress passed was not as bold as Collier had wished, it still provided a vital mechanism for tribes to establish governments with federally recognized control over internal affairs. It was a great step forward for Indian sovereignty. And yet the reforms were not totally responsive to Indian advocates. In drafting his proposal, Collier consulted with a number of Indian organizations and tribal councils. It is not clear how far Collier went in incorporating these viewpoints; a significant number of tribal councils were very critical of Collier's bill (Prucha 1984, 954–955).

D. TERMINATION

This trend toward acknowledging self-determination was a shaky one, and it faced notable interruptions along the way: most notably, with the appearance of termination policy in the 1950s. As leadership changed in the Bureau of Indian Affairs and the Department of the Interior after the Roosevelt administration, federal Indian policy took on a new cast. The push began to terminate the powers and legal status of tribal governments. Federal assistance to reservations would end, tribal governments would be stripped of their authority, and states would assume all jurisdiction over Indian lands. The initial termination legislation applied to a subset of tribal governments, with plans to terminate many more tribal governments over time. While termination was intended as a new nationwide policy, as opposition rose, its implementation was limited.

The newly ascendant termination policy resembled the once-favored assimilation policy in some ways, but not in others. In the end, both schools of thought centered on the repudiation of tribal sovereignty. Assimilationists wanted to trample sovereignty in order to impose new cultural practices. Termination supporters wanted to trample sovereignty in order to end the distinct legal status of tribal governments and to rid the federal government of related encumbrances.

In the face of this threat, which persisted through the 1960s, American Indian leaders renewed efforts to shape the federal policies. In this new context, the push for federal policy reform intensified but not always in high-profile ways. American Indian advocates continued to work at a range of strategies for altering federal relations.

Cowger (1999) and Philp (1999), in their analyses of the history of the National Congress of American Indians (NCAI), documented the NCAI's role in bringing tribal leaders together. (For similar accounts, see also Drinnon 1987, Fahey 2001, and Wilkinson 2005.) The NCAI was formed to preserve and extend the advances in federal policy from the 1930s. In the 1950s the NCAI proved largely successful in staving off a series of proposed termination policies. Most of this process involved battling over bureaucratic policy changes: for example, new BIA rules about what powers on-the-ground federal agents could delegate to reservation governments and new BIA rules about tribes' ability to employ outside legal counsel. Some of the fight against termination policy occurred in Congress: there, tribal advocates succeeded at stopping a good amount of termination legislation but not all of it. Yet many important fights occurred in quieter realms, as tribes sought to out-maneuver new restrictions from the federal bureaucracy. Tribal leaders at the turn of the century had learned to keep a careful eye on their local federal agents and to push back against their policies wherever possible; by mid-century, tribal leaders were applying these lessons both to their local agents and to relations with bureaucrats in D.C.

The battles over termination both galvanized and crystallized tribal strategies for federal relations. As Cornell (1988, 124–125) noted, the experience brought about even greater awareness of the need to monitor and react to federal policy-making. The early stages of termination policy began in the late 1940s; it would be over two decades before the policy ended fully (in 1970). Tribes' efforts to stave off the implementation of this new agenda took effect slowly, but they brought important results in the end.

All the same, legacies of termination persist. Public Law 280 was a related initiative; it awarded jurisdiction over reservations to select states, with a plan to spread the practice to other states. A number of tribal governments still function today under the state government authority that P.L. 280 created (Cohen 1988, Wilkinson 2005). In some ways, the 1950s and 1960s became lost decades; what Deloria and Lytle (1984) called "the barren years." In important ways, the progress of tribal governments halted. Tribal leaders weren't working on ways to make conditions better; they were consumed by making sure things didn't get worse.

In this same era, some tribal efforts to shape federal policy occurred outside the debate over termination. For example, in the 1940s the Navajo Nation began intense efforts to influence decision-making in the Department of the Interior and in the Bureau of the Budget. Among their various objectives, Navajo leaders sought a new framework for federal relations, and they won a degree of accommodation of those demands. Philp (1999, 67) noted: "During the Truman years, the Navajos made significant progress toward self-determination. They reaffirmed their government-to-government relationship with the United States by insisting that federal officials consult with them on all important matters." The Navajo Nation wanted to restructure the terms of federal relations, and they began a slow process of seeking change that would pay off for the tribe over the decades.

E. SELF-DETERMINATION

Since the 1960s, however, the trend toward self-determination has been more constant. Not surprisingly, the growing emphasis on self-determination has been coincident with the rising political power of American Indian communities. American Indian political organizations grew in number, size, and presence through the mid-20th century. In this same time frame, tribal officials gained experience in governance and politics; Native Americans' access to higher education expanded; and Indians' exposure to broader social institutions grew with wartime military service and with increased movement to urban areas.[3]

Castile (1998) stressed how change in federal Indian policy in the 20th century fit into national political trends and broader policy goals. In the 1960s, federal initiatives like the War on Poverty provided new forms of assistance to Indian communities. Prucha (1984, 1094–1095) noted, "Grants were made directly to Indian groups, who used the money for programs they chose and developed themselves."

In 1970, President Nixon officially repudiated the policy of termination and declared that the aim of federal Indian policy was Indian self-determination. Nixon proposed numerous legislative initiatives to facilitate self-determination. Partial enactment of these proposals came in 1975, with the passage of the Indian Self-Determination and Education Assistance Act. The Nixon administration had envisioned that tribal governments would assume management of federal reservation-based programs and that the federal government would provide funding and technical assistance to support this transfer of authority. The bill that eventually passed was a diluted version: it permitted federal departments to contract with tribes to deliver some or all of their programs. The act was a step forward, as it improved opportunities for tribes to build their own programs and capacities. Still, the measure was not a full realization of the goal of devolving authority (Prucha 1984).

Tribal criticisms ensued about federal bureaucratic resistance and insufficient technical assistance. The critiques resulted in amendments in 1988 and 1994, "in both instances to speed up what appeared to be a considerable reluctance on the part of the Bureau [of Indian Affairs] to cooperate in its own withering away" (Castile 1998, 179).

Other significant progress occurred in this same time frame. The passage of the Indian Child Welfare Act (ICWA) in 1978 is one example of these other successes. The act granted tribal governments control over custody and adoption matters involving member children. In addition, ICWA "authorized the secretary of the interior to make grants to Indian tribes and organizations for the establishment of child and family service programs on or near reservations and for the preparation and implementation of child welfare codes" (Prucha 1984, 1156).

Where the federal government's relationship with native peoples was once extremely paternalistic and bent on forced assimilation, today tribes exercise a fair amount of autonomy through their reservation governments. By and large, federal Indian policy over the 20th century moved away from treating American Indians as dependent wards and toward greater independence from federal control (Berkhofer 1979, O'Brien 1989).

F. THE STRANGE HISTORY OF THE BUREAU OF INDIAN AFFAIRS

This history has delivered into the present day a curious relationship between tribes and the Bureau of Indian Affairs. Ultimately, the Bureau is a perch of (a certain degree of) power. BIA power can be directed in tribes' favor and against them. For much of its history, the BIA worked against American Indian self-determination. BIA power was partly redirected with the Indian Reorganization Act, but then abruptly turned back against Indian power in the late 1940s with termination policy. It would take many years for Indian leaders to steer the agency back to a policy of self-determination. Furthermore, at many moments when BIA officials have promoted Indian self-determination, it has been for expediencies of increasing the agency's powers and without a long-term commitment to tribal sovereignty. An enduring suspicion of the BIA is well-founded in its history.

When self-determination became official federal policy, BIA leadership changed, but the agency's services did not adjust so readily. Indian preference in hiring, instituted by Collier in the 1930s, meant that BIA policy was implemented by native peoples. Top-level BIA appointees after the late 1960s had a history of involvement in Indian advocacy. Yet the new leadership faced "bureaucratic inertia." Efforts at reorganization produced unimpressive results, yielding "a decade of shuffling and reshuffling" (Prucha 1984, 1120, 1121). With time, as tribal leaders advocated transferring more and more BIA functions to tribes themselves, the agency has naturally had a certain ambivalence about participating in its own "withering away," in Castile's terminology.

On top of all of this, the Bureau of Indian Affairs faces serious operational challenges. The agency is known for its troubles with poor management. David Lewis (2007) documented the agency's underperformance.[4] These are not new problems; Daniel Carpenter (2001, 328) noted the Interior Department's "deep structural flaws" in the early 20th century, including "bureau-stifling procedures."

Yet despite the BIA's troubling history and contemporary failings, it is point of entrée for Indian advocates, and it is staffed with personnel who are sympathetic to their aims. BIA personnel are spread across the country and in close proximity to many reservations. In some places, BIA and tribal government offices are actually just a short walk from one another. To be sure, some BIA personnel are indifferent, power-grabbing, frustrated, or unenthusiastic; but there are many BIA employees who want to make a difference. Furthermore, the agency's stated mission is to improve the well-being of native peoples. In the end, its performance measures will always be linked to the interests of Indian nations. In short, the BIA is a promising, limited, and dangerous resource all at once.

G. INTO THE PRESENT DAY

By 1990, federal Indian policy included some moments of tribal success, but it also contained some sizeable defeats. It is important to draw a distinction between the types of support that tribes can and cannot gain from institutional niches within the federal government. American Indian advocates have not succeeded at the wholesale reinvention of federal Indian policy. The U.S. Commission on Civil Rights (2003) noted the many needs of American Indians that are neglected or underfunded in federal policy. Indeed, tribes have experienced devastating setbacks in federal policymaking in recent decades. Most notably, the 1980s brought severe budget cuts to the programs serving Indian populations, and federal funding has remained anemic over time. Roger Walke (2000) of the Congressional Research Service calculated that spending on Indian programs, in constant 1997 dollars, rose from $2.9 billion in 1975 to $4.9 billion in 1980, and then declined steadily back down to a low of $3.0 billion in 1989. Over the 1990s the rate of growth in spending on Indian programs was far behind the rate for the overall nondefense budget. Per capita spending on the overall U.S. population climbed relatively steadily from around $2,600 in 1975 to around $3,300 in 1989 (again in constant 1997 dollars), while per capita spending on Indian programs fell from around $5,000 in 1975 to a low of less than $2,800 in 1989. Indian per capita spending was relatively flat over the 1990s (at $2,891 by 1999), while overall per capita spending rose almost 30%—to $4,276—in the same window. Table 2.1 summarizes Walke's analysis and shows that funding for Indian programs from 1975 to 2001 did not keep pace with spending to provide other services in comparable policy areas. Note that Indian programs all had lower growth rates than other comparable programs.

Furthermore, Indian communities experienced legislative defeats beyond the annual appropriations battles. The passage of the Indian Gaming Regulatory Act (IGRA) in 1988 gave state governments powers to regulate (and in some circumstances wholly restrict) tribal gambling enterprises. The dichotomy in federal Indian policy in recent decades led Wilkins (2002, 117) to remark that, "[b]y the late 1980s, federal policy was a bizarre and inconsistent blend of actions that, on one hand, affirmed tribal sovereignty and, on the other, aimed at severely reducing tribal sovereign powers."

These political challenges are compounded by tribes' limited access to forums where they can articulate their political objectives. Stereotypes of American Indian political leaders have persisted over time; various media distort and devalue the political aims of Indian advocates. Mainstream press outlets often provide scant coverage of tribes' perspectives.[5] Over time, American Indian advocates have faced a thorny choice. They can attempt to undo existing frames about their values, but the odds of failure are high. Or they can express their priorities within existing frames, but in the process risk losing control of their own identity. For example, in the 1970s, the American Indian Movement (AIM) embraced a media-centered political strategy, but the demands of that approach pushed AIM away from its initial mission and ultimately fed the organization's decline and perhaps detracted from its policy impact (Sayer 1997, Castile 1998). These unsavory options add to the daunting challenges that tribal governments face as they seek political success.

H. REFLECTIONS ON HISTORY

Undoubtedly, American Indians—under present-day circumstances and, indeed, for the foreseeable future—are often not well positioned to win major political victories. Traditional political analysis might end the story here, explaining tribes' political successes in the 20th century as a result of simply drafting in the wake of a broader civil rights movement. But there is another layer that explains the unexpected victories. Since the late 19th century (and sometimes even earlier), some tribal governments have found ways to use certain federal programs as institutional niches. Policy change did not result from a sudden wave of benevolence engulfing the federal government. Rather, a militarily subjugated people pushed slowly to redefine their relationship with powerholders.

The continuing application of such strategies benefits from a bevy of intertribal organizations that can serve as coordinating mechanisms for tribal governments. Table 2.2 illustrates a dense web of networks: 29 major national intertribal organizations and 21 major regional intertribal organizations. Tribal leaders have created a variety of settings where they can pool ideas and share lessons.

It would be a great overstatement to say that tribes have "captured" federal bureaucracies—but considering that oppression was the starting point, the hard-fought transition is remarkable. Generations of tribal leaders learned painful political lessons from the brutal experiences of their communities. Those leaders also discovered and refined tactics for political resilience along the way. In the end, the accumulation of small, quiet changes has had profound effects.

II. Research Design and Case Selection

A. REGIONS INCLUDED

This analysis focuses on tribes in the Southwest, Pacific Northwest, and Upper Plains. Regional variation allows me to consider some ways in which different histories shaped tribal governments. Today, the Pacific Northwest has fewer Native American citizens and less land under tribal control than the other two regions. Its reservations are more likely to have small populations and small land bases, although this is not universally true. The Upper Plains has more Indian citizens and more Indian lands, and those lands are more likely to be concentrated in larger reservations. The Southwest captures perhaps the widest spread—a great many reservations are small, but it also contains some of the largest reservations in the country.

This variation reflects differing histories of Indian-white conflict. In the Pacific Northwest, a critical mass of treaties was settled by 1855. The Pacific Northwest never had a fierce military resistance or an iconic figure of military resistance. In

TABLE 2.1

Federal Spending on Indian Programs and on Comparable Programs, FY 1975 to FY 2001

Program Name	Average Level (in millions)	Annual Change (in millions)	Annual Change as % of Average Level
Education			
Indian Spending			
Indian Education Office	$95.8	-$2.5	-2.57
BIA education programs (Interior)	$474.8	$2.3	0.47
Spending in Comparable Areas			
Overall education	$49,093.1	$432.4	0.88
Department of Education	$26,131.7	$563.2	2.16
Health			
Indian Spending			
Indian Health Service	$1,525.0	$60.0	3.93
Spending in Comparable Areas			
Overall health	$76,495.0	$4,890.2	6.39
HHS, excluding Social Security	$212,298.8	$12,098.8	5.70
Housing (calculated with budget authority, not outlays)			
Indian Spending			
Indian Housing Development Program	$474.4	-$48.9	-10.30
Spending in Comparable Areas			
Overall housing assistance	$24,141.4	-$1,215.6	-5.04
	$31,170.6	-$1,592.2	-5.11
Economic Development, Training, Employment			
Indian Spending			
Administration for Native Americans	$46.3	-$1.7	-3.57
BIA economic development programs	$82.6	-$4.0	-4.79
Indian & Native American Training & Employment	$127.4	-$10.1	-7.91

Spending in Comparable Areas	Overall community development	$11,750.2	-$288.3	-2.45
	Overall employment	$9,601.2	-$393.6	-4.10
	Department of Labor	$39,504.3	-$725.6	-1.84
Natural Resources				
Indian Spending	BIA natural resources programs	$145.2	$0.6	0.43
Spending in Comparable Areas	Overall natural resources	$21,010.8	$86.6	0.41
	Department of Interior	$7,024.6	$30.9	0.44
Overall				
Indian Spending	BIA & Office of Special Trustee for American Indians	$1,686.3	$2.2	0.13
	Overall Indian programs	$3,947.5	$15.2	0.39
Spending in Comparable Areas	Overall federal budget, excluding defense & interest on debt	$872,738.6	$24,972.5	2.86

Calculated in 1997 constant dollars, from Walke (2000, 293).

TABLE 2.2

NCAI Directory of Intertribal Organizations, 2004

National and International Tribal Organizations

- AMERIND – Risk Management
- American Indian Higher Education Association
- Americans for Indian Opportunity
- California Rural Indian Health Board
- Center for World Indigenous Studies
- Council of Energy Resource Tribes
- First Nations Development Institute
- Indian & Native American Employment & Training Coalition
- Indian Law Resource Center
- Intertribal Agricultural Council
- Intertribal Timber Council
- Intertribal Trust Fund Monitoring Association
- Native American Finance Officers Association
- National American Indian Housing Council
- Native American Journalists Association
- National Indian Child Welfare Association
- National Indian Council on Aging
- National Indian Court Judges Association
- National Indian Education Association
- National Indian Gaming Association
- National Indian Health Board
- National Intertribal Tax Alliance
- National Indian Justice Center
- National Indian Women's Health Resources Center
- National Native American AIDS Prevention Center
- National Tribal Environmental Council
- National Tribal Environmental Research Institute
- National Tribal Justice Resource Center
- Native American Rights Fund

Regional Tribal Organizations

- Affiliated Tribes of Northwest Indians (ATNI)
- Alaska Federation of Natives
- Alaska Inter-Tribal Council
- All Indian Pueblo Council
- American Indian Health Commission for Washington State
- Association of Village Council Presidents
- California Indian Lands Office
- Indian Art Northwest
- Intertribal Bison Cooperative
- Indian Tribal Council of Arizona
- Intertribal Council of Nevada
- Las Vegas Indian Center
- Montana-Wyoming Tribal Leaders Council
- Native American Fish & Wildlife Society

- California Nations Indian Gaming Association
- Columbia River Inter-Tribal Fish Commission
- First Alaskans Institute
- Great Lakes Intertribal Council
- Northwest Indian Fisheries Commission
- Northwest Portland Area Indian Health Board
- United Southern and Eastern Tribes

the Upper Plains, a critical mass of treaties was not finalized until 1880s. In the Southwest, the framework for a large part of Indian-U.S. relations was from the Spanish legal framework, which had first been laid in the 1600s. Furthermore, since treaties were negotiated (or dictated, as the case may be) in each region by different federal agents and at different times, there was regional variation in the boilerplate language in treaties.[6]

Of vital importance is the substantial regional difference under the 1887 General Allotment Act. In some places, the Act transferred reservation lands from collective ownership to individual homesteads for tribal members. The Act also declared much reservation land to be "surplus" after a reservation was carved up into individual homestead tracts for tribal members, opening the "surplus" lands for white settlers. And if individual Indian owners found themselves overwhelmed by financial hardship, unfamiliar with the practices of private land ownership and thus easily conned by outside land speculators, or unable or unwilling to take up farming, they could sell their land plots. Many did. (Harvard Project on American Indian Economic Development, 2008, 96; Wilkins 2002, 110–112). The consequence today is "checkerboarded" reservations, where Indian lands are interspersed with plots of lands owned by non-Indians. Imagine the governance nightmare for any sovereign power of a land base filled with parcels of land over which it does not have authority. Checkerboarding is far more common in the Upper Plains. Tribes in the Southwest and Pacific Northwest are much more likely to possess consolidated land bases.

Native communities in different parts of the country have different cultural heritages. Those cultural heritages have consequences for social and political organization, of course (Cornell and Kalt, 1998). Also, geography shapes the details of issues that are relevant in any place—be they contestations over salmon fisheries in the coastal Pacific Northwest, scarce water supplies in the arid West, mining for minerals in the Southwest, or control of the Black Hills in the Upper Plains.

B. DATES INCLUDED

This analysis focuses on the years 1990 through 2000, although occasionally I dip into materials from the late 1980s and early 2000s. The 1990s are an opportune decade for study, for several reasons. They capture some key policy changes. By the 1990s federal policies of self-determination were well underway, but important growth in those programs occurred over the decade. Contracting with tribes continued to expand in this time period, particularly under the Consolidated Tribal Government Program and Self-Government Compacts. Thus, we have the opportunity to see how tribes made use of some new opportunities contained in federal policy, both at their earliest stages and as they developed further. Furthermore, the 1990s were the era of the growth in Indian gaming. These data speak to conditions before, during, and after proliferation of the political negotiations and dollars resulting from gaming. Of course, the era captures some interesting national political variation as well, with its Republican and Democratic presidents and its Democratic and Republican congresses.

C. CRITERIA FOR CASE SELECTION

The analysis focused on 12 tribes. To capture variation in tribal circumstances, I examined tribes that were in differing conditions at the start of the sample period. First, I differentiated cases based on *government institutionalization*. More precisely, I looked to tribal governments that have achieved greater functional specialization, which we can also think of as greater differentiation of the tribal government. They stand in contrast to tribes where officials function as generalists and operate in less routine ways. I want to evaluate whether tribal governments with greater in-house specialization have greater expertise to start and thus have better tools for cultivating and deploying expertise as support becomes available. We find smart, hard-working leaders across all levels of institutionalization. I join others in arguing, however, that for governments to best utilize and sustain individual talents, and for government agencies to disseminate best practices, institutionalization plays a critical role. Generalists who wear many hats and who function in less routine ways face serious performance constraints.

Additionally, I evaluate whether well-established *economic development* matters. Here, I can consider whether a certain infusion of funds makes it easier to start building up expert capacity, by allowing tribes to bring in additional staff or build new programs, which can complement outside support for cultivating expertise. Essentially, independent funds may give tribes greater ease in adapting their governments. Note that tribal economic development almost always takes the form of tribally owned and tribally operated enterprises. Also, it is important to keep in mind that tribal economic development does not necessarily translate into big changes in the personal income of tribal members.

Cornell and Kalt have stressed repeatedly in their work that institutions matter for effective tribal governments. Specifically, they have directed attention to the importance of "rules and procedures that delegate and delimit authority" (1992; see also Harvard Project on American Indian Economic Development 2008). We find these same themes in Polsby's work on political institutionalization, which he argued is necessary for effective "resource allocation, problem solving, conflict settlement, and so on" (1968, 144). Polsby specified three key features of institutionalization: (1) structures that are well-bounded and differentiated from the broader environment, (2) complexity and functional specialization, and (3) universalistic, automatic rules and criteria. He continues, "the total impact of a cadre of specialists operating over the entire spectrum of public policies is a formidable asset for a political institution" (166). Along the same lines, Stinchcombe (1990) argued that, where there is differentiation of tasks, workers can more easily develop specialized, context-specific skills and routines for information processing. Organizations, he argues, need decentralization in order to understand their environments and to promote innovation.

We find routinization, differentiation, and specialization in the traditions of both indigenous and European-derived governments. For example, Biolsi (1992, 35–36), drawing on Wissler (1912, 7–11) and Walker (1982), documents patterns in mid-19th century Oglala Lakota society. There were distinct roles for decision-making across bands, selected through stable procedures. He describes how the *naca ominicia*, a body composed of most older men, selected seven *wicaśa it'ancan* (men chiefs) to serve lifelong, usually hereditary terms. Those seven then selected four others to oversee hunting and campsites. Another body that served one-year terms then appointed *akicita it'ancan* (soldier chiefs), who in turn appointed a police force. Even if certain institutions today are borrowed from Westerners, it does not mean those particular practices are incompatible with traditional values. As Alfred (1999, 3) notes, "[m]ost acknowledge that all Native structures will have to incorporate modern administrative techniques and technologies." Rather, Alfred argues, the distinction between indigenous and European-derived governments lies with features such as the role of government in society and the nature of the consent of the governed.

I want to evaluate whether tribes that differ across key qualities then behave in ways that are consistent with changing opportunities to accumulate expertise. I draw here on Elisabeth Clemens's (1997) insight that innovative strategies will emerge among those who are marginalized but not too marginalized. In other words, if groups are not doing all that well under existing arrangements, they will be looking for new approaches. But within that subset, those with more means will be better able to implement new strategies: in this case, strategies for cultivating expertise and institutional niches. Clemens's framework points to the expectation that these strategies will be most common among tribes with some advantages, but they should be visible occasionally among the least endowed. Consequently, the analysis can identify how strategies differ and how they remain the same for tribes in varying circumstances.

D. OPERATIONALIZING CASE SELECTION

Figure 2.1 summarizes case selection. I selected three tribes with both constrained economic development and constrained government institutionalization. I then selected three tribes with both developed economies and institutionalized governments. I also selected six tribes whose circumstances are a mixed bag. Specifically, I selected three tribes with developed economies but constrained governments and three tribes with institutionalized governments but constrained economies. These categories capture basic differences in tribal circumstances as identified in previous scholarship on American Indian politics (see Lopach, Brown, and Clow 1998).

Cases in the Southwest

	More Developed Economy	Less Developed Economy
More Institutionalized Government	Navajo Nation: Most Endowed	Tribe A: Moderately Endowed
Less Institutionalized Government	Tribe B: Moderately Endowed	Tribe C: Less Endowed

Cases in the Pacific Northwest

	More Developed Economy	Less Developed Economy
More Institutionalized Government	Tribe D: Most Endowed	Tribe E: Moderately Endowed
Less Institutionalized Government	Tribe F: Moderately Endowed	Tribe G: Less Endowed

Cases in the Upper Plains

	More Developed Economy	Less Developed Economy
More Institutionalized Government	Tribe H: Most Endowed	Tribe J: Moderately Endowed
Less Institutionalized Government	Tribe K: Moderately Endowed	Tribe L: Less Endowed

FIGURE 2.1 Cases Selected for Analysis

Also, I selected tribes so that critical features of regional politics did not line up with the tribal characteristics that I examine. As a result, key traits of neighboring communities—such as how urban or rural they are, how politically liberal or conservative they are, and how affluent they are—are distributed across the cases. Finally, to provide comparability among cases, I eliminated from consideration tribes located in very remote areas. Specifically, I only included reservations that were near at least one non-Indian community. In some cases, these nearby non-Indian communities were very small, with only a few hundred residents. I believe these controls allow more meaningful comparisons on the variables at the heart of my analysis: region, economic development, and government institutionalization. To identify the six tribes with stronger economic bases, I looked for reservations with very profitable economic development enterprises: most commonly, extensive natural resources extraction operations (four tribes) and/or a large casino (three tribes). While four tribes had notable commercial development—such as resorts, shopping centers, other retail services, and manufacturing—in all but one case, commercial development was preceded (and presumably funded to a degree) by natural resources extraction or casinos.

The sources of information about government institutionalization are far from uniform. I turned to existing narratives and documentation for a variety of indicators; I selected the six institutionalized tribes on the following bases:[7] (1) for all six tribes, there was functional specialization within tribal government; (2) for five tribes, there was praise by outside analysts for units within the tribal government for specialized, effective skills; (3) for four tribes, the number of tribal employees was much larger than for the other tribes in the sample; (4) for four tribes, staff had played key roles in intertribal organizations; (5) departments within several of the tribes have received recognitions, such as Honoring Nations awards from the Harvard Project on American Indian Economic Development; (6) all six tribes received funding from the Bureau of Indian Affairs (Bureau of Indian Affairs, 1992–1999) in ways that suggested more effective governments. If tribes are willing and able to operate their own government programs, they can opt into certain BIA grants. Four tribes received especially large grants from the BIA. Three tribes persuaded the BIA to allocate funding through block grant programs where BIA oversight is less, including the Consolidated Tribal Government Program and the Self-Government Compacts.

I identified the six less institutionalized governments by the following features of existing narratives and documentation: (1) All six tribes lacked the following traits in the early 1990s: functional specialization, large staffs, key roles in intertribal organizations, programs that won prominent awards, and Self-Government Compacts from the BIA. (2) Two tribes received federal recognition fairly recently, which meant that their governments were less experienced at key tasks. (3) Four of the tribes had Indian populations living on the reservation of less than 200 people. With such a small population, it is hard to justify staffing beyond a handful of people, which of course then makes specialization and differentiation impracticable.[8] (4) The BIA has guidelines for minimal budgets for tribal governments to sustain basic operations (Bureau of Indian Affairs 1998, BIA-60). Two tribes were below that threshold and two were only slightly above it. (5) For two tribes, I found praise of the tribal government by outside analysts, but that praise centered on particular personalities and not on organizations or structures.

Why would any tribe end up with developed economies but constrained governments, or institutionalized governments but constrained economies? The easiest cases to explain are institutionalized governments with constrained economies. All three tribes in these circumstances face massive disadvantages of geography. None sits atop highly profitable natural resources. None is very close to metropolitan areas or busy interstates, which means they lack a customer base for a highly profitable casino. All have fostered multiple economic development initiatives—such as small-scale natural resource extraction, agriculture, casinos, retail services, and programs to help tribal artists. These initiatives generated jobs for tribal members, but none generated large revenue surpluses for tribal government.

How does a tribe end up with a developed economy but a less institutionalized government? In at least one case, the tribal government had only fairly recently been recognized by the federal government, which meant that tribal leaders began the 1990s still trying to hammer out basic operations. In two cases, very small tribal populations resulted in governments with very small staffs, making it more difficult to specialize and differentiate. In all three cases, flourishing economic activities were relatively more recent developments. As the 1990s unfolded, tribes with economic advantages and government constraints invested in their governments. By the final years of the sample, at least two of the tribes had staff with roles in intertribal organizations. Two tribes won federal funding that was more overall and/or more flexible, and at least two tribes initiated programs that would go on to receive awards as they matured. Yet institutionalization can be a slow process, and these three tribes pursued it carefully.

E. KEEPING TRIBES UNNAMED

In the text that follows, I do not specifically name most of the 12 tribes. When I spoke to tribal officials about this project, many were enthusiastic to have more written on this topic, but some tribal officials asked that I avoid naming their tribes in print. I want to honor these wishes. These officials were worried that information on some particular details could be damaging to them. None asked me to suppress information about their actions or decisions, but they were concerned that since the project dealt with 12 tribes and three regions of the country, it could not possibly capture all the nuance and context of each community. I certainly agree with that assessment; I have very consciously chosen to trade off some place-specific nuance in order to provide a more comprehensive view. I do not consider this book to provide the complete or definitive assessment of any one tribe. Some tribal officials feared, however, that policymakers with a superficial understanding of their tribes might make conclusions based on this book without learning more or without consulting anyone in the tribe. I concur that such actions would result in ill-formed policy that would serve no one's interests.

I do not want to draw attention to those particular tribes that requested that they not be named, so I avoid naming others as well. To the extent that it is necessary for the analysis, I provide place-specific details about the tribes in the sample, but I have obscured enough particulars to make it difficult to pinpoint an exact tribe. That would not be impossible to figure out, with enough research into the records that I reference and into other sources of information about local and national politics. In that process, however, such an industrious reader would encounter volumes more of information about a particular tribe and thus have at hand a trove of contextual, nuanced information.

There are names of tribes and tribal officials that appear in the text that follows, however. In some instances, I introduce brief profiles of some intertribal organizations or I include an example with a passing reference to one or two tribes. My hope is that even an incautious reader would recognize that a few sentences or even a few pages of text are just a starting point, and in no way an ending point, for understanding a particular government or organization. Those short profiles and passing references may or may not include mention of the 12 tribes in this analysis; I will remain silent on that topic.

I do make one exception among the 12 tribes. The Navajo Nation is one of the cases that I include from the Southwest, and it operates in a set of extraordinary circumstances. There would be no way of discussing even basic details of the Navajo Nation without its identity becoming quite plain to anyone with a modicum of knowledge about tribal governments in the Southwest. Navajo is by far the largest Indian Nation in the United States. The Navajo reservation covers over 16 million acres in Northeastern Arizona, Northwestern New Mexico, and Southern Utah. According to census data, there were 175,000 American Indians living on the reservation in 2000. Extensive natural resource extraction operations—mostly oil, gas, and coal mining—have existed on the reservation since the early 20th century. The tribal government has over 4,000 employees, allowing a high degree of specialization of tasks. This is true not only for the tribal bureaucracy but for elected officials as well: political leaders are paid for their job and have staff to assist them (Navajo Nation 1998; Sturtevant 1983, 624–658; Tiller 1996).

The Navajo people have taken an extraordinary journey; their experiences have much to teach. The Navajo Nation's unique circumstances make it a useful case for understanding what tribal governments can accomplish in the most promising of circumstances and also what conditions are shared across many Indian communities. The fact that the Navajo Nation continues to have much in common with other tribal governments speaks very powerfully.

Furthermore, for readers and analysts who want to understand the Navajo Nation, there is a vast quantity of additional information available. My university library has shelf after shelf filled with books on the Navajo Nation. Many Navajo writers and artists have documented their lives and communities with great honesty and insight. The Navajo Nation produces a large volume of written materials, which it makes available online at navajo.org. I will say here that anyone who wants to understand the Navajo Nation and only reads my book is a very sloppy researcher indeed. (And no, you can't just pick up a Tony Hillerman novel to get out from under that charge.)

F. METHODS OF DATA COLLECTION

This analysis draws on records about tribal government activities generated by tribal officials, tribal governments, state and local governments, and the federal government. In the process of this research, I conducted many off-the-record interviews with tribal officials. The evidence that I present to make my case, however, is all from written materials. When the research began, I was astonished by the volume of detailed tribal government documents that I encountered. As far as I have found, these records have been entirely untouched by social science researchers. I decided to focus much of my attention on illuminating these rich troves of tribal written materials, which have allowed me chart in great detail many specific events and practices. All these documents are public records, although many are rarely accessed and have accumulated a notable layer of dust.

A number of tribes—in varying economic and government contexts—have produced newsletters and newspapers that have been retained in tribes' own archives or in other libraries. A number of tribal governments—again, in varying economic and government circumstances—retain written tribal council minutes and other documents related to council proceedings. Like bureaucrats everywhere, tribal officials write memos and reports. Not all tribes chose to make these records publicly available, but many do. Furthermore, many tribes belong to intertribal organizations that produce comparable volumes of documentation. Finally, I was very fortunate to access the papers of former Navajo Nation president Peterson Zah, which are housed in the Labriola National American Indian Data Center at Arizona State University.

Keep in mind that I did not select tribes for this study on the basis of available written records; rather, I selected cases based on government and economic features and then searched for information relevant to those places. I was able to locate written records for the preponderance of these tribes and across the tribal conditions that I examine. These sources may not always be continuously available, as funding for tribal newspapers or for records management programs may falter at times, but I have found tribally generated records covering lengthy periods of time.

Furthermore, tribes have shared with federal agencies a great deal of information on their governmental activities and most of these records become available to researchers after the passage of some time. I also drew on other voluminous federal, state, and local government records and archives to fill in what those sources have to say about their interactions with American Indian tribes. Thus, I can detail the perspectives of the feds, states, and localities. Another particular advantage of state and local records is that they can have fairly uniform formats across place, which facilitates more comparisons of state and local policymaking among all 12 cases.

In short, I turned to a range of diverse sources in order to triangulate among multiple perspectives. I pulled in materials that varied by level and type of government, by the policy areas addressed, by the type of authors, by intended audiences, and by the circumstances of the communities that they covered. In situations where the structure of records differed noticeably over time and from place to place, I concentrated on qualitative analytic approaches that allowed me to more fully account for differing structures.

As a result, I have had the great privilege of hearing in remarkable detail from a host of tribal officials about their needs, opportunities, and agendas at precise moments in time. I have spent a great deal of time with these many voices—some of whom are still at work in public service, some of whom have now retired, and some of whom have passed on. I invite you to hear what they have said.

G. AN INVENTORY OF SOURCES USED

Given the wealth of materials available, I did not access every possible source. Instead, I focused on materials that could provide the widest scope of cases, the best theory testing, and the greatest clarity and comprehensiveness. Note that for most tribes, available records exceed the records that I collected. Of course, for some tribes, records were less extensive than for others. In general, there were more documents among which to choose for tribes with institutionalized governments. Records were the most scant for less institutionalized governments in the Upper Plains.

Some sources capture trends in systematic and comprehensive ways but not necessarily fine-grained detail. For example, a typical tribal newspaper or newsletter ranged from 4 to 16 pages long and was published weekly or monthly. It could not capture all the particulars of government activities. Other sources capture strategies and attitudes at particular moments in remarkable clarity but do not always indicate overall trends. In some of these instances, records could have provided more comprehensive information, but my access to a particular archive or office was limited. In those moments, I had to be very selective about the portions of records to review. The documentation that I discuss in this paper is follows:

1. *The papers of Navajo Nation president Peterson Zah*, who served in office from 1991 to 1994. His papers are extensive; with a thorough review, I extracted content from the 1990s that was most pertinent to Navajo Nation operations, Navajo Nation external relations, and advocacy by intertribal organizations in which the Navajo Nation participated. Among those intertribal organizations, the National Congress of American Indians is most notable.

2. *Reports from the Navajo Nation Divisions of Natural Resources, Public Safety, and Economic Development.* All Navajo Nation divisions provide quarterly reports to the Navajo Nation Council. Typically, a department's report is 4 to 15 pages long. This type of reporting was launched in the early 1990s. I collected reports from 1992 to 2000. I selected these agencies because, throughout this book, I focused on these three policy areas when records were extensive and non-indexed. For each division, there are some reports that have been misplaced over time, particularly for the early years. Although the reports were submitted to the Navajo Nation Council as a single bound volume, many of the reports have been retained in their initial form, as separate documents for each agency. Therefore, it is unusual for reports to be missing for all three agencies for a given date.

3. *Federal grant records from Tribes A and C:* two Southwest tribes with limited economic development. Tribe A has a more institutionalized government; Tribe C's government is less institutionalized. I was able to access the two tribes' reports to federal funders from the mid and late 1980s. The typical report is 2 to 4 pages long. The files contain applications for funding, updates from police chiefs about program operations, and related tribal council resolutions. In all, I analyze 23 reports.

4. *The newspaper of Tribe E:* a Pacific Northwest tribe with relatively limited economic development but a widely respected government. I was able to access the newspaper from 1998 to 2001.

5. *The newspaper of Tribe F:* a Pacific Northwest tribe with a developed economy and a less institutionalized government. I accessed the newsletter from 1990 to 2000. Since this trove of newspapers was extensive and

non-indexed, I selected samples among the years for my analysis. Subsequent chapters detail the samples drawn for a given part of the investigation.

6. *Tribal council minutes for Tribe F.* I accessed minutes from the mid-1980s up into the early 2000s. Since the minutes were extensive and non-indexed, I selected samples among the years for my analysis. Subsequent chapters detail the samples drawn for a given part of the investigation.

7. *The newsletter of Tribe G:* a less institutionalized, less developed Pacific Northwest tribe. I accessed the newsletter from the mid-1980s to the mid-1990s. Since this trove of newsletters was extensive and non-indexed, I selected samples among the years for my analysis. Subsequent chapters detail the samples drawn for a given part of the investigation.

8. *The newspaper from Tribe H:* an Upper Plains tribe with both government institutionalization and economic development. I reviewed issues from 1990. While the paper has been retained over a long time span, the issues themselves are detailed but non-indexed, and the logistics of identifying and extracting any given issue are cumbersome.

9. *Tribal council minutes Tribe J:* an Upper Plains tribe with government institutionalization but with limited economic development. I reviewed segments of the minutes from 1990 to 2000. While minutes have been retained over a long time span, they are detailed but non-indexed. Also, it was not possible to spend a very long time in the records repository.

I examined specific records of two intertribal organizations. Of course, as table 2.2 showed, there are lots of intertribal organizations; many have produced newsletters and publicly available reports over time. I selected this pair of organizations for three reasons. First, they track to different regions in the sample: one serves a consortium of Northwest tribes; the other includes strong representation among a variety of Southwest tribes. Also, one of the organizations focuses on natural resources policy; the other focuses on public safety. The policy areas were appealing because, throughout my analysis, where available records were vast and unorganized, I concentrated on finding documentation in the policy areas of natural resources, public safety, or economic development. Third, each organization involves active participants from tribes across a range of economies and governments.

10. *Northwest Indian Fisheries Commission News.* The Commission represents 20 tribes in Western Washington.[9] The organization serves as a key pathway for advocacyforNorthwesttribesacrossarangeofgovernmentinstitutionalization

and economic development. I accessed the newsletter from 1990 to 2000. The newsletter was produced quarterly; a typical issue was 12 pages.

11. *Documentation from the Indian Country Law Enforcement Section in the International Association of Chiefs of Police (IACP).* The IACP is perhaps the preeminent organization of police chiefs in the United States. The Indian Country Law Enforcement Section has included strong representation from a variety of Southwest tribes, whose police chiefs have played key leadership roles in the Section. I reviewed materials from a major conference that the IACP organized in 2001 on Indian Country policing: specifically, the conference's final report and newsletter articles that offered further detail on the conferees' concerns and objectives.[10]

Another category of records was generated by other governments. Mainly, I used these sources to document federal, state, and local officials' responses to tribal advocacy. Sometimes, these records did include materials that were authored by tribal officials and then transmitted to the agency in question.

12. *Bureau of Indian Affairs archives from the Department of Interior's American Indian Records Repository (AIRR).* The AIRR contains the archived records of the Bureau of Indian Affairs. These materials offer an insightful profile of BIA deliberations. Access to the AIRR was particularly limited when I visited. A Department of Interior attorney had to review every document that I requested before I could see it. None of the documents that I requested failed to make it through the review, but of course it resulted in a slow and cumbersome process. Also, my ability to make photocopies was restricted. I targeted files that seemed to offer the most detail on responses to tribes' advocacy from the regions in the sample and the policy areas of greatest interest.

13. *The Environmental Protection Agency's documentation of its American Indian programs.* The EPA offers a useful contrast to BIA's patterns of interactions with tribal governments. The EPA has developed programs on Indian reservations since the 1980s but without the same legacy as BIA programs. Of course, this is in part due to the fact that the EPA has only existed for a few decades now. The EPA produces regular reports on its activities on Indian lands; I accessed five reports from the early 1990s.

14. *Bureau of Indian Affairs annual appropriations hearing.* Starting in 1992, when the Bureau of Indian Affairs provided testimony for federal annual appropriations hearings, it attached a report that detailed amounts and types of funding to each tribal government. These reports allow for detailed profiles of federal support for any given tribe.

15. *County Council minutes* and attachments for the 12 counties within which the 12 tribes in the sample are located, for a review of tribal-county relations. I accessed minutes from 1990 to 2000. My review focused on the policy areas of natural resources, public safety, economic development, and elections and office-holding. Some minutes contain transcripts of discussion and/or a large collection of attachments. I supplemented my analysis by occasionally reviewing a few local newspaper articles in order to flesh out examples.

16. *Legislative records from eight states*, which allowed a review of tribal-state relations. I reviewed proceedings from 1990 to 2000. The states are from the Southwest, Northwest, and Upper Plains.

None of these sources tell a complete story on its own. In combination, however, they are quite powerful. Please note that when I quote these written records, I have corrected any typographical or grammatical errors.

III. Summing Up

The historical record offers key insights into the nature of American Indian tribal government, the political obstacles that tribal leaders have faced, and the strategies that tribal advocates have used over time. Tribal leaders have turned to some enduring approaches to protect their nations' status in the face of varying assaults on their communities. Specifically, since the late 19th century, tribal leaders have pushed over the long term for incremental, low-profile adjustments in the terms of their relationships with federal powerbrokers.

In the analysis that follows, I examine such approaches in the present day. I access a range of sources—sources that span region, types of economic development and government institutionalization, audiences, and authors. I consider tribes' own voices and the responses from other governments, producing a thorough evaluation of tribes' contemporary political strategies and the consequences that they bring.

3   Quiet, Yet Ever-Constant Advocacy

HOW AMERICAN INDIAN TRIBAL GOVERNMENTS HAVE CONFRONTED AND CHANGED FEDERAL INDIAN POLICY

I. Introduction

A. RECAP OF THE ARGUMENT

This chapter examines how American Indian tribal governments win particular kinds of external assistance—via institutional niches in the federal government— that provide small but needed subsidies for the cultivation of expertise about policy and politics. Groups that typically face daunting odds in politics can some- times find institutional niches, which help with developing technical policy exper- tise, providing opportunities to get to know the external environment, and offering exposure to a variety of strategies and organizational forms. Groups can maintain and improve a niche's support by seeking modest yet serial adjustments in their access to officials, in overall policy frameworks, and in specific procedures. My argument identifies political tools that are often underappreciated or simply unrecognized.[1]

Niches can emerge and thrive in highly variegated institutional environments, such as the American federal system and the many separations of powers it con- tains. In such a context, the costs to any actor of monitoring all spaces would be extraordinary, so nuanced decision-making is more apt to fall to particular, sheltered nodes. [2] Tribes and other similarly situated actors are able to capitalize on these arenas of discretion.

In essence, tribes employed two techniques to maximize modest federal support: they focused on particular forms of assistance and they were attentive to the policy environment shaping that assistance. To restate the definition provided in chapter 1: niches brought multiple benefits. With the development of technical policy expertise, tribes could accumulate detailed knowledge of specific problems and policies, and of tools of evaluation and remediation. With opportunities to get to know the external environments, tribes gained skills at building networks, understanding outside interests, and developing demonstration or pilot projects that could be persuasive to potential outside supporters. With exposure to strategies and organizational forms, tribes encountered new organizational repertoires. Consequently, they accessed new tools of program management, planning, and of envisioning frameworks. Furthermore, I observe tribal advocates that focused on obtaining outside assistance that covered fixed (lump-sum) needs for expert organizations. With this approach, tribes could build expertise that could endure even if aid faltered in the future. This approach covered a broad range of critical start-up costs.

Second, tribal leaders cultivated niches in ways that buttressed outside help. Through long-term relations with agencies and legislators, tribes gained access to learn about political obstacles and opportunities and to advocate for program adaptations. Also, tribes could work to slowly adjust frameworks that would more fully acknowledge tribes' importance and endorse collaboration and consultation. And as tribes gradually altered federal procedures, more favorable, flexible, simple, and stable standard operating procedures could emerge. Furthermore, the programs that tribes accessed did not attract much attention beyond the bureaucrats who directly administered them and a small circle of legislators who oversaw them. As a result, changes in these programs needed consent from only a small number of actors and escaped the view of many others.

B. ORGANIZATION OF ANALYSIS

The discussion of the findings is split into two sections. Section II explores in detail the first part of tribes' strategy; specifically, the sorts of federal assistance that tribal officials tended to seek: lump-sum assistance with capacity building. Afterward, section III details the second part of this strategy: the ways that tribes interacted with federal bureaucrats and legislators to achieve policy revisions. Of course, these strategies were interconnected, and some officials talked about both at once and interwove their thinking about both.

My analysis is grounded in sources of information that capture a wide range of tribal circumstances, contexts, and audiences. I draw on records from a great range of tribes, tribal organizations, and federal officials. The features of the data are described in detail in chapter 2.

This chapter employs a multilayered approach. Some of my analysis tallies categories of tribes' actions, when records were well suited to that approach. With this coding, I capture overall patterns and frequency of behaviors, without necessarily spelling out microfoundations and mechanisms. Some of my analysis presents case studies with rich detail on motives, logic, internal calculations, and importance.[3] The case studies do not necessarily capture the frequency of behaviors. The combination of coding and case studies allows me to consider a wide range of sources, despite varying formats. Even more importantly, the combination allows me to analyze tribal-federal relations on two levels: broad processes and the dimensions within those processes.

Hypothesis tests begin by considering individual tribes from my sample. First, there is the example of the Navajo Nation, and in particular the papers of Navajo Nation president Peterson Zah from the 1990s. In many ways, the Navajo Nation is one of the tribes that was best positioned to influence federal policy, given its significant government institutionalization and economic development.

The next tasks are to test whether strategies seen with the Navajo Nation carry across varying tribal endowments and audiences. A second test considers whether patterns carry to tribes in the Southwest that face limitations, especially in their economies. In particular, I compare Tribes A and C—specifically, their federal grant applications. Both Tribes A and C faced limitations in their economic development and shared many features in common, but Tribe A had notably more government institutionalization.

A third test evaluates whether comparable patterns can be found in the Northwest and when tribes face varying governments and economies. Specifically, I explore the tribal newsletters of Tribes E, F, and G, and the tribal council minutes of Tribe F. Tribe E had less economic development but an institutionalized government; Tribe F had more economic development but a less institutionalized government; Tribe G had neither advantage.[4]

The fourth test evaluated more variation by region—whether patterns carried into the Upper Plains—and varying limitation on economies. Specifically, I compared the tribal newsletter of Tribe H, which had government institutionalization and economic development, and the tribal council minutes of Tribe J, with government institutionalization but less economic development.[5] In sum, with this series of tests, I incorporate variation across three regions, across types of economies and governments, and across four formats of information: personal papers, direct communication with federal officials, tribal newspapers, and tribal council records.

But how to know the results aren't unique to the tribes in my sample? To rule out this possibility, the tests extend to intertribal organizations and to federal officials. Intertribal organizations are important for a couple of reasons. A good portion of tribal governments' advocacy occurs through intertribal organizations. Also, intertribal organizations are sources of diffusion among tribes. If intertribal organizations employ the approaches that I describe, it helps explain why many individual tribes use parallel tactics.

Therefore, a fifth test examines the behavior of the National Congress of American Indians (NCAI), the preeminent organization of American Indian tribal governments. Specifically, I draw on records from the Zah papers and federal documents on NCAI's advocacy. Of course, I want to be sure the NCAI's unique status doesn't result in unique tactics. To this end, I consider other intertribal organizations that differ by region, policy domain, and records format. A sixth test looks to the Northwest Indian Fisheries Commission (NWIFC) and its newsletter. A seventh test evaluates advocacy by the Indian Country Law Enforcement Section within the International Association of Chiefs of Police, which includes strong representation from Southwest tribes.

The final domain is federal records. I can verify the effects of tribes' advocacy in federal officials' documentation. An eighth test examines the papers of Bureau of Indian Affairs (BIA) officials. A ninth test moves to other agencies and policy arenas; it evaluates reports and deliberations from within the Environmental Protection Agency's and the Department of Justice's Indian programs.

In sum, my analysis spans regions, tribal traits, authors, and audiences. I can conduct rigorous tests of whether certain political strategies cross domains. The formats of records do not make it possible to use all nine tests for evaluating both two components of my argument: the nature of the assistance that tribes sought and the strategies they used to stabilize that assistance. Yet for each component, I can employ the preponderance of the tests and offer extensive evaluation of the pervasiveness of behaviors.

C. SPECIFICS OF THE ANALYSIS

Where I tally the frequency of tribes' behaviors, there are several features worth noting. First, keep in mind that the level of detail in source materials varies from tribe to tribe. As a result, it is inappropriate to compare the raw number of initiatives from one tribe to another. Instead, I compare relative frequencies: out of a given number of initiatives, what was the relative importance of various types?

My criteria are as follows. I document the frequency of the three strategies for building independent expert organizations: help with technical policy expertise, the external environment, and strategies and organizational forms. Also, starting in section III, I document the frequency of the three components for nudging federal policy: reshaping access, frameworks, and procedures.

Additional behaviors fall into two sets of categories. The first set encompasses aid that complements independent expert organizations: physical infrastructure, potential self-determination funding, and other lump-sum discrete projects. Physical infrastructure can include buildings, other facilities, and equipment. Some physical infrastructure projects are quite small, but in any case, discrete physical building blocks can bolster independent expert organizations. Next, potential self-determination spending could be used to develop expertise, but tribal officials do not always clearly identify that objective. For example, a grant to run a new tribal program could contribute to skills and experiences that could endure even if federal funding dried up at some point. Probably tribal officials recognize that advantage, but if they don't say so, I can't be sure. Next are other lump-sum, discrete projects. Here, federal aid can expand the accomplishments and experiences of independent tribal organizations without long-term reliance.

The final category includes behaviors that do not appear to build or complement independent expert organizations. Instead, tribes seek federal policies that serve their interests but do not improve their own capacities. Sometimes, tribes seek change in a federal regulation that they dislike or they seek a favorable new federal regulation. These requests or opposition to regulations are distinct from nudging federal policy toward more favorable procedures. In the former case, tribes seek regulatory change with immediate and narrow application to their interests. In contrast, with procedural change, tribes seek changes with wider and less direct impacts: new rules that don't necessarily provide much of big gain right away but with consequences that will play out over time. Lastly, in some cases, tribes seek ongoing federal spending or services, without a mechanism for building their own capacities along the way.

Of course, some initiatives are multipronged. When a proposal included elements from multiple categories, I tallied the proposal in all the relevant categories.

II. Seeking Particular Kinds of Federal Assistance

There are two puzzles in institutional niches. Here, I address the first: how can modest assistance with building expert organizations accumulate into anything substantial?

A. NAVAJO NATION

The papers of former Navajo Nation president Peterson Zah, from the early 1990s, offered clear and frequent illustrations of the strategies for building independent expert organizations. One striking example was a position paper on initiatives to build a Navajo Department of Education.[6] This document laid out tactics that will appear in multiple contexts.

In this case, Navajo Nation officials highlighted areas where federal aid could help build program capacities within tribal government. The authors showed a remarkable talent to paint broad ambitions while also setting goals for targeted assistance with segmented, specific capacities. The position paper articulated a bold agenda—to build integrated, independent education programs that respected the Navajo Nation's special needs and taught Navajo culture:

> What the Navajo Nation seeks from the government of the United States and the governments of the states is the means of accomplishing the Navajo Nation's goal of Navajo control of Navajo education. These means include authorizing laws and interpretations of existing laws needed to vest a Navajo Department of Education with state education agency-level authority. They also include funding to develop the plan for a Navajo Department of Education and to start up implementation of such a plan. Finally, this effort will require intergovernmental agreements with the states, encouraged by federal priorities, transferring state education agency-level decision making authority to the Navajo Nation and its education department.

A massive federal allocation and redesign for educational initiatives would be warmly welcomed should it arrive—but after the authors articulated broad goals, they turned their attention to 28 particular reforms. The authors were even more focused on using outside support to build skills, gather information, and plan in specific ways: training for teachers and administrators, curriculum development and pilot programs such as a teen pregnancy program and intergenerational learning services tailored to the Navajo Nation. The tribe wanted "develop a model of Head Start services and classroom delivery" for which federal officials would "support Navajo specific (and tribally specific) modifications to the basic program." The Navajo Nation also sought to implement needs assessment for special education and develop a master plan for which "IHS should be a diagnostic and therapeutic resource." In all, 18 of the 28 items focused on targeted support for program design and strategy for implementation; 4 of the items focused on training and technical assistance.

The authors were acutely aware of the advantages that high-level changes could offer. Later in the memo, the authors remarked that if larger-scale reforms were won:

> [T]he piecemeal efforts Indian people are now engaged upon to amend this law, change that regulation, get clarification of one program and revision of another would be replaced by a comprehensive review of the real world working of the relationship between Indian nations and the United States.

But the authors held out only slim hope for sweeping change, and they suggested pursuing such an approach only if stymied in smaller arenas. The Navajo analysts focused on winning lump-sum aid for capacity-building that could be delivered through the adaptation of existing programs.

Of course, as described in chapter 2, the Navajo Nation has far more resources than many other tribes—in the form of government institutionalization and economic development—to pursue these approaches. How do we know that these tactics aren't specific to an unusual set of resources? I address this question by examining the behavior of tribes in very differing circumstances. By doing so, I find a great variety of tribes engaging in strikingly similar strategies.

B. EVIDENCE FROM SOUTHWEST TRIBES

I begin by evaluating two other Southwest tribes with less economic development and varying government institutionalization. These two tribes shared much in common, including a shared cultural heritage. Yet there were differences between the places that mattered. Tribe C had a less developed economy and a less institutionalized government; Tribe A had more specialized personnel and was seen as a source of regional leadership.

BIA records of tribal grant requests showed in great detail how the tribes strove to structure federal assistance. The records document the two tribes' efforts to win BIA funding through its Self-Determination grants in the late 1980s. The Self-Determination program was a substantial BIA function. All the same, funding under the program fluctuated. Did tribes manage to tailor their proposals to the program's constraints, and if so, how exactly?

The requests from Tribe A focused nearly exclusively on concrete tasks, not on support for continuing activities, as table 3.1 shows. Half of their requests pursued tools for building expert organizations. In particular, the tribal government was

TABLE 3.1

Types of Federal Aid Sought by Tribe A

	Percent of aid sought
Building independent expert organizations	52%
Getting to know external environment	12%
Strategies and organizational forms	28%
Technical assistance or training	12%
Complement to independent expert organizations	44%
Physical infrastructure	32%
Potential self-determination spending	12%
Lump sum, discrete project	0%
Other	4%
Opposition to a federal regulation	0%
Request for new federal regulation	0%
Ongoing funding or services	4%
Number of times aid was sought	25

Source: Federal grant applications from late 1980s.
Percentages may not add to 100% because of rounding.

interested in building independent expert organizations; most notably, envisioning and planning organizational forms that could deliver on their goals. For example, a series of grant applications each targeted particular steps to develop new economic development plans:

- Reviewing old economic development plans and their performance
- Researching and drafting a new economic development plan
- Evaluating funding alternatives for desired projects

Furthermore, Tribe A sought more than dollars in building these capacities: one application noted the community's desire for BIA technical assistance in getting an employment assistance program underway.

Tribal officials also requested aid with physical infrastructure, such as building additional fire hydrants and building an office complex for tribal programs. There were a few realms where this tribe was willing to run the risks of funding continuing needs with unstable dollars. In FY87, it requested funds to hire a tribal administrator and to provide that person with a small staff. The grant application noted that this new administrator would explore other sources to fund his position over the longer term, but this discussion is brief and vague. This instance, although focused on capacity-building tasks, was a notable departure from the overall pattern of seeking lump-sum aid.

Tribe C focused preponderantly on lump-sum capacity-building as well, as table 3.2 shows. Three quarters of their proposals centered on tools for building expert organizations. A 1987 grant application highlighted some overarching needs:

> Acquire necessary management skills and experience in dealing with all levels of government (federal, state, local, etc.)....
>
> Become knowledgeable in how the bureaucratic system and political process work at the federal and state level and how changes in the administration and policies affect [Tribe C].

The tribe wanted support for management, planning, and needs assessment in some specific areas, such as aid with researching substance abuse on the reservation and writing a program plan. Along comparable lines, the tribe pursued, over the course of three years, a series of steps to train staff on new computer

TABLE 3.2

Types of Federal Aid Sought by Tribe C

	Percent of aid sought
Building independent expert organizations	76%
Getting to know external environment	10%
Strategies and organizational forms	38%
Technical assistance or training	29%
Complement to independent expert organizations	14%
Physical infrastructure	10%
Potential self-determination spending	5%
Lump sum, discrete project	0%
Other	10%
Opposition to a federal regulation	0%
Request for new federal regulation	0%
Ongoing funding or services	10%
Number of times aid was sought	21

Source: Federal grant applications from late 1980s.
Percentages may not add to 100% because of rounding.

software. The proposal noted that the tribe had acquired already basic computer equipment and training with Administration for Native Americans (ANA) and Housing and Urban Development (HUD) grants; in subsequent phases it wanted to upgrade the system and the related human capital.

Both Tribes A and C valued federal aid with skills and structures. Furthermore, both seemed to understand that lump-sum assistance with program infrastructure would better serve their interests. Support for research on economic development, for writing a procurement policy, and for computer training were hardly impressive federal benefits. They were notable, however, for the groundwork that they and many other efforts could help lay.

C. EVIDENCE FROM THE PACIFIC NORTHWEST

Do these patterns extend beyond the Southwest? I find that they do. The trends observed in the Southwest showed up in the tribal newsletters and tribal council minutes of several tribes in the Pacific Northwest. Specifically, I looked to the records of three native nations. Tribe E had limited economic development but impressive government capacities; for this tribe, I turned to the tribal newsletter and tribal council minutes from 1998 through 2001. Tribe F began the 1990s with a developed economy and a less institutionalized government that experienced growth over the course of the decade. For this case, I referred to Tribe F's council minutes and tribal newsletter from 1990 through 2000. The third case was Tribe G, with a less developed economy and a less institutionalized government; I made use of its tribal newsletter from 1985 to 1995. The three governments operated within very different circumstances, but the parallel strategies were striking.

1. Tribe E: An Impressive Government

Tribe E—with limited economic development but impressive government capacities—focused on lump-sum projects that fit into continuing goals of capacity-building. 48% of initiatives sought support for independent expert organizations, as table 3.3 shows. Perhaps the most significant effort in this time frame was gaining more control over federal programs on the reservation, thus building the tribe's experience with program management and delivery. Of the ten initiatives of this type, the records document five cases where Tribe E was in the process of contracting out an existing federal program. In another three cases, Tribe E was striving to adjust features of the existing contracting relationship. On two more occasions, tribal leaders were pushing for some sort of shared administration of a program. These changes in control were designed to endure over time, but staff stressed the tangible background

TABLE 3.3

Types of Federal Aid Sought by Tribe E

	Percent of aid sought
Building independent expert organizations	48%
Getting to know external environment	11%
Strategies and organizational forms	22%
Technical assistance or training	15%
Complement to independent expert organizations	39%
Physical infrastructure	30%
Potential self-determination spending	7%
Lump sum, discrete project	2%
Other	13%
Opposition to a federal regulation	0%
Request for new federal regulation	2%
Ongoing funding or services	11%
Number of times aid was sought per year	11.5

Source: Tribal newspaper over the course of four years.
Percentages may not add to 100% because of rounding.

that they were gaining along the way in program development and implementation. In other words, these federal transfers of funds offered opportunities to build capacity and experience, which could persist even if federal dollars faltered.

Some of the most detailed portions of the records illustrate the capacity-building process. For instance, reports on Tribe E's housing programs sketched the concrete, distinct steps in program development. The tribe's housing authority offered the following assessment at the end of its first year of operations: "The first year has been spent navigating the waters: trying to define what can be done with what, what should be, and what could be." The housing authority noted that it would be important to refine policies and procedures after a year of field-testing.

In another example, work on landfills was multistage and combined technical assistance, contact with the outside environment, and familiarity with new organizational strategies. By the end, tribal staff had built important new capacities. Initial efforts included EPA technical assistance for environmental impact assessment of an existing landfill and possible remediation. Subsequent evaluation of the landfill occurred in concert with EPA, BIA, and the state government. A tribal official described the process:

We began by putting together a landfill team here at the tribe. We then took a look at who our advisors were in this process. We were unhappy with what we found and set about to correct things. We identified money to hire consultants and attorneys specializing in these matters to help us become better informed and to more fully examine our options. At this point we met with state and county officials to inform them of our immediate intentions. We told them they would simply have to wait on a number of issues until the Tribe had a reasonable opportunity to become more informed and could then establish a framework for decision making.

It did not take too long for this to occur. A lot of information came to us and a lot of things quickly became clearer to the Council. We are now operating with better understanding of the problems we face. In the coming years we will now be able to make informed responsible decisions for the welfare of our Tribe.

Here, Tribe E became a genuine player in regional planning because of the independent expert organization that it built.

To be sure, there were some moments that fell outside of prevailing tendencies. There were some cases where tribal leaders sought to generate federal funding for ongoing tribal initiatives, rather than focusing on lump-sum assistance. In theory, such initiatives could be structured in ways to build independent skills and experience, but there was no indication in the records at hand.

2. Tribe F: Economic Development and Limited Institutionalization

Next, I examine two Northwest tribes with less impressive government institutionalization. Did the patterns persist? They did.

Tribe F—with a strong economic base but a less institutionalized government—was focusing on building up its government and reservation. Compared to other places, it gave relatively greater emphasis to ongoing federal support that wouldn't build or complement independent expert organizations; ongoing aid was a third of the tribe's interactions, as table 3.4 shows. All the same, the tribal officials turned serious attention toward assistance with policy expertise and management skills. For example, Tribe F pursued funding for planning native language programs and child health education programs.

There were a variety of areas where Tribe F pursued BIA technical assistance. Over the course of one year in the mid 1990s, the tribe had meetings with the BIA and with an outside accountant, to get technical assistance on improving financial procedures and ultimately to build internal skills in this area. With this

TABLE 3.4

Types of Federal Aid Sought by Tribe F

	Percent of aid sought
Building independent expert organizations	33%
Getting to know external environment	8%
Strategies and organizational forms	13%
Technical assistance or training	13%
Complement to independent expert organizations	31%
Physical infrastructure	18%
Potential self-determination spending	8%
Lump sum, discrete project	6%
Other	34%
Opposition to a federal regulation	15%
Request for new federal regulation	6%
Ongoing funding or services	14%
Number of times aid was sought per year	48

Source: Tribal newspaper. One year in early 1990s; one year in late 1990s.
Percentages may not add to 100% because of rounding.

support the tribe designed and implemented a system for monitoring long-distance phone calls. Tribe F also sought support for the physical infrastructure needed to support independent expert organizations: in one instance, tribal leaders tapped BIA funding in order to acquire a variety of office equipment for the tribal government.

3. Tribe G: A Constrained Tribe

Tribe G—with limited economic development and government institutionaliza-tion—was overwhelmingly interested in improving its expertise, like many other governments that we have seen so far. Table 3.5 shows that support for building independent expert organizations was 46% of the aid that the tribe pursued.

Tribe G sought a number of federal grants and training to develop better management practices, such as to design new procedures for financial management, program evaluation, procurement, property management, recordkeeping, per-sonnel rules, accounting, and auditing. Other forms of technical assistance in specific program areas included police officer training and evaluations of the health system.

TABLE 3.5

Types of Federal Aid Sought by Tribe G

	Percent of aid sought
Building independent expert organizations	46%
Getting to know external environment	15%
Strategies and organizational forms	19%
Technical assistance or training	12%
Complement to independent expert organizations	42%
Physical infrastructure	25%
Potential self-determination spending	6%
Lump sum, discrete project	10%
Other	12%
Opposition to a federal regulation	4%
Request for new federal regulation	3%
Ongoing funding or services	4%
Number of times aid was sought per year	33.5

Source: Tribal newsletter. One year in early 1990s; one year in mid-1990s.
Percentages may not add to 100% because of rounding.

Tribe G also sought aid with improvements in the physical plant of certain programs, which again followed the tendency of seeking a series of lump-sum pieces of assistance. These included a series of improvements to water and irrigation systems, divvied up into some components as small as asking for two outside water faucets, in one instance, and equipment for public safety programs (such as car seats to distribute on one occasion and a patrol car at another time.)

In short, all three Northwest native nations used federal aid for capacity-building, with aid tailored to their circumstances at a given time. They saw benefits from knowledge of technical issues, external environments, and organizational strategies. Tribes acquired many small pieces for solving the bigger of puzzle of finding their own voice and priorities.

D. CAPACITY-BUILDING IN THE UPPER PLAINS

The patterns described thus far extended into the Upper Plains as well and across varying economic development in the region, offering further evidence of the wide spread of the same approaches. I examined two tribes in the Upper Plains: Tribe H, with both government institutionalization and economic development, and Tribe J, with the former but not the latter. Both sought help with program infrastructure, including support for designing administrative and bureaucratic procedures. Tables 3.6 and 3.7 show that about half of each tribe's desired aid centered around support for building independent expert organizations.

In one case, a group of Upper Plains tribes worked on a program to support the development of reservation cattle ranching. The tribal council minutes of Tribe J recorded that the BIA had provided technical assistance and supported data analysis for developing a plan of operation, and the tribes' leadership was seeking more assistance as it eyed a next stage of pursuing congressional funding for the demonstration project. The tactic of gradual support appeared to be working: later in the year, one of the U.S. senators from the region reported back about additions to the Farm Bill that would fund new, more expansive technical assistance for the project. The tribes' next goal was federal funding for low-interest loans; correspondence from a member of Congress from the area noted that the member had introduced a bill that would provide such funding. In this instance, the tribes patched together interconnected, multiphase bureaucratic and legislative strategies for program design and development.

TABLE 3.6

Types of Federal Aid Sought by Tribe H

	Percent of aid sought
Building independent expert organizations	51%
Getting to know external environment	22%
Strategies and organizational forms	21%
Technical assistance or training	13%
Complement to independent expert organizations	28%
Physical infrastructure	16%
Potential self-determination spending	4%
Lump sum, discrete project	7%
Other	21%
Opposition to a federal regulation	7%
Request for new federal regulation	5%
Ongoing funding or services	9%
Number of times aid was sought per year	111.7

Source: Tribal newsletter. Ten months in early 1990s.
Percentages may not add to 100% because of rounding.

TABLE 3.7

Types of Federal Aid Sought by Tribe J

	Percent of aid sought
Building independent expert organizations	48%
Getting to know external environment	17%
Strategies and organizational forms	21%
Technical assistance or training	11%
Complement to independent expert organizations	33%
Physical infrastructure	12%
Potential self-determination spending	11%
Lump sum, discrete project	10%
Other	19%
Opposition to a federal regulation	3%
Request for new federal regulation	5%
Ongoing funding or services	10%
Number of times aid was sought per year	77.5

Source: Council minutes. 12 months in early 1990s; 8 months in mid-1990s; 4 months in late 1990s. *Percentages may not add to 100% because of rounding.*

E. EVIDENCE FROM INTERTRIBAL ORGANIZATIONS

A great deal of tribal advocacy happens through coordinated initiatives and intertribal organizations. Are the strategies that I described unique to individual tribal pursuits? I find that they are not.

One powerful example from within the National Congress of American Indians (NCAI) allows us to glimpse these mechanisms at play in coordinated intertribal policy initiatives.[7] As the Department of Defense implemented base closures in the early 1990s, American Indian tribal governments that were adjacent to these bases wanted to be included among local actors eligible to obtain control over those lands. To that end, they pursued federal help with outside interactions and management needs.

A small group of tribal leaders—from the Muckleshoot Indian Tribe, San Manuel Band of Mission Indians, San Carlos Apache Tribe, Shoshone Wind River Tribe, Gila River Indian Community, and Navajo Nation—organized a session on base closures at the annual conference of the National Congress of American Indians (NCAI). The working group circulated a position paper that outlined their strategy. They sought aid for capacity-building and they identified approaches for winning the regulatory change that could make such aid become available:

The most effective method for Tribes to acquire properties is through the "excess" federal screening process. However, given the expeditious manner President Clinton proposes to transfer properties to local communities, it is highly doubtful that a federal agency, particularly BIA, can meet the President's 30-day screening process. Consequently, it is imperative that a strategy be developed by which a Tribe can streamline current BIA Area and Agency office responsibilities for the preparation of initial property transfer documents and which would allow for the Tribes to meet directly with the BIA Central Realty and Property office.

Whether the Tribes elect to seek property under the "excess" or the "surplus" procedure, the Department of Defense needs to be fully supportive of Tribes' efforts by: 1) providing Office of Economic Adjustment (OEA) planning grants specifically for Tribes who have an interest in property and were not included in the local reuse planning efforts; 2) providing assistance to the Tribes in processing the necessary documents needed for real and personal property transfers as well as acquiring transition and community assistance funds identified in the President's Five Point Plan; and 3) assisting Tribes in educating the local governments of the Tribe's rights to actively participate in the reuse planning and base disposal process, including property acquisition.

These tribes identified small adjustments in federal aid that could make sizeable differences. Their agenda was to win specific, one-time improvements in specific subject area knowledge, in outside relations, and in understanding relevant and effective planning approaches.

This approach carried over to intertribal initiatives beyond the NCAI. We see another example of these patterns of seeking specific, lump-sum assistance with tribal capacities in the experiences of the Indian Country Law Enforcement Section of the International Association of Chiefs of Police (IACP). The Indian Country Law Enforcement Section brings together tribal police chiefs and representatives of federal law enforcement agencies operating on and near Indian lands (Reina 2002).

The Section persuaded the IACP to focus its 2001 annual policy summit on Indian Country, bringing together policymakers and IACP members. This was a major event and clearly a major accomplishment by one section within a large organization which, as of 2010, had 18 sections representing over 20,000 member law enforcement professionals.[8] At the end of the summit, a series of proposed changes were identified, most of which could be implemented or facilitated by federal actors:

a. 9 steps to streamline jurisdiction in Indian Country, both through changes to law and also on-the-ground strategies: "Tribal, federal, state and local law enforcement agencies should pursue cross-jurisdictional cooperation whenever and however it is possible."

b. 21 specific policy reforms to improve resources for Indian Country police, courts, and social services; resources that translate into "manpower, training, facilities, equipment, program development, research and evaluation, and community outreach."

c. 8 particular steps to improve coordination between law enforcement agencies.

d. 8 ways to better support crime victims, including information-sharing among agencies, training for victim support providers, and a "review and potential adjustment" of existing federal funding programs.

e. 4 policy changes to improve crime prevention, based on "strategic, problem-solving, community-oriented policing and prevention approaches." (IACP 2001)

Note that these concrete steps would not necessarily require continuing or sweeping federal action. Considering what a unique and high-profile moment this policy summit offered, its focus on modest and rather technical policy changes was striking. Broad goals are broken down into 52 targeted proposals, most of which could be addressed in rather modest initiatives—but they all helped tribal police departments improve their problem-solving capacities, their relations with other law enforcement agencies, and their access to information.

F. THE FEDS' PERSPECTIVE

Tribes' own records, across a dizzying array of circumstances, show a consistent pattern of seeking federal aid for building independent expert tribal organizations. But do federal officials acknowledge this pattern, especially when their comments are unlikely to be seen by tribal officials? I find that these pervasive efforts to build independent program infrastructure and skills were also captured in the words of federal officials.

In one case in the mid-1990s, the BIA began drafting a report on the restructuring of its area offices and it compiled status updates from various area offices. The plans from BIA's area offices revealed the offices' understanding of tribes' vision for how BIA restructuring could improve tribal capacity building. The Albuquerque Area Office reported, and did not resist, tribal governments' proposal to convert the office into a Regional Technical Services Center and devolving the area office's functions to sub-offices that were smaller, decentralized, and in closer proximity to the reservations themselves. The Eastern Area Office reported, likewise without any objection, that tribal governments in the region wanted to maintain the basic existing area office structure but to increase resources "to better provide the technical assistance required by the Tribes."[9] In short, BIA officials reported back that, at least in some places, they were hearing tribes' agenda for supporting independent expert organizations.

The responses were uneven: not all the area offices reported back, and the Aberdeen and Billings Area Offices (housed in South Dakota and Montana, respectively) reported that they had not so far undertaken significant tribal consultation on planning. Billings noted:

> The Area Director submitted a restructuring plan for the Area Office, but this plan does not necessarily reflect what the Tribes want as there was no consultation with or participation by the Tribes. The Area Director's plan is directed toward meeting NPR [National Performance Review] guidelines to reduce middle-management layers and to increase the supervisory rates.

This exception is notable. It shows that the patterns I describe were not absolute. It also offers some reassurance that the records here were not tidied up for outside eyes.

Acknowledgments of tribal priorities of building expert organizations were not unique to the BIA. In 1984, the U.S. Environmental Protection Agency (EPA) began a project supporting environmental activities on Indian reservations. The program was slight: $22 million and 155 work-years in FY 1990; $35 million and 168 work-years by FY 1993. But if the quantity of support was slim, the characteristics of the support were telling: again, aid flowed in large part toward tribes' underlying capacities. The FY 1990 and FY 1992 reports included detailed categorization of that support (EPA 1991a, 1992, 1993, 1994). Table 3.8 presents those categories.

The FY 1993 report provided greater detail on EPA's networking role; the specifics were quite striking.[10] One project brought together EPA Region 5, the Federal Emergency Management Agency, and tribal governments in the Mississippi River Basin to coordinate on flood damage. In a parallel fashion, EPA Region 10 coordinated a solid waste network—a "multi-agency technical assistance team"—with involvement from BIA, IHS, and HUD. The network had partnered with the Confederated Tribes of the Umatilla Reservation and was initiating new work with the Spokane and Makah Tribes.

To a large extent, EPA's limited resources attended to construction: not just of buildings, but also of skills, networks, and program design. These features also

TABLE 3.8

EPA Aid to Tribes

	Technical assistance or training	Outreach	Financial assistance	Direct implementation of services
1990				
Dollars (in millions)	$2.6	$0.7	$18.3	$2.8
Work years	33	21	41	44
1992				
Dollars (in millions)	$4.1	$0.5	$24.3	$5.6
Work years	48	10	47	82
Examples	Assistance for developing regulations, scientific assessments, and training.	Facilitating outreach and interactions with other agencies.	Funds for management, planning, program development, facility construction, and ongoing programs.	Scientific assessment or remediation on behalf of a tribe.

Categories set by EPA. Note that some projects fit into more than one category.

showed up in additional documentation of Radon Programs on Indian Lands, which sought to improve tribes' "program strategy and extend program management capability" and "establish an effective program infrastructure."

G. IN SUMMARY

Certain threads ran through the variety of initiatives described in preceding pages, despite their authors' widely varying circumstances. Tribal governments pinpointed forms of federal assistance that could develop the building blocks of programs. Furthermore, they sought to structure this support as series of lump-sum investments. With specific and often subtle forms of help, these tribes worked to expand their tools for assessing tribal needs, navigating opportunities and constraints, and implementing new tribal initiatives. Particular demands varied by circumstances, but the similarities across context were remarkable.

III. Laying the Groundwork in Bureaucratic Relationships

The above analysis described the forms of federal assistance that tribes pursued. Now, I turn to the relationships that tribes built with federal bureaucrats and legislators. Put differently, we've explored what tribes want. Next is the inquiry into how to get it.

Specifically, tribes maintained and even improved institutional niches over time by seeking modest but serial adjustments to access, frameworks, and procedures. Undergirding specific policy requests were relationships built on repeated interactions, through which tribes pushed regularly for changes to make programs better suited to their needs. Many of these changes involved merely adjusting bureaucratic procedure or tweaking legislation. Other changes were of greater—although sometimes seemingly abstract—scope, which might first seem like empty rhetoric or organizational shuffling. Furthermore, interactions were not just with bureaucrats. Tribes also maintained regular contact with a select number of legislators who conducted oversight, usually in policy-specific, low-profile settings. In short, the tribes examined sometimes expanded the scope of conflict slightly, in order to bring sympathetic legislators or statutory change into the mix.

A note about methods of analysis: some of the sources that I use offer enough consistency over time to allow for coding. For these cases, I evaluate the frequency of nudging access, frameworks, and procedures. Do tribes pay attention to overall dynamics that shape how to get what they want? Or do they focus on what they want and leave how to get it as an afterthought? I answer these questions by examining the ratio between the frequencies of these two groups of behavior. If the ratio is closer to zero, tribes' attention to what they want far exceeds attention to how to get it. If the ratio is closer to one, tribes pay comparable to attention to what they want and how to get it. If the ratio exceeds one, tribes' attention to what they want is surpassed by attention to how to get it.

Other sources that establish an unambiguous pattern of repeated, long-term policy revision are richly detailed but do not cover a wide sweep of time or place. My analysis of these sources does not focus on the frequency of these approaches; instead, it shows their importance and their microfoundations. I consider a series of questions for each example: Does it involve a significant policy issue or a trifling one? Is policy reform a long-run process or a one-shot exertion? Are access, adjustments in frameworks, and procedural change, on their own, characterized as important outputs or as trivial steps? I am not claiming that tribes buttress all prospective institutional niches to the exclusion of other approaches. The question is whether tribes devote considerable effort to a set of strategies that at first may appear to yield little.

A. NAVAJO NATION: THINKING SMALL, THINKING LONG TERM

In a prior example, Navajo Nation officials sought to build an independent expert Navajo Department of Education and broke the agenda into specific, discrete steps. The memo detailed what the tribe wanted. It also described the tribe's strategies for how to get those things:

> [T]o first seek support for Navajo education goals through administrative action—either policy directive or administrative rule change. If the executive department or agency is not prepared to use its rule making and interpretive powers in a way supportive of Navajo education goals, however, change in the law would be sought from the Congress.[11]

Furthermore, the Navajo strategy gave careful attention to ways to cultivate aid: persuading federal bureaucracies to adapt existing programs to new aims. Along these lines, the position paper noted:

> In some cases, new laws at the federal or state level will be required to make the federal or state program supportive of and consistent with Navajo educational goals. In other cases, amendment of existing state or federal laws may be required.

In many cases, however, what is needed is an interpretation of existing laws and authorities within federally funded and federal or state administered education programs, which is more supportive of Navajo education goals (and the education goals of other Indian nations), than current interpretations by officials administering the programs. Some new interpretations will require regulatory change. In others, a simple shift in policy emphasis, reflected in policy directives of the executive branch agency involved, would accomplish the necessary change. In many cases, as described below, the strategy of the Navajo Nation is to first seek support for Navajo education goals through administrative action—either policy directive or administrative rule change. If the executive department or agency is not prepared to use its rule making and interpretive powers in a way supportive of Navajo education goals, however, change in the law would be sought from the Congress.

The authors went on to offer examples of the precise administrative obstacles that needed attention: "uncreative and intransigent adherence to existing program structures" on the part of some managers in federal substance abuse programs and

[Federal bureaucrats who] need to be directed by their superiors to favor and support Navajo specific (and tribally specific) modification to the basic program and to cease trying to incorporate Navajo and other tribally operated Head Start Programs into a regional framework.

Overtime, such nudging toward more flexible procedures could accumulate into something bigger.

Other papers of the Navajo Nation president showed comparable tendencies. Arguably, the Navajo Nation was one of the best positioned governments to pursue an aggressive agenda—it had both the finances and the staff to develop and implement a lobbying strategy. Yet the tribe devoted considerable attention to nudging federal programs toward greater accessibility and flexibility.

In 1994, the Navajo president outlined his entire legislative agenda. In this document, the tribe's description of what it wanted and how to get it were particularly intertwined, so it makes sense to consider both steps together. There were, of course, some exceptions, but the Navajo Nation was remarkably concerned both with building expert organizations and nudging practices.[12]

As table 3.9 shows, the Navajo Nation's agenda devoted considerable attention to assistance of the sort described in section II: training, external environments, and strategies and organizational forms. But the table also shows that the Navajo

Nation had more proposals for nudging federal policy than for building independent expert organizations. For example, one item would clarify the roles of various federal agencies in cleaning up abandoned mine lands. In all, the Navajo Nation sought resources for building independent expert organizations in 57% of cases. The ratio between nudging underlying policy and seeking such aid was 1.25; the ratio between nudging underlying policy and seeking any kind of aid was 0.71.

TABLE 3.9

The Navajo Nation's Agenda for Federal Policy Change, 1994

	Percent of aid sought
Building independent expert organizations	57%
Getting to know external environment	19%
Strategies and organizational forms	5%
Technical assistance or training	33%
Complement to independent expert organizations	14%
Physical infrastructure	5%
Potential self-determination spending	10%
Lump sum, discrete project	0%
Other	29%
Opposition to a federal regulation	5%
Request for new federal regulation	10%
Ongoing funding or services	14%
Number of times aid was sought	21

Strategies for Obtaining Aid	
Ratio between nudging underlying policy	
...and building independent expert organizations	1.25
...and all initiatives*	.71
Tactics for nudging underlying policy	Percent of total
Increase access	33%
Alter frameworks	27%
Adjust procedures	40%
Number of attempts at nudging underlying policy	15

Source: Briefing document prepared for members of Congress.
**Includes building independent expert organizations, complements to independent expert organizations, and all other federal aid sought.*
Percentages may not add to 100% because of rounding.

More context came a year later, in an internal memo where Navajo Nation lobbying staff asked for tribal department directors for information on desired "statutory reauthorizations…regulations, policies, directives, new initiatives, and other issues affecting your departments which require congressional attention *outside of any appropriations concerns.*" [Emphasis in original.] Attached was a form where division heads were asked to fill in needs in the categories of "A. Reauthorizations B. Federal Regulations, Policies, Directives C. New Initiatives, Other Issues" In sum, the lobbying staff prioritized favorable changes to existing programs over new programs or big changes in funding.[13]

Another attached document from 1994 showed that strategies of the Navajo Nation were consistent with priorities across the Southwest. It described the legislative agenda of a consortium of the Southwest Tribal Leaders Legislative Forum. Table 3.10 summarized the Forum's priorities. The Forum was not as attentive to nudging federal policy as the Navajo Nation, but they still gave substantive attention to such efforts. For instance, the Forum sought a new framework that would declare tribal governments as the primary authority to regulate underground storage tanks and dumps on reservations. They sought training and technical assistance for tribal courts, which "culminates nearly six years of work by tribal leaders and judges." The tribes' efforts may have looked like dribs and drabs in a single shot, but the potential over-time effort—of accruing access, better procedures, and reconceived frameworks—was wider-ranging.

B. THE UPPER PLAINS

This appreciation carried over to other individual tribes. My precise point here is to offer examples that span a wide range of circumstances. (Readers are free to move on to Section IV as soon as they are persuaded on this point.) The onslaught of examples demonstrates that the motif repeats often and cannot be ignored.

Tribe H was more likely to give attention to nudging policy than to obtaining specific resources for building independent expert organizations, as table 3.11 shows. In one instance, the newspaper described how the tribal government had worked with federal legislators to adjust program procedures that would ease and expand the reporting of child abuse.

Tribe J was also strongly inclined to nudge federal policy. Table 3.12 demonstrates that Tribe J worked on nudging federal policy at the same frequency as it pursued aid with building independent expert organization. In 1990, a staffer from BIA's alcohol and substance abuse program met with Tribe J's council and provided a remarkable example of the insights that access could deliver. The program staffer

TABLE 3.10

Southwest Tribal Leader Legislative Forum's Agenda for Federal Policy Change, 1994

	Percent of aid sought
Building independent expert organizations	73%
Getting to know external environment	9%
Strategies and organizational forms	9%
Technical assistance or training	55%
Complement to independent expert organizations	0%
Physical infrastructure	0%
Potential self-determination spending	0%
Lump sum, discrete project	0%
Other	27%
Opposition to a federal regulation	0%
Request for new federal regulation	0%
Ongoing funding or services	27%
Number of times aid was sought	11

Strategies for Obtaining Aid

Ratio between nudging underlying policy	
... and building independent expert organizations	.75
... and all initiatives*	.55
Tactics for nudging underlying policy	Percent of total
Increase access	17%
Alter frameworks	33%
Adjust procedures	50%
Number of attempts at nudging underlying policy	6

Source: Briefing document prepared for members of Congress.
*Includes building independent expert organizations, complements to independent expert organizations, and all other federal aid sought.
Percentages may not add to 100% because of rounding.

discussed in a frank and familiar way the most effective tactics to write grants and to structure programs so that they had a greater chance of funding.

There was an exchange over how to match the federal program's flexibility to Tribe J's existing policy priorities. One council member asked about this particular program's grants "if the money is earmarked just for juveniles." The staffer replied

TABLE 3.11

Tribe H's Strategies for Obtaining Federal Aid

Ratio between nudging underlying policy	
...and building independent expert organizations	1.38
...and all initiatives*	.69
Tactics for nudging underlying policy	Percent of total
Increase access	55%
Alter frameworks	19%
Adjust procedures	26%
Number of attempts at nudging underlying policy per year	111.6

Source: Tribal newsletter. 10 months in early 1990s.
Includes building independent expert organizations, complements to independent expert organizations, and all other federal aid sought.
Percentages may not add to 100% because of rounding.

TABLE 3.12

Tribe J's Strategies for Obtaining Federal Aid

Ratio between nudging underlying policy	
...and building independent expert organizations	.95
...and all initiatives*	.46
Tactics for nudging underlying policy	Percent of total
Increase access	38%
Alter frameworks	28%
Adjust procedures	34%
Number of attempts at nudging underlying policy per year	35.5

Source: Council minutes. 12 months in early 1990s; 8 months in mid-1990s; 4 months in late 1990s.
Includes building independent expert organizations, complements to independent expert organizations, and all other federal aid sought.
Percentages may not add to 100% because of rounding.

yes; he also noted "but if they wanted to have an adult training program... it could be used to help families to stop the cycle of alcoholism."

The staffer also offered insights into how to navigate other federal programs. The tribe had negotiated an agreement where the Indian Health Service (IHS) would pay for the construction of a new substance abuse facility on the reservation. The BIA representative warned the tribal council to be careful that

IHS wouldn't take this funding out of other expenditures it might otherwise have, and he cautioned the tribe to get IHS's commitment in writing:

> [M]ake sure the language and the position that they [IHS] have taken is available both to the Senate Committee [on Indian Affairs] and the [House] Interior and Insular Affairs Committee, so when the issue does surface later on and somebody wants to talk about it they will know what their position is.

The staffer also described some HUD programs that could be of interest to the tribe and referred tribal staff to a particular contact person of his in the agency. The mutual benefits of the information exchange became clear. After delivering his insider's understanding, the BIA official highlighted programs where funding was scarce and where he encouraged Tribe J to ask Congress for more BIA funding. This particular case illustrated the opportunities that Indian nations discovered in building long-term relationships: insights into bureaucratic machinations and into ways to leverage existing programs.

C. NORTHWEST TRIBES: PATTERNS THAT CARRY ACROSS CONTEXT

These patterns—of buttressing institutional niches through gradual policy adjustment—showed up in an even wider range of circumstances. The newsletters and tribal council minutes of the three Pacific Northwest reservations captured the frequent pursuit of access, procedural revision, and frameworks.

1. Tribe G: A Disadvantaged Tribe

The toughest test of my hypothesis comes from the case of Tribe G—a highly marginalized Northwest tribe with a less developed economy and a less institutionalized government. The hypothesis holds up, as table 3.13 demonstrates. In fact, Tribe G was more likely to nudge federal policy than to focus on particular resources for independent expert organizations. Tribe G's personnel met regularly with the staff from federal agencies that delivered programs and granted dollars on their reservation. Not all meetings would serve Tribe G's aims—federal bureaucrats often dictated record-keeping and accounting procedures to tribal grantees, but I did not include those meetings in my tally here. I only considered meetings that involved program consultation of the tribe's choosing.

This disadvantaged tribe got federal agencies to reshape practice by drawing on precedents set by other tribes and advice from intertribal organizations. Most notably, the tribal government reached a partnership with the U.S. Forest Service.

TABLE 3.13

Tribe G's Strategies for Obtaining Federal Aid

Ratio between nudging underlying policy	
…and building independent expert organizations	1.35
…and all initiatives*	.63
Tactics for nudging underlying policy	Percent of total
Increase access	57%
Alter frameworks	36%
Adjust procedures	7%
Number of attempts at nudging underlying policy per year	21

Source: Tribal newsletter. One year in early 1990s; one year in mid-1990s.
Includes building independent expert organizations, complements to independent expert organizations, and all other federal aid sought.
Percentages may not add to 100% because of rounding.

Tribal officials observed that USFS had negotiated these types of arrangements with several tribes in the region. In another moment, an intertribal advocacy group advised Tribe G on how protect and hunting rights. The organization's representative suggested breaking down the larger goal into smaller adjustments to procedures and consultation. He wrote, "I think the best approach for [Tribe G] to take would be to discuss thoroughly what it wants and to prioritize those wants.... If there are certain deer herds that used to be on or near the reservation or migrate through it, perhaps the Tribe would be interested in having a say in the management of those herds." The author went on the recommend that tribal leaders then match specific subgoals to a specific federal agency with which Tribe G had an ongoing relationship, noting, "I understand that the tribe has worked with the Forest Service in the past on root gathering sites. The Tribe may want to talk to the BLM and Forest Service regarding the proposed land swap between the two agencies and what impact that will have on the management of those gathering sites." In other words, the approach was not about immediate big wins. Rather, Tribe G wanted to push, bit by bit, for a more hospitable federal approach.

2. Tribe E: An Effective Government

Tribe E—with a weaker economy but a well-regarded government—invested in ongoing federal relationships and used those relationships to push for a host of reforms. Tribe E worked on nudging federal policy more frequently than on

TABLE 3.14

Tribe E's Strategies for Obtaining Federal Aid

Ratio between nudging underlying policy	
... and building independent expert organizations	1.36
... and all initiatives*	.65
Tactics for nudging underlying policy	Percent of total
Increase access	63%
Alter frameworks	7%
Adjust procedures	30%
Number of attempts at nudging underlying policy per year	7.5

Source: Tribal newspaper over the course of four years.
Includes building independent expert organizations, complements to independent expert organizations, and all other federal aid sought.
Percentages may not add to 100% because of rounding.

specific aid to build independent expert organizations, as table 3.14 shows. Tribal officials interacted regularly with the managers of federal programs affecting them. Tribal officials reported back that detailed discussion of federal program design and operation occurred at these meetings. Most of the accounts depicted meetings in a collaborative light. But the attendees described also some moments of conflict, when Indian representatives made clear to federal officials that they would approach members of Congress, if necessary, to gain program changes that they desired.

3. Tribe F: A Developed Economy and Less Institutionalized Government

The third Pacific Northwest tribe, Tribe F—with a strong economy and a less institutionalized government during the 1990s—had similar repeated interactions with federal bureaucrats, which it used as a channel for seeking change. Table 3.15 shows that Tribe F nudged federal policy more frequently than it attempted to gain specific resources to build independent expert organizations. As with other tribes, there were regular meetings between tribal officials and their counterparts in federal agencies. In one moment of familiarity, the BIA asked for Tribe F's recommendation of whom to hire as the new BIA regional director when the position became vacant, and the tribal council suggested an official already in the BIA with whom they felt they had a strong working relationship. Additionally, the tribal council minutes provided evidence of notable

TABLE 3.15

Tribe F's Strategies for Obtaining Federal Aid

Ratio between nudging underlying policy	
... and building independent expert organizations	1.78
... and all initiatives*	.59
Tactics for nudging underlying policy	Percent of total
Increase access	63%
Alter frameworks	19%
Adjust procedures	18%
Number of attempts at nudging underlying policy per year	28.5

Source: Tribal newspaper. One year in early 1990s; one year in late 1990s.
Includes building independent expert organizations, complements to independent expert organizations, and all other federal aid sought.
Percentages may not add to 100% because of rounding.

frameworks for federal collaboration. Tribe F reached agreements with the U.S. Forest Service and the Bureau of Land Management on coordinated land management planning. The tribal official who led these efforts noted, "[t]his agreement opens the opportunity for Tribe F to have the authority to write a management plan, coordinate efforts with the Forest Service, and to implement the plan on federal lands."

D. NCAI: PREEMINENCE OF FRAMEWORK

These strategies weren't just employed by the occasional tribe here and there. They were core objectives for major intertribal organizations. Indeed, over the course of the 1990s, the NCAI consistently described access, frameworks, and adjustments to existing approaches as vital priorities.

As the Clinton administration prepared in December 1992 to assume power, the NCAI made the case to the transition committee for some key objectives. In the transcripts of an internal conference call of the NCAI, the first item considered was political appointees; the team wanted to ensure the placement of officials who were both knowledgeable about and sympathetic to tribal governments and NCAI priorities. The conversation then moved to economic development proposals and how to fit them into the administration's existing goal—essentially, how to cast NCAI's goals as adjustments to existing practices rather than as new programs. NCAI's executive director remarked, "We might like to tag onto their [the incoming administration's] agenda to create jobs." NCAI's treasurer, who would later serve as NCAI president, remarked, "I think it's politically astute to ride the tide of the administration." Furthermore, he emphasized a framework for federal relations, noting:

> [O]ne of the primary objectives that we should request is a better government-to-government mechanism for the federal/tribal relationship. Whether they take any of our initiatives or not, they won't work effectively unless the government-to-government mechanism is firmly in place.[14]

The other participants agreed. They didn't treat the declaration of a new relationship as window dressing. To the contrary; they thought it was important to change the stated frames for interaction.

The theme continued in 1994, when a range of Indian advocates organized a Federal Listening Conference, a forum where tribal leaders could communicate their priorities to federal officials. In the conference's aftermath, NCAI President gaiashkibos wrote a memo to President Clinton outlining NCAI's policy objectives. Most of these initiatives focused on frameworks. The memo remarked:

> We have concluded that the key to building an effective relationship between your administration and the tribes is to focus on the day-to-day contact between federal agencies and tribal governments. Far too many federal officials are totally ignorant of the most basic protocols which should govern such a relationship....

The letter went on to remark that "an Executive Order providing such simple and direct guidance to all federal officials to provide Indian tribes due process, notice of federal actions impacting trust properties, and basic respect for their rights of self-government would be truly historic." Other parts of the letter encouraged adjustments to access, roles, and procedures, such as:

- Amending enterprise zone legislation to permit tribal governments to participate in the same way that states and localities could and supporting "a special task force to be created within the Community Enterprise Board which you established."[15]
- For natural resources, "we ask that our tribal governments have a 'seat at the table' as federal resource management decisions are made. Further we seek your support for the rights of Indian tribes to exercise primary jurisdiction over natural resource management within the boundaries of our reservations."

- For health insurance reform, as the administration contemplated its plans for large-scale change, "we must upgrade the capabilities of the Indian Health Service in order for it to be able to provide a benefit package comparable to that offered to the general population. A national 'Indian Board of Directors' representing the tribes should be appointed to supervise this effort and provide ongoing direction."
- Adjusting procedures of the Office of Management and Budget to provide more "uniformity and predictability" in existing federal allocations to reservations by reorganizing some accounting and reporting procedures, as part of the administration's broader effort to streamline federal agencies.

In short, the NCAI pushed for gradual adjustment in consultation, formal status, and existing programs.[16]

The NCAI gave special emphasis to structures for transmitting information. The year 1992 saw the creation of the Joint Tribal/Bureau of Indian Affairs/Department of the Interior Advisory Task Force on Bureau of Indian Affairs Reorganization that involved leaders from the NCAI. In the Executive Summary of a progress report, the Task Force spotlighted how the absence of information could be an important impediment in tribes' efforts to shape federal policy, and it gave priority to adjustments that could reduce that obstacle. Specifically, the Task Force pushed for making permanent a recent set of changes in BIA budgeting procedures. The Task Force noted, "Utilizing the new budget format, tribes were provided with more complete information about the BIA budget than ever before and were afforded an opportunity to participate in budget planning."[17]

In a 2000 letter to the assistant secretary of Indian Affairs, this same approach was articulated again by NCAI advocates.[18] The NCAI wanted formal and unencumbered access to a high-level BIA official with decision-making authority who could "understand the constraints and positions of the BIA on data collection and management issues; be knowledgeable about the budget formulations process." They suggested specific BIA officials who could serve as an advisory team for such a position.[19] The objective was access alongside a new framework that acknowledged the importance of tribes' right to information. From 1992 to 2000, NCAI leaders sketched a long-run plan: reform frameworks, gain access and information, gain gradual influence, then repeat. The stability of the strategy is remarkable.

E. EXAMPLES FROM NORTHWEST INDIAN FISHERIES COMMISSION

The NCAI is a very unique—and uniquely important—organization, but its strategies are not isolated. In another striking example, the newsletter of the Northwest

Indian Fisheries Commission (NWIFC), *Northwest Indian Fisheries Commission News*, chronicled that organization's efforts to influence salmon habitat regulation in the 1990s.[20] In this series of interactions, we can observe patterns of long-term communication. The NWIFC took a page from the NCAI playbook. (Or perhaps it was vice-versa.) Through enduring relationships, NWIFC fought for formal acknowledgment of tribes' important role in the policy process. With that official status in place, it pushed for further policy change.

In the mid 1990s, NWIFC was pushing the National Marine Fisheries Service to avoid classifying some particular salmon stocks as endangered species. NWIFC wanted federal agencies to support extensive habitat restoration outside of the regulatory setting of the Endangered Species Act. The National Marine Fisheries Service met this demand in 1995, deciding to study salmon populations rather than to impose reclassification.[21]

Indeed, Chairman Billy Frank, Jr., of the Northwest Indian Fisheries Commission juxtaposed the ability of tribes to win bureaucratic accommodation against their difficulties in winning other policy changes.[22] In the summer of 1995, the Senate Interior Appropriations Subcommittee had just voted to cut the BIA's proposed budget for the upcoming fiscal year by 26%. (Ultimately, a sizeable portion of the reduction was restored, but some cutbacks did occur.) At the same time, the Commission had just realized a major accomplishment. The chairman noted: "It's the For the Sake of the Salmon Charter, and it is potentially the most far-reaching comprehensive cooperative commitment to salmon restoration and protection to come along in many years." Specifically, the National Marine Fisheries Service had agreed to fund an initiative that would facilitate stakeholder dialogue, provide technical assistance to local watershed protection program, and develop new programs, including "a monitoring system that tracks progress toward measurable salmon recovery objectives," and "a regional package of proposed incentives for private landowners." By establishing a new framework, the Charter enabled access to technical assistance, outside environments, and new organizational forms.

In 1997, NWIFC's newsletter described tribes' ongoing collaboration with federal and state authorities.[23] The Commission joined representatives of the National Marine Fisheries Service, the EPA, state officials, and timber industry representative in negotiations over updating state regulations of the timber industry. Even more importantly, NWIFC was involved in reshaping the basic terms of federal-tribal interactions over fisheries policy. NWIFC and federal actors were drafting a secretarial order that acknowledged some key powers of Indian nations to regulate fisheries—that the federal government would "give deference to tribal conservation and management plans for tribal trust resources that govern activities on Indian lands"—and specified some supportive roles that federal agencies would play,[24] "the culmination of a year-long effort involving tribes from across the United States who met several times to develop language."[25] Once more, new frameworks developed in a setting of repeated interactions.

Some of the bigger-ticket items that tribes pursued for habitat restoration ran into snags. For example, efforts to obtain federal funding for removing dams on the Elwha River became snarled in the legislative process.[26] But by 1999, the "decades-long struggle" to tear down the dams paid off and the removal process began. The article on dam removal concluded by noting the continuing process:

> Michael Langland, Elwha River restoration coordinator for the [Lower Elwha Klallam Tribe] had little time to celebrate. Just a few days later, Langland was headed back to Washington, D.C. to meet with leaders from the National Park Service, the Bureau of Reclamation, and other key officials with hope of keeping up the [salmon habitat] restoration momentum.[27]

NWIFC worked hard to win a seat at the table when the federal agencies supervising fisheries made decisions. As a result of these efforts, NWIFC and member tribes did far more than seek out ways to benefit from set federal programs: they developed methods to reshape gradually those programs to better serve their needs.

F. IN SUMMARY

In short, tribes didn't find ongoing institutional niches by luck; they made their own luck through hard, persistent work. They tugged and leaned with the oftentimes limited weight they had. The kept a sharp eye on overall structure and on possible footholds. They didn't leave their powerful federal partners alone or unattended for very long. They appreciated the potential of each seat at the table and place in the process.

IV. Playing Federal Actors against One Another

Tribal leaders, in their own words, attached value to slowly reinforcing institutional niches within the federal government. Did federal officials respond to the priorities that tribes communicated to them? First, I illustrate the incentives that federal officials saw in responding to tribes' objectives. Second, I examine whether internal BIA communications showed that federal officials worried about tribes' priorities—for reasons of good will, fears of retribution, or both. Third, I explore how tribes kept the scope of conflict small and low-profile but also pulled in other actors to hold bureaucratic power in check.

A. BUREAUCRATS AS ALLIES

First, what did bureaucrats stand to gain from collaboration? For starters, tribal officials could help make the case for a program before appropriators. Tribe J's president highlighted this opportunity frequently in comments in tribal council proceedings. "The Tribe is also testifying on behalf of the Bureau of Indians Affairs because they aren't allowed to lobby," he remarked in 1993.

Sometimes, tribal advocacy helped promote particular expansions of bureaucratic power. In the early 1990s, the president of an Upper Plains tribe noted that the pilot cattle ranching program that the tribe was promoting "is proposed as a demonstration model which could serve as the basis for a new BIA Indian Agriculture program." In effect, tribal governments' advocacy could help federal agencies claim new turf. Furthermore, agencies could claim some credit for reservations' successes before stakeholders. Tribe H's newspaper noted in the early 1990s that its substance abuse treatment center, which IHS's local area office described as "exemplary, innovative and positive," would be showcased by the area office at a national IHS meeting.

EPA had incentives to expand its own reach by affirming tribal powers; it noted one case where:

> [The EPA was working with the Suquamish Tribe] at a site not technically within its jurisdiction, but which is on land where the Tribe has hunting, fishing, and gathering rights. This decision sets a precedent for enhancing participation of Indian Tribes in Superfund responses. (1993, 8)

In short, by leveraging tribal jurisdictional claims, EPA could gain entrée on new lands and new projects. In discussing a pesticide program on the Leech Lake Reservation, the report remarked:

> The project ... will allow the Tribe to gain experience enabling it to advise members *and non-members* of possible pesticide-related concerns with fish taken from the lakes and potentially used as a major food source for both members and *non-members*. [Emphasis added.] (1993, 9)

When an EPA report discussed its initiative to promote tribal radon programs, it again saw tribal allies as a way to influence policy at the local level. The report observed that not only would new tribal programs be sharing with EPA the data that they gathered, but also "grantees are not prohibited from (and do not have to disclose) activities intended to encourage local entities to adopt the EPA model construction standards."[28]

Perhaps it is not a coincidence that many of the programs described here were not located in particularly powerful bureaucracies: either they faced anemic funding and marginal support (the Bureau of Indian Affairs most notably; the Indian Health Service as well) or were younger organizations still seeking to carve out their place (the Environmental Protection Agency, the Department of Justice's Office of Tribal Justice). For more vulnerable programs, allies are useful, even if those allies sometimes push back—and push back hard.

B. TRIBAL PRESSURES ON BUREAUCRATS

In line with these incentives, we see federal bureaucrats who worried about tribes' priorities. Perhaps the toughest tests come from federal bureaucrats' willingness to support tribal priorities in the face of countervailing pressures. Along those lines, federal records offered many examples of coordination between Indian nations and federal agencies on legislative relations. Here, I rely exclusively on records where federal officials address other federal officials and not on tribes' records.

In one case in the late 1990s, an exchange of faxes showed communication between tribes and the BIA about a bill that would have limited tribes' hunting rights. In one fax, the Northwest Indian Fisheries Commission provided a staffer in the BIA's D.C. offices with planned testimony that would oppose the bill at a congressional hearing. The fax cover letter stated: "This is draft testimony—Hope it's helpful." The second fax, from the Yakama Indian Nation to the same federal official, included a proposed settlement between tribal and state governments on the issue. The fax cover page commented: "1st cut rough and unedited draft → let me know what you think....comments, suggestions, etc. Thanks." [ellipses in original] Several weeks later, the Northwest Indian Fisheries Commission, the Yakama Indian Nation, and BIA's Deputy Assistant Secretary testified in opposition to the bill at a congressional hearing.[29]

Internal communications show how BIA officials felt compelled to serve tribes' preferences before Congress. In one instance in the late 1990s, BIA's Office of Congressional and Legislative Affairs (OCLA) solicited feedback from BIA area offices on a bill that would hand some tribal authority over water to state governments. The area offices were unambiguous in their recommendations. After receiving the feedback, OCLA then expressed opposition to the bill to BIA's Legislative Counsel.

Nine area offices condemned the bill. The Portland Area Office reacted most strongly; its response termed the bill "simplistic" and "not reasonable" and the attached comments on the bills from the Kootenai Tribe.[30] The Eastern Area Office's explanation of its opposition was based solely on tribes' preferences. The office's recommendation built solely on what tribes wanted, not on anything characterized as an independent assessment. Their sentence structures are telling; every sentence that justified their conclusion was about tribes' priorities: "We are all aware that Indian tribes are strongly opposed.... Indian tribes are still opposed.... The tribes believe.... [The proposed legislation] was and still is viewed by Indian tribes.... [T]he Indian tribes feel.... Indian tribes believe.... The tribes would prefer.... In view of these findings, it our recommendation that the Bureau of Indian Affairs strongly oppose this proposed legislation."

That same year, area offices and BIA headquarters shared more faxes and e-mails about a broader matter, the Department of Interior's Legislative Plans for the 105th Congress.[31] It was a detailed and lengthy document, with a variety of items of consequence to reservations. Many of the proposals would expand tribal authority and resources.[32] A controversial item, however, was tucked in the BLM's multipronged proposals under its largely innocuous Omnibus Antiquated Laws Act. The proposal would have removed a century-old, seldom-used procedure whereby individual Indians could acquire farmland with federal help. BIA leadership reacted strongly and noted that the perils of ignoring tribes' preferences. An e-mail from the BIA Office of Trust to OCLA made a strong critique of the BLM proposal and observed: "The BIA should strongly object to this legislative plan. If this gets introduced and tribes learn that the BIA knew about it prior to introduction and did not object, they will be upset to say the least." Subsequently, OCLA wrote to the Office of General Counsel with a strong critique of the bill. BIA headquarters spoke strongly against BLM's initiative, whether for reasons of policy affinity with tribes, fear of tribal reprisal, or both.

Another item that generated heat was an Indian Land Consolidation Act that BIA headquarters proposed. BIA wanted to address issues of fractionated heirship, where multiple individual Indian descendants hold a tiny share of control over a parcel of reservation land, which then makes any changes to land use extremely difficult. BIA proposed buying up those shares when heirs were willing to sell them and then returning the land to the tribe once all the individual claims were settled.

At the same time, the Act would also limit individuals' ability to further subdivide their claims among subsequent heirs. The Portland Area Office commented with strong language on prospects for implementation, calling the bill "an accounting nightmare." Also, the office's director worried that "[m]ost Indian people have a special attachment to the land. Although they might have a minuscule interest, it is important for them to retain this interest and be able to transfer it to their heirs."

The voices within BIA's internal deliberations were not totally uniform, however. This is hardly surprising; it is a large agency. The findings illustrate tribes' need for a multipronged strategy: work with bureaucrats where possible but sometimes also seek legislative constraints on bureaucrats. The Aberdeen Area Office's director argued that the current proposal did not go far enough; the director's reactions were grounded in the office's own administrative headaches. The area director commented:

> The repeal of this law would eliminate time and resources expended for its administration, eliminate the misconception by the public [that the BIA is responsible for these complications], thus reducing congressional inquiries; it is for these reasons we feel the law should be repealed.

The Aberdeen Area Office argued that the Indian Land Consolidation Act did not propose action that was bold enough to fix the problem of fractionated interests, and its director went on to make a rather amazing suggestion:

> Why can't we deal with the problem from the standpoint of Congress exercising its right of eminent domain, through a declaration of taking?...It seems if just compensation, based on the current value of the land, not income generated, was paid to the current owners, then the state should be able to take it. It would appear that the United States could give a good argument for the taking of these fractionated interests, based alone on the current funding now required to administer them, which impacts the public's economic stability.

This remarkable proposal—that it would be easier if the federal government seized Indian lands and then offered compensation of the federal government's choosing—was offered without any comment on what the past 500 years of a not-entirely-dissimilar policy would have to say about its continued use.

This recommendation was not embraced by other units within BIA and by the agency's chief legislative liaison; they had a very different vision of how to deflate criticisms of their agency. Nonetheless, this dissenting view reflected a real tension. The proposal fit with a bureaucrat's desire to make her job simpler and to eliminate daily criticisms. This tension is real, and it shows that tribal governments can never completely or naively trust the BIA to always promote tribal governments' priorities.

C. HOLDING BUREAUCRATS IN CHECK

This tension—in moments where federal bureaucrats and tribal leaders diverged—drove the other side of tribes' political strategy. Members of Congress and other agencies provided an important check on bureaucratic power. Tribes played legislators against bureaucrats and bureaucrats against bureaucrats. Actors within small nodes of the federal government faced differing incentives, constraints, and opportunities; these federal actors were also to an extent in inherent competition with each other for power. These facts did not escape the attention of Indian leaders.

1. . . . With Congress's Help

Tribal leaders carried some issues to the legislative arena because those changes would not be possible for bureaucrats to achieve—perhaps because bureaucrats were unwilling, perhaps they were unable, perhaps there was a confluence of the two motives. Federal records captured a number of moments where members of Congress constrained the BIA according to tribal priorities. In 1996, strongly worded letters passed between the Navajo Nation President Albert Hale and the office of Ada Deer, head of the BIA. Hale objected pointedly to language in a BIA budget proposal with consequence for the Navajo Nation. BIA's response, through the deputy commissioner of Indian Affairs, was chilly in places, but it ended by remarking, "It [BIA's proposal] was clearly a mistake. You will be glad to know that the House Appropriations Committee denied the Bureau's request. . . . The Committee stated they would have no objection to a reprogramming request upon assurance" that several requirements be met, all of which were Hale's priorities. BIA was hardly pleased with the situation, but they accepted the outcome begrudgingly because Congress had taken the Navajo Nation's side.[33]

In December 1997, a similar exchange occurred from the Upper Plains, this time between the Aberdeen Area Office and Senator Tom Daschle. Given the Aberdeen Area Office's proposals detailed in the prior section, there is certainly reason for some skepticism about suggestions that the office might make. The Aberdeen Area Office's letter was worded frostily: "We are very disappointed in the lack of coordination by your staff with our Aberdeen Area Office staff.... We believe that many of these issues can be resolved by rewriting passages that are incorrect, confusing, or vague." The text that follows wasn't diplomatic; the Aberdeen Area Office made nine pages of detailed comments that were worded as directives, not suggestions. It's a surprising tone for mezzo level bureaucrats to take with their state's senior senator and the Senate minority leader. Senator Daschle fired back, observing that "I was disappointed by the tone of your letter," and that "I was informed by the Corps of Engineers that it is Administration policy that federal agencies not comment on draft legislation." Daschle continued:

What is particularly troubling for me is the perception that the BIA is actively attempting to substitute its judgment for those of the elected tribal leaders who have chosen to endorse this approach and who were instrumental in crafting the language of this bill. To suggest that these tribes are incapable of making independent judgments about what is best for themselves strikes me as both patronizing and unconstructive, and an inappropriate role for the BIA to play.

The Aberdeen Area Office replied with a hasty, contrite apology: "We commend you on the efforts you have made to bring together all parties involved in this legislation and apologize if our comments were misinterpreted and were the cause of distress for your staff."[34] In this instance, the legislative ally put the bureaucrats in their place.

2.... By Playing One Bureaucrat against Another

Tribes could also play bureaucrat against bureaucrat. As Indian nations cultivated a few new—but fairly small—programs beyond BIA and IHS, these programs served not only to address Indian concerns directly but also to check and balance traditional sources of federal Indian policy. Most certainly, BIA and IHS were still at the center of the room. But select engagements by other bureaucracies brought new forces to bear on the two mainstays.

As EPA provided overviews of its new and growing tribal programs, it was explicit about the opportunities it saw from coordinating with Native Nations.[35] Recall the EPA initiatives from Section IV.A in pursuit of broader, interagency networks. EPA could make important gains for its own agenda when it brought other agencies to its negotiating table. In particular, EPA noted that it could reach its goals more quickly and easily if it could urge voluntary compliance with its standards.

In another instance, in the mid 1990s, Indian advocates coordinated with the U.S. Department of Justice (DOJ) to organize a Federal Listening Conference, where tribal leaders presented their concerns to DOJ leadership and used the process as a foundation for building a DOJ program on tribal affairs. A DOJ internal strategy memo on the conference discussed the space that a new DOJ program would fill.[36] The author argued for the design of overarching DOJ policy on Indian affairs. The memo contended that Justice could help unify and clarify the legal issues at the heart of many tribal concerns—and many bureaucracies— and thus make an important contribution "in building tribal institutional capacity." The author observed specifically that this new framework set forth by DOJ would entail significant interaction with the Department of Interior. These were small endeavors within DOJ. Yet in the process, the agency made its own contribution to defining frameworks and serving tribal capacity-building in ways that would constrain other agencies. It introduced a new source of influence on the existing practices of the BIA.

D. RECAP OF BUREAUCRATIC RELATIONS

To a large degree, all the agencies described here couldn't afford to ignore tribes. First, tribal leaders were talking about issues and programs that fit squarely in their agencies' missions and goals. Second, tribal leaders wouldn't leave them alone and kept showing up everywhere. Third, tribes found leverage to push these agencies to accommodate their demands. Fourth, there was something to be said for allies, even if they occasionally turned to being critics. Tribal leaders posed threats, but they also offered potential for profitable partnerships.

V. Conclusions

Tribes are aware of the precariousness of their federal relationships and of the need to manage those relationships astutely. A councilmember from one Pacific Northwest tribe captured that sense in a July 1999 statement, where he remarked:

> For future survival as a people we must become more involved in economic development. Already old foes like Senator Slade Gorton threaten to cut off

federal funds to tribes that do not conduct themselves like he thinks we should. We need to earn money from economic development that is not subject to interference from well-placed political Indian fighters. We must find ways to avoid total dependence on federal funding.

Another tribal official echoed these same themes in 2000, when he noted:

I believe tribal governments have a real obligation to plan for economic self-sufficiency, in recognition that the mood in Washington, D.C. toward tribal people could change at any time and funding could be slashed or cut completely. I believe our ultimate solution to this potential problem lies in the development and strengthening of our own economies exclusive of federal government support.

These comments were not empty rhetoric: the tribe was undertaking a large initiative to expand tribal enterprises and to pursue greater economic development on the reservation. There are no illusions about federal aid being constant or about federal programs being constantly aimed at native peoples' best interests: history has hammered home that lesson.

All the same, the tribal governments in this analysis, operating across time and in range of circumstances, appeared to have learned that federal programs could be managed in careful, nuanced ways. American Indian advocates have not succeeded at the wholesale reinvention of federal Indian policy. However, tribal governments won subtle forms of support, situated in continuing interactions, which buoyed tribal efforts to build independent expert organizations. Furthermore, tribal governments in a variety of contexts found political means to mold these federal programs in subtle ways and over long-term trajectories, and thus enhance the assistance that they provide. This support must be managed astutely and targeted strategically, but it is possible to win unobtrusive yet meaningful benefits as a result.

To summarize, tribes sought support from institutional niches for the following activities: the development of technical expertise that allowed tribes to understand particular problems and solutions; getting to know the external environment in order to understand outside interests, interact with them, and persuade them; and exposure to organizational strategies and forms in order manage, plan, and frame with new repertoires at hand. Tribes secured this assistance over time through the following approaches: seeking access to officials as a means to share information and gain political insider insight; pursuing changes in frameworks that acknowledged tribes' role as important participants and collaborators; adjusting and stabilizing procedures to produce regulations that were more favorable, flexible, and simple.

It is easy to overlook victories that occur in low-visibility settings. If we miss these successes, however, our view of how tribal governments participate in politics becomes fundamentally skewed. Capacity-building has dramatic consequences. As the next chapter will illustrate, tribal leaders who have built greater expertise see their problems and see solutions in vastly different ways.

4 Expertise-Centered Behaviors
HOW KNOWLEDGE CHANGES ORGANIZATIONS AND HOW TO KNOW WHEN IT'S THERE

I. Introduction

A. THE ARGUMENT

The previous chapter illustrated how tribes gained assistance with capacity-building from federal actors. Here, I show the benefits that expert organizations can bring. This chapter turns attention to the internal dynamics of tribes. This analysis highlights the significance for tribes of identifying processes that drive outcomes and of imagining new solutions to problems.

To restate the basic argument advanced here and in previous chapters: political actors stand to gain if they can build expertise about policy problems and political environments. The more a group possesses specialized knowledge about problems, problem-solving routines, and environments, the better a group is positioned to envision and implement new strategies. In this chapter, I examine how tribes use expertise to engage in four critical behaviors. Two expertise-centered behaviors are manifestations of analytic capacity: *diagnosing* and *anticipating*. Two others are manifestations of capacity for action: *initiating* and *partnering*. Greater expertise increases these behaviors. Consequently, it improves abilities to light upon solutions and to guide those solutions through implementation.

An extensive qualitative scholarship on both public and private organizations argues that effectiveness improves with learning and knowledge. This chapter continues in that tradition. It also addresses a puzzle in existing literature, by proposing new criteria for measuring expertise. Much work to date has assessed expertise through thick description of decision-making within organizations. This technique has had great benefits for building nuanced theory, but it is difficult to apply to analyses of larger numbers of cases. I propose an alternate approach. While it is very difficult to observe expertise itself, expertise translates into certain behaviors that are more easily identified: *diagnosing, anticipating, initiating*, and *partnering*. Greater expertise increases the frequency of all these behaviors.

This chapter takes advantage of three natural experiments. First, I compared Tribes A and C, discussed in chapters 2 and 3, that share much in common but have long-standing differences in their government institutionalization. Second, I examined Tribe F—with less government institutionalization but solid economic development—that changed over time. Third, I examined three units in the Navajo Nation that faced very different opportunities for federal funding. The lessons are consistent across the comparisons. Tribes with better means to build expertise displayed greater skills. Expertise had wide-ranging consequences for their effectiveness.

B. RELATED THEORIES IN EXISTING LITERATURE

There is a vast literature brimming with models of learning and with sensitivity to the many challenges in defining and measuring knowledge.[1] Despite the differing views on the details, researchers have converged on some broad common understandings about organizational learning. Some scholars who have synthesized much of this literature argue that learning organizations cycle through a conceptual phase and an operational phase (Kim 1993, Mukherjee et al. 1998, and Lapre et al. 2000). There are many models based on two phases of evaluating then acting, although they vary in their specifics.[2] In short, while existing literature on organizational learning has not agreed fully on nuanced measures of knowledge or on the exact cognitive processes involved in learning, scholars have been remarkably consistent about the basics of a two-stage process by which knowledge is used. Organizations must analyze their environment first (described variously as observing, assessing, reacting, judging, scanning, interpreting, filtering, or processing) and then forge new courses of action (by designing, implementing, inventing, producing, generating, intervening, acting, or adapting). Here, I leverage the behavioral implications from the areas of consensus.

Much of the existing empirical work on expertise centers on detailed case studies. Such an approach makes rich contributions. It builds nuanced theory with great sensitivity to context. It unveils microfoundations and microprocesses. Unfortunately, it is not a research design that can be applied in all cases where learning and expertise may matter. Scholars are left with the puzzle, then, of whether analyses of multiple cases can actually capture learning. I offer a solution to that anxiety. In short, I highlight the behavioral implications of the underlying cognitive processes described in prior literature, in order to analyze expertise through new, more generalizable methods.

C. A NEW APPROACH: FOUR EXPERTISE-CENTERED BEHAVIORS

Each of the behaviors that I highlight is easily observed, even when the underlying cognitive processes are not. I measure four expertise-centered behaviors: *diagnosing, anticipating, initiating,* and *partnering*. Both diagnosing and anticipating are indicators of expertise-centered analysis, while initiating and partnering are indicators of expertise-centered action.

First, I consider the frequency with which actors *diagnose*: in other words, whether they assess or identify mechanisms driving outcomes. When actors diagnose, they move beyond simply seeing the problems that they confront and they progress to seeing the processes that produce those problems. Causal language can indicate diagnosing. In a second, related vein, I tally how often actors *anticipate*: whether they foresee consequences, reactions, and other future outcomes. When actors anticipate, they display understanding of the forces in an environment, the interrelationships between those forces, and the effects that they will precipitate. Anticipating can take the form of predicting what the future holds. If actors just talk generally about next steps, I do not classify that discussion as anticipating. But if actors provide detailed discussion of next steps—details of program activities, timelines, or expenses—I define that behavior as anticipating.

Third, greater expertise leads to more ability to *initiate*: to pursue new solutions to problems. Simply, expertise makes it easier to craft new strategies, because expertise makes it easier to see the forces causing problems and to identify pathways that can mitigate those problems. Finally, greater expertise leads to more ability to *partner*: to identify other actors with shared interests and with valuable resources, to work with them, and to function oneself as a valuable partner. Partnering does not include adversarial relations; nor does it include contracting out for services or analysis. Contracting can complement capacity-building in certain contexts, of course: for tasks that are newer or rare, for isolated tasks that require unusually specialized skills, for tasks where the tribe can learn important skills that will carry forward in time once the contract is done. When a unit contracts out certain core skills repeatedly, and expertise has to be purchased on a project-by-project basis, it is a powerful indicator of limitations on capacity-building opportunities.

My approach stood up to two possible critiques. The first concern is that less expert organizations might engage in just as much diagnosing, anticipating, initiating, and partnering as anywhere else—however, they would engage in inaccurate analyses and fruitless actions. Second, perhaps more learned organizations engage in *less* diagnosing, anticipating, initiating and partnering—after all, once you've built better circumstances, there's more risk from change and less urgency to act differently.[3] I find, however, that my measures of expertise-centered behaviors avoid these pitfalls. In places where organizational learning was poorer, leaders were keenly aware of their limitations. They diagnosed, anticipated, initiated, and partnered less. They weren't sure of either the nature of their problems or the steps that could improve their lot. They described their frustration with their own limited analyses and actions. In places where organizational learning was stronger, leaders embraced the idea that there was always room for improvement.

D. METHODS FOR THE INVESTIGATION

My analysis employed qualitative and quantitative approaches. For each test, I examined a small set of records in order to produce a qualitative description of expertise-centered behaviors. Then, I coded expertise-centered behaviors for a wider case base. Qualitative analysis focused on records with a high level of detail and very consistent formatting. Coding was better able to accommodate content with less detailed description and varying formats.

I examined various written records from four tribes whose particular circumstances generated clear a priori expectations about their level of expertise. In short, I explored whether, in conditions where expertise flourishes, officials were then more adept at analyses and action. Also, the information available on these tribal governments allowed both for detailed description of particular moments in time and for quantitative analysis over a broader range.

The cases included in this analysis were *not* selected on the basis of written records available. I investigated the eight tribal governments in the sample from the Southwest and Pacific Northwest. One tribe was excluded because available records were quite limited. Three were excluded because, although available records were sufficient, the circumstances of these tribes did not provide compelling natural experiments. There was greater theoretical leverage from the circumstances of the four remaining tribes.

As a bonus, the written records of these four tribes each addressed different audiences. One set of documents spoke primarily to external grantmakers, another to tribal members, and another to tribal officials. This fortuitous variation provided a check on whether displays of expertise were unique to some audiences but not others. Another circumstance that allowed for a rigorous test: the particular authors of documents from a specific tribe changed over time. Yet despite variation in audience and author, expertise-centered behaviors still revealed themselves as expected.

E. PREVIEW OF FINDINGS

First, I compared Tribes A and C that shared much in common but possessed differing levels of institutionalization. Greater institutionalization helps to harness expertise: organizational learning would be a slower, harder slog without functional specialization. The results were as expected; there was a clear difference between the tribes' expertise-centered behaviors. The analysis of Tribes A and C also showed, however, that even very disadvantaged tribes can build skills with the right help. The disadvantaged tribe did not lack entirely the means to analyze and act, and it still managed to build some skills worth noting.

Secondly, I evaluated Tribe F that experienced improvements in institutionalization and in funding over time. I would predict that expertise grew as circumstances improved. The analysis showed that when external hindrances on government institutionalization and economic development lessened, those endowments grew and helped facilitate more expertise-centered behaviors. Outside partnerships—including federal partnerships—were key building blocks for translating opportunity into accomplishments.

Finally, I examined three subunits in one tribe, the Navajo Nation, where one of the subunits had a great deal less federal support than the third. I would expect that the units with more federal aid cultivated and harnessed more expertise, resulting in more new ideas and new strategies. The analysis showed that continuing barriers to outside institutional niches had negative consequences for expertise, even when other endowments were strong. The Navajo agencies that operated in policy domains with a stronger federal presence built more skills through federal interactions. The Navajo Nation agencies in policy domains with a weaker federal presence still made use of the Nation's other advantages, but they encountered greater struggles.

In short, the data at hand accomplished two things. First, they showed that expertise matters. Ultimately, greater expertise facilitated new abilities to plan, implement, and successfully complete activities. This is not to say, however, that less advantaged groups lacked insights entirely. Expertise-centered behaviors also occurred for less-endowed tribes, although they occurred less frequently. In short, settings that impeded capacity did not stifle it completely.

II. Test 1: The Comparison of Two Similar, Neighboring Tribal Governments

First, I compared Tribes A and C. These two tribes shared much in common, but one of them—Tribe A—had a more institutionalized government. Specifically, it has had a larger, more specialized government for decades; a strong, long-standing reputation for high program performance; and leadership roles in intertribal initiatives.

In the 1980s and 1990s, both Tribe A and Tribe C were receiving grant monies from the Bureau of Indian Affairs to help with certain government programs. The two tribal governments submitted detailed grant proposals to the BIA and, once grants were awarded, provided regular briefings on programs. I was able to access Tribes A and C's police reports and grant proposals for overall tribal administrative programs for several years in the late 1980s. I compared the two tribes' federal reporting to evaluate expertise within the two governments. I would expect that Tribe A would display more expertise-centered behaviors; I used qualitative description alongside coding of expertise-centered behavior to evaluate that expectation.

A. A CASE STUDY OF TRIBES A AND C

There were, of course, some obvious similarities between the tribes. Both tribes noted their constrained resources. In various policing reports, the police chief from Tribe C (with less institutionalized government) observed that one patrol car needed to be replaced, that the department lacked funds to send an officer to a law enforcement training program, and that "[t]he police department cannot buy any uniforms, needed equipment, and necessary supplies for the police officers." Similarly, the police chief from Tribe A (with the more institutionalized government) noted that his police department was unable to offer competitive pay for the region; was understaffed; was struggling to cover the high costs of detention services; and lacked needed equipment such as computers, a television, a VCR to play training videos, and police radios.

Beyond these shared traits, however, notable differences existed. To a limited degree, Tribe C's police chief was managing to understand his environment, the needs of his department, and how to best meet those needs. In contrast, Tribe A's police chief engaged in these activities on a wholly different scale.

1. TRIBE C: LESS INSTITUTIONALIZED GOVERNMENT

The reports from Tribe C's police chief were filled mostly with cataloguing the department's recent activities: the number and type of cases investigated.

Diagnosing did occur, most frequently tied to a request for additional funds. For example, in one instance the police chief noted that officers "have been attending as many training sessions as possible but we currently need some training or refresher courses in 1) firearms, 2) side handle baton, and 3) radar." He also diagnosed why relations with other policing agencies could not address all the department's needs: "[This reservation] is a small isolated area.... Backup from the State Police and County Sheriff's Department would take about 25 minutes to get to [here]."

Anticipating. The police chief also anticipated sometimes: for example, at one moment he noted that the tribe was opening a convenience store, museum, and restaurant soon, and there would be greater patrolling needs as a result.

Partnering. Tribe C's police department was involved in partnering. The police chief noted, "[w]e have been assisting the State Police, the County Sheriff's Department, and [a nearby jurisdiction's] Police Department with emergency and non-emergency calls and they have been assisting us."

Initiating. However, no behaviors appeared that could be described as initiating. Tribe C's police chief did not describe any new approaches or strategies he had undertaken.[4]

2. TRIBE A: MORE INSTITUTIONALIZED GOVERNMENT

While the reports from Tribe C were dominated by tallies of recent activities; reports from Tribe A were dominated by analysis. Tribe A's police chief devoted more attention to identifying causal dynamics and possible solutions.

Diagnosing ran throughout Tribe A's reports. One of the police chief's reports not only described recent crimes but also identified which policing needs had been unusually high that month (such as juvenile vandalism, process serving, prisoner transports) and which needs had been consistently high over time (such as citations for driving while intoxicated, also known as DWIs). On another occasion, Tribe A's police chief assessed the best way to acquire new police cars, noting that leasing vehicles from the federal government was proving more expensive up front but more cost-effective in the long run.

Anticipating. Tribe A's police chief predicted trends in the demands on officer time. He remarked in one case, "DWI arrests slowed down some, but the threat is still active. In view of the warm weather ahead, more drivers will be out on the highways." He projected that funding for the DWI Program would likely be cut soon, but he stated that, nonetheless, he would continue to allocate officer time to DWI interdiction because he foresaw an urgent need. He also noted the challenges that the entire tribal government was facing in budgets for the upcoming year, and the police chief predicted that he probably would be unable to replace any departing officers or pay competitive wages until additional outside funding was identified. He pointed to one officer's departure to join a nearby local government's police department, as an indicator of a looming trend.

Partnering came through as an important priority in Police Chief A's narratives. He noted that tribal police were assisting the state police: "Our police officers, now knowledgeable in investigating motor vehicle accidents, were relied upon by the State Police to assist in the investigation of a sizeable number of motor vehicle accidents within our jurisdiction." Furthermore, he described how tribal governments in the region came together to create a new intertribal police association "to combine all our resources to assist each other in many ways" and that he would have an important leadership position in the new association.

Initiating. In contrast to Tribe C, Tribe A's reports were full of initiating. On one occasion, the chief reflected on improvements in officer training, achieved both through more internal training and with off-site training as well. The chief designated an official training officer on his force who would train both police officers and fish and game wardens. That officer was sent to a series of BIA training courses, with the intent that he would then train other officers afterward.

Furthermore, there were examples of the synthesis of these skills sets, as when the chief described a set of activities that drew on all four of the expertise-centered behaviors:

> We continue to highlight alcohol-related crimes. We are finding that almost all motor vehicle accidents are alcohol or drug related here. Recently, we were informed that [the reservation] is experiencing an alcohol abuse epidemic.
>
> We now believe many of our problems caused by alcohol abuse need the attention of service programs, including law enforcement. [We] are engaged in enforcing the laws on DWI as a primary effort to control our highways. Secondly, we are assisting in the education process by doing school presentations. We are now looking at the general public. Hopefully, we will receive as

much input as necessary to engage on a much greater scale to address the alcohol problem.

Here, the department engaged in diagnosing—accumulating and processing information on the nature of crime on the reservation—as a first step in a chain of actions.[5] Furthermore, the chief envisioned a trajectory of intervention and anticipated next steps that could further serve this effort. Next, Police Chief A implemented a variety of policy reforms. Some of those reforms involved independent action. Others—working with schools—required partnerships in order to implement.

Expertise, and the behaviors centered on it, changed in many ways what was possible for Tribe A. This community faced severe budgetary limitations, and there were many problems to address with few resources at hand. But Tribe A's police chief brought to these problems expertise-based problem-solving skills.

B. TALLIES OF EXPERTISE-CENTERED BEHAVIORS FOR TRIBES A AND C

I measured expertise-centered behaviors in the police reports and also in a set of grant proposals that Tribes A and C submitted. Tables 4.1 and 4.2 present the results. The two sets of documents allowed evaluation of different circumstances. In the police reports, the tribes reviewed their activities within established programs. In the grant proposals, the tribes discussed plans for new programs. It seems reasonable to expect that the grant proposals would be heavier on initiating and partnering—since the point was to pursue new courses of action—while the police reports would be heavier on diagnosing and anticipating—since the point was more to discuss existing operations.

For the full set of police reports examined, Tribe A (with the more institutionalized government) was more likely to engage in expertise-centered analyses and the effect is significant at the 10% level. When the forms of expertise-centered analysis were disaggregated, we see that Tribe A engaged in much more diagnosing (significant at the 1% level). Contrary to expectations, Tribe C engaged in slightly more anticipating, but the difference was insignificant and about one-fifth of the magnitude for diagnosing.

For expertise-centered action, there was almost no difference. Tribe A initiated more—indeed, Tribe C presented no initiatives. But Tribe C partnered more than A. The two effects counteracted each other nearly perfectly, and the overall difference for expertise-centered action is near zero and insignificant.

TABLE 4.1

Expertise-Centered Behaviors in Police Reports from Tribes A and C

	Tribe A: Less Institutionalized Government	Tribe C: More Institutionalized Government	Difference between Tribes C and A
Expertise-Centered Analysis	1.67 (1.15)	3.80 (1.30)	2.13* (0.92)
Expertise-Centered Action	3.00 (0.00)	2.80 (1.48)	−0.20 (0.88)
Diagnosing	0.33 (0.58)	3.00 (1.00)	2.67*** (0.64)
Anticipating	1.33 (0.58)	0.80 (0.45)	−0.53 (0.36)
Initiating	0.00 (0.00)	1.40 (1.67)	1.40 (1.00)
Partnering	3.00 (0.00)	1.40 (0.55)	−1.60*** (0.33)
Number of reports	3	5	

For differences, significance at the 1%, 5%, and 10% levels is indicated by ***, **, and *, respectively. Standard deviations in parentheses for tribes; standard errors in parentheses for differences. Expertise-centered analysis=diagnosing and anticipating. Expertise-centered action=initiating and partnering. *Totals per report.*

For the grant proposals examined, the differences in expertise-centered actions were rather astonishing. Tribe A put its greater government institutionalization to good use. Tribe A was far more likely to engage in expertise-centered actions; the difference was large and the overall effect was significant at the 1% level. For expertise-centered analysis, the difference was negative, but small in magnitude and nowhere close to significance.

The *ex ante* expectation was that Tribe A, with its greater government institutionalization, would display more organizational expertise. The results fit with that expectation. The police reports showed that Tribe A engaged in notably more expertise-centered analyses. In the grant proposals, where the tribes were asked to tout new endeavors rather than discuss existing operations, Tribe A displayed vastly more expertise-centered actions.

At the same time, in some domains, Tribe C kept apace of Tribe A. Most notably, while Tribe C struggled greatly with individual policing initiatives, it

TABLE 4.2

Expertise-Centered Behavior in Grant Proposals from Tribes A and C

	Tribe A: Less Institutionalized Government	Tribe C: More Institutionalized Government	Difference between Tribes C and A
Expertise-Centered Analysis	3.43 (2.94)	2.67 (3.06)	−0.76 (2.05)
Expertise-Centered Action	3.43 (1.51)	9.00 (2.00)	5.57*** (1.14)
Diagnosing	2.29 (2.75)	2.00 (2.00)	−0.29 (1.78)
Anticipating	1.14 (1.68)	0.67 (1.15)	−0.48 (1.08)
Initiating	2.71 (1.38)	5.00 (2.65)	2.29* (1.23)
Partnering	0.71 (0.76)	4.00 (4.58)	3.29* (1.64)
Number of reports	7	3	

For differences, significance at the 1%, 5%, and 10% levels is indicated by ***, **, and *, respectively. Standard deviations in parentheses for tribes; standard errors in parentheses for differences. Expertise-centered analysis-diagnosing and anticipating. Expertise-centered action=initiating and partnering. *Totals per report.*

engaged in multiple partnered endeavors. In this relatively short time frame, the question remained open of whether partnerships in one time period would help Tribe C with the next round of analyzing and acting. Fortunately, the discussion below of Tribe F's experiences can help answer that question. As the examination of Tribe F will show, partnerships can help foster expertise-centered behaviors over time.

III. Test 2: A Comparison of Changes over Time in Tribe F

One way to identify the impacts of differing expertise is to contrast two tribes such as Tribes A and C. Another approach is compare a single tribe—one that experienced change—over time. Tribe F provided such an opportunity. Tribe F experienced limited government institutionalization in the early 1990s, due to some specific exogenous obstacles that abated somewhat with time. Over the course of the 1990s, Tribe F's government saw some growth in its functional specialization, specialized skills, and accumulated experience. Also, while the tribe's economy was strong to begin, casino growth expanded its economic opportunities over the decade. As in chapter 3, I draw on Tribe F's tribal newsletter and tribal council minutes for my analysis. I begin with thick description of a subset of council minutes. Next, I expand the case base and apply the measures of expertise-centered behavior in a quantitative manner.

The qualitative analysis focused on three time periods: a period in the early 1990s, a middle time period after some growth in government institutionalization, and a late time period well into the casino's growth. I examined tribal council minutes for eight months in the early time period, for eight months in the middle time period, and six months in the late time period.

The results below fit with the motifs that run throughout this chapter. First, it helped to have government institutionalization and economic development, which meant that Tribe F improved its abilities to understand problems and to find solutions. Even within a few short years, growth in these two endowments started to make a difference. Furthermore, it helped to have partners, including federal institutional niches. A notable building block in Tribe F's expertise was early and continued partnerships with many actors, including the federal government.

A. TRIBE F'S EARLY YEARS

At the earliest date, tribal officials still had much to learn about operating their organization. Early tribal council minutes showed a tribe striving to build up basic government operations. This model offered a compelling example of how inexperienced, resource-strapped organizations can find their way—by focusing on partnerships for capacity-building.

Partnering. There were a variety of areas where Tribe F pursued Bureau of Indian Affairs (BIA) technical assistance. For one, tribal officials consulted with BIA personnel about designing procedures to manage tribal enrollment and how to best structure contracts with attorneys. The minutes revealed interactions with eight intertribal organizations: some regional, some national. Tribe F followed up on intertribal connections to gain help, for example, with grant-writing in one instance and in another case to receive formal and informal training from a tribal department on another reservation.

Diagnosing and Anticipating. Tribe F was not doing much diagnosing or anticipating on its own in these early records. Instead, it needed to hire a variety of outsiders to help with those tasks. The tribe was contracting out much of its legal assistance and management planning. Additionally, the tribe was contracting out its accounting functions, since tribal officials were struggling with basic financial management procedures. They had trouble anticipating whether programs would be in the red or the black when the fiscal year ended and why: tribal officials had encountered several moments where they didn't know how much was being spent on a given program and for what purposes. A key tribal official misplaced a check from the BIA one time; he didn't have a clear sense of how this happened.

Initiating. The tribe launched some endeavors with limited scale. The tribe began planning for its own health programs, and it compiled health statistics and a demographic profile to use in the planning process. With BIA help, Tribe F began small steps to carry out its financial management: it designed and implemented a system for monitoring long-distance phone calls.

In short, these early years were replete with very promising partnerships—but diagnosing, anticipating, and initiating weren't as impressive.

B. CONSEQUENCES OF GROWING GOVERNMENT INSTITUTIONALIZATION

In the next period observed—occurring several years after the first time period, but before casino revenues had their greatest effects on the tribal government's budget—much of Tribe F's behavior had changed. Expertise within the tribal government had expanded. Partnerships continued to be important, but relationships based on a one-way stream of advice were gone. Furthermore, Tribe F now possessed skills that better enabled it to diagnose, anticipate, and initiate.

Partnering remained a frequent activity, but the tenor had changed. Relationships with federal actors also continued to matter. The tribe sought the Administration for Native American's support for updating the tribe's comprehensive plan and for improving administrative facilities. The tribe won BIA block grants where there was less BIA oversight and more tribal discretion in program administration.

Bilateral partnerships, with expertise on both sides, were more the norm. On one occasion, a local sheriff sought the tribal council's input into a resource guide that his department was preparing. Participation in intertribal organizations remained a prominent activity; officials were active in at least eight intertribal organizations. The tribe's relationship with one of those organizations captured much of the change that had occurred. While Tribe F turned to that organization for advice in the early time period, now the roles were reversed: a tribal official was assisting with a performance evaluation of the organization's executive director.

Initiating. Perhaps even more importantly, there were new initiatives. The tribal attorney had just completed successfully some notable litigation; legal expertise had been built in-house. Expertise-centered initiatives occurred in other arenas as well: the tribe was drafting a natural resource management plan, water system improvements, and housing and wildlife ordinances.

Diagnosing and Anticipating. One department reported its assessment of the possible construction of a new facility and recommended that the tribal council move forward. They stated that "preliminary feasibility analysis has been completed as well as the first phase of planning and design. Operations can be funded with available resources and collected revenue without requiring any tribal subsidy." They projected a 16-month timeline for completion.

Not every skill possible had been captured within tribal government, however. For instance, the tribe contracted out for an evaluation of its treatment center. And some rather basic tasks were still being addressed: the elections division was just getting around to purchasing a secure, fire-proof cabinet to store "ballots and other sensitive materials."

C. TRIBE F'S CAPACITIES AT THEIR GREATEST: GROWTH IN GOVERNMENT AND ECONOMY

The final time period examined, after the casino's full flourishing, offered the fullest display of tribal capacities.

Initiating had been modest in the middle time period; now it was more extensive. For example, the tribal natural resources program conducted reforestation, thinning, and fire protection operations and was drafting a long-term management plan. The tribal council approved significant expansions in the ethics code. Tribe F launched a cultural resources program that was monitoring sacred sites, repatriating remains and sacred objects, and archiving tribal photographs.

Partnering. The tribe maintained relationships and pursued joint initiatives with other tribes, nearby governments, and federal agencies. The tribe drew on some degree of federal support for six different programs in the time period: for example, to launch a fish hatchery program, undertake a dental health education campaign, and run a reservation housing program. Tribe F was active in at least four intertribal organizations. In addition, the tribe was jointly managing two particular projects with nearby governments: one for water system improvements, the other for a vocational rehabilitation program.

Diagnosing and Anticipating also appeared more frequently. For example, casino officials monitored the enterprise's performance carefully. One report illustrated these abilities to diagnose and anticipate:

> Marketing efforts are being put into place to counter the outside competition from [casinos in another state] and due to the saturation of gaming activities

via the lottery and Indian casinos. However, [last year's] profits were 14% higher than budgeted.... [There was an] 83% occupancy rate at [the hotel] for January, which is 15% ahead of budget. Comment cards from guests have been consistently positive.... New [advertising] campaigns will be proposed and surveys are out to gain feedback on whether to consider providing bus service to the casino....

Natural resources programs were another area where the tribal government possessed particular diagnostic skills. The activities of the wildlife program included monitoring species, assessing environmental conditions and whether they met needs for species protection, and identifying vulnerable natural areas on the reservation.

All the same, Tribe F still faced some constraints. There were areas where the tribal government lacked capacities to carry out desired tasks. For example, the tribe hired outside consultants to research tribal history, to conduct environmental assessment of a waterway on one occasion and of a tract of land another time, and to "perform a review of employee/management relations." In another instance, Tribe F had started a new firm, but the business was unprofitable and staff was unsure what, if anything, to do differently.

If there is a lesson to draw from Tribe F's experience, it is the value of building partnerships. Tribe F began with a notable degree of partnering. In the middle time period, partnering continued, initiatives grew, and more diagnosing and anticipating emerged. In the final time period, expertise-centered behaviors were even stronger. Federal actors, neighbors, and other tribes all helped Tribe F to learn new skills and to accomplish new tasks.

D. TALLIES OF EXPERTISE-CENTERED BEHAVIORS FOR TRIBE F

I expanded the findings by coding expertise-centered behaviors. Here, I examined all coverage in the tribal newsletter on various tribal government activities (including coverage of tribal council meetings), rather than just limiting analysis to the tribal council minutes. Also, I expanded the time periods included; I examined four different 12-month periods. The evaluation began with an earliest period. Next was Period 2, where government institutionalization had progressed but the very impressive casino revenues had not yet arrived. Then, I considered Period 3, where government institutionalization continued and shortly after new economic expansion that could be attributed to the casino. The Period 4 came after several years of strong casino revenues. Tables 4.3a and 4.3b present the findings.

For the most part, the format of the tribe's newsletter was consistent over time. Between Periods 2 and 3, however, the paper expanded: it doubled the number of pages that it printed. There are good reasons to conclude that this growth in the paper wouldn't have consequences for the way that a particular story might be written: presumably as the tribe grew, the pages needed to offer comparable coverage of tribal government grew as well. At the same time, the change in length was such a large jump and a one-time occurrence; it is possible that once-terser articles were filled subsequently with more details in order fill the space. Tables 4.3a and 4.3b present the data in two formats, as a robustness check: actual average monthly volume of coverage, and average monthly volume of coverage adjusted for overall newsletter length.

The changes over time comported with expected patterns. From Period 1 to Period 2, expertise-centered analysis jumped. The difference was substantial and statistically significant at the 1% level. Most particularly, diagnosing increased both substantially and significantly. There was literally no change in expertise-centered actions: the volume was exactly the same between the two years. The coding confirm that both partnering and initiating were already fairly common in the earliest years.

From Period 2 to Period 3—when institutionalization continued and revenues started to grow—expertise-centered action expanded substantially. The effects were significant at the 5% level in one model and at the 1% level in the other model. The two specifications of the model diverge on the prevalence of expertise-centered analysis (diagnosing and anticipating): the effect is positive and significant when considering overall coverage, but negative and insignificant when considering coverage adjusted for newsletter length. Note that this is the only moment when the key predictions of the two models diverge. As noted above, Tribe F increased its analyses from Period 1 to Period 2. In Period 3, as government continued to become more specialized and more financing become available, it appears that the tribe's greatest thrust was translating analysis into actions.

Finally, from Period 3 to Period 4, both expertise-centered analysis and action increased substantially and at the exact same rate. Both effects were significant at the 5% and 10% levels, respectively. These results were precisely what the thick description found as well: all kinds of expertise-centered behaviors flourished after governmental and economic change accumulated.

Tribe F's experience offers insight into pathways of organizational growth. The analysis tracked outcomes as some particular external hindrances on this tribe's governmental institutionalization abated and as the nationwide casino industry flourished. Because these changes happened in a compressed time frame, when the other contexts that the tribe faced did not change dramatically, it was especially easy to see the consequences of expertise. Tribe F found ways to do more to shape the future of its people; expertise-centered behaviors had very real

TABLE 4.3A

Expertise-Centered Behaviors in Tribe F's Newsletter

	Period 1	Period 2: growth in government begins	Period 3: growth in economy begins	Period 4	Difference between Periods 1 & 2	Difference between Periods 2 & 3	Difference between Periods 3 & 4
Expertise-Centered Analysis	1.67	5.00	7.33	12.25	3.33***	2.33**	4.92**
	(1.56)	(3.25)	(2.10)	(6.45)	(1.04)	(1.12)	(1.96)
Expertise-Centered Behavior	2.50	2.50	10.08	15.00	0.00	7.58***	4.92*
	(3.09)	(2.28)	(5.11)	(7.31)	(1.11)	(1.61)	(2.57)
Diagnosing	0.75	3.33	4.33	8.58	2.58***	1	4.25***
	(1.22)	(2.61)	(2.27)	(4.46)	(0.83)	(0.98)	(1.44)
Anticipating	0.92	1.67	3.00	3.67	0.75	1.33**	0.67
	(1.16)	(1.44)	(1.48)	(2.42)	(0.53)	(0.59)	(0.82)
Initiating	1.42	1.58	5.08	7.83	0.17	3.50***	2.75*
	(1.78)	(1.51)	(2.35)	(4.22)	(0.67)	(0.81)	(1.39)
Partnering	1.08	0.92	5.00	7.17	-0.17	4.08***	2.17
	(1.56)	(1.31)	(3.69)	(3.97)	(0.59)	(1.13)	(1.57)
Number of months	12	12	12	12			

For differences, significance at the 1%, 5%, and 10% levels is indicated by ***, **, and *, respectively. Standard deviations in parentheses for tribes; standard errors in parentheses for differences. Expertise-centered analysis=diagnosing and anticipating. Expertise-centered action=initiating and partnering. *Average monthly volume.*

TABLE 4.3B

Expertise-Centered Behaviors in Tribe F's Newsletter, Adjusted for Newspaper Length

	Period 1	Period 2: growth in government begins	Period 3: growth in economy begins	Period 4	Difference between Periods 1 & 2	Difference between Periods 2 & 3	Difference between Periods 3 & 4
Expertise-Centered Analysis	1.67 (1.56)	5.00 (3.25)	3.67 (1.05)	6.13 (3.23)	3.33*** (1.04)	-1.33 (0.99)	2.46** (0.98)
Expertise-Centered Action	2.50 (3.09)	2.50 (2.28)	5.04 (2.55)	7.50 (3.66)	0.00 (1.11)	2.54** (0.99)	2.46* (1.29)
Diagnosing	0.75 (1.22)	3.33 (2.61)	2.17 (1.13)	4.29 (2.23)	2.58*** (0.83)	-1.17 (0.82)	2.13*** (0.72)
Anticipating	0.92 (1.16)	1.67 (1.44)	1.50 (0.74)	1.83 (1.21)	0.75 (0.53)	-0.17 (0.47)	0.33 (0.41)
Initiating	1.42 (1.78)	1.58 (1.51)	2.54 (1.18)	3.92 (2.11)	0.17 (0.67)	0.96* (0.55)	1.38* (0.70)
Partnering	1.08 (1.56)	0.92 (1.31)	2.50 (1.85)	3.58 (1.99)	-0.17 (0.59)	1.58** (0.65)	1.08 (0.78)
Number of months	12	12	12	12			

For differences, significance at the 1%, 5%, and 10% levels is indicated by ***, **, and *, respectively. Standard deviations in parentheses for periods; standard errors in parentheses for differences. Expertise-centered analysis=diagnosing and anticipating. Expertise-centered action=initiating and partnering. *Average monthly volume.*

consequences for the community. Furthermore, Tribe F offered the lesson that partnerships were a notable element in laying the groundwork for growth in expertise. In particular, federal partnerships were important resources with consequences for internal skills and external relations. Furthermore, Tribe F's economic successes did not mean that dollars simply substituted for expertise cultivation. Rather, the tribe's economic engine was harnessed to feed governmental capacities.

IV. Test 3: A Comparison on Three Divisions within the Navajo Nation

When we turn our attention to the Navajo Nation, we see another scale of information-processing, problem-assessment, and problem-solving. The Navajo Nation has the biggest reservation in the United States and one of the largest tribal memberships. Its government is highly specialized. The tribe has natural resource extraction enterprises that provide the government with an impressive economic base. Chapter 2 provides more background on the tribe. Capacities do vary, however, among different parts of the Navajo Nation. I examined Navajo Nation's Divisions of Economic Development, Public Safety, and Natural Resources over the 1990s. Navajo Nation budgets showed that expenditures for public safety and natural resources were consistently about five times greater than for economic development. I would expect that these systematic budgetary constraints on the Division of Economic Development would translate into meaningful impediments to expertise accumulation, and indeed they did.

For this analysis, I used quarterly briefing reports that the three divisions provided regularly to the tribal council. The reports revealed systematic differences in expertise-centered behaviors that accorded with the differences in federal help available. The qualitative analysis focused on reporting in July 1993. The coding for expertise-centered behaviors encompassed a larger case base, examining seven reports from seven different years.[6]

A. FUNDING FOR THE THREE DIVISIONS

Walke (2000) documented variation in federal spending on economic development, natural resources, and public safety on all reservations. From 1975 to 2001, the federal government, in an average year, spent $82.6 million on Indian economic development programs, compared to $145.2 million on Indian natural resources programs.[7] Walke did not examine Indian public safety spending directly, but he included it in the overall category of tribal services, on which $465.2 million was spent in an average year. Furthermore, the over-time trajectory (from 1975 to 2001) in federal economic development spending was more anemic than in the other policy areas. Allocations to Indian economic development declined an average of $4 million a year. In contrast, federal spending on Indian natural resources was increasing an average of $0.6 million a year. Expenditures on tribal services were also rising: an average of $15.2 million a year.

These differences in spending were apparent in Navajo Nation budgets, as table 4.4 shows. The Division of Economic Development received far less federal support and the tribe did not find or use other funding sources to compensate. On average throughout the 1990s, the Division of Economic Development operated with less than 1% of the federal support that Division of Natural Resources or Division of Public Safety received. Natural Resources enjoyed generous support from the federal government as well as from all other sources.[8] Public Safety and Economic Development differed vastly in their federal dollars, although funding from other sources was fairly comparable.

TABLE 4.4

Budgets of Three Navajo Nation Divisions from Select Years, in Millions			
	Division of Natural Resources	Division of Public Safety	Division of Economic Development
1990 Total budget	$11.02	$18.28	$1.77
Federal funding	$6.01	$14.89	$0.04
All other funding	$5.01	$3.39	$1.73
Federal as % of total	55%	81%	2%
1992 Total budget	$23.00	$20.34	$4.23
Federal funding	$9.64	$13.61	$0.05
All other funding	$13.36	$6.73	$4.18
Federal as % of total	42%	67%	1%
1994 Total budget	$26.74	$26.27	$5.00
Federal funding	$11.63	$20.19	$0.00
All other funding	$15.11	$6.08	$5.00
Federal as % of total	43%	77%	0%
1996 Total budget	$33.74	$28.82	$5.81
Federal funding	$13.08	$23.99	$0.35
All other funding	$20.66	$4.83	$5.46
Federal as % of total	39%	83%	6%

Source: Budget of the Navajo Nation.

B. OVERVIEW OF THE THREE DIVISIONS

I begin with a discussion of what these divisions had in common. First, Navajo Nation divisions displayed remarkable capacities. In the January 1998 report, the Division of Economic Development's activities included formulating tourism projects, developing private housing, and finalizing financing for an agricultural processing plant. Activities of the Division of Natural Resources included developing new water systems, negotiating multimillion dollar royalty agreements with mining companies, and implementing multiple abandoned mine reclamation projects. The Division of Public Safety, among other things, was assessing the feasibility of building a jail, winning grants to fund new police officers, and drafting a community-oriented policing plan.

Yet all these divisions faced significant challenges. The Division of Economic Development noted that the tribe had yet to meet fundamental infrastructure needs that limited economic development severely. Old, leaking underground storage tanks were found across the reservation and most of the water system was inadequate. The Division of Natural Resources noted that it been unable to enforce logging restrictions and was having trouble providing basic sanitation at recreation areas. Lastly, a court ruling had found that the sorry state of Division of Public Safety's detention facilities was in violation of prisoners' rights. Organizations with these kinds of fundamental shortcomings would hardly be the paragon of public administration, and the lean budgets on which these divisions ran myriad programs would not earn the envy of most administrators. In spite of their constraints, these agencies managed to carve out notable successes by using expertise-centered problem-solving skills.

C. THE DIVISION OF NATURAL RESOURCES (DNR)

For the Navajo Division of Natural Resources, much of its mission focused on technical services and technical assistance. The division conducted a great deal of outreach to tribal members on land use practices and it implemented a variety of surveys and inspections of land conditions. This work required specific forms of expertise, as the analysis below will show.

Anticipating. In July 1993, the office repeatedly identified the interplay of forces and their possible future consequences. For example, the agency was assessing the possible impacts of a proposed water system. Also, staff evaluated future forestry needs as they drafted a 10-year Forestry Management Plan.

Diagnosing. In partnership with the U.S. Bureau of Reclamation, DNR was evaluating reservation irrigation systems. DNR's offices of Historic Preservation, Fish and Wildlife, Parks and Recreation, Grazing, Environmental Protection, Minerals, and Land Administration were all assessing the performance of their respective resource management plans and drafting revisions.

Diagnoses helped guide initiatives. For example, in one situation the division noted:

> Given the extraordinary Hopi interest in a pipeline from Lake Powell—which can only be funded and built with Navajo Nation support—to supply Hopi water needs, an effort is now being made to combine issues in the Land and Water Rights disputes with the Hopi into a single comprehensive settlement strategy and approach.

DNR was well-informed about needs throughout the region, so it could envision new approaches to issues and to other actors.

Initiating. Upgrades to water systems—irrigation, wells, dams, and sewage lagoons—were in progress. The reclamation of abandoned mines was ongoing and one project had been recognized "as one of the top ten AML [Abandoned Mine Lands] projects nationwide."

Partnering. DNR's actions frequently involved other actors—especially federal actors—as in the following case:

> The [Water Resources Management] Department sponsored a joint meeting at Birdsprings Chapter with the U.S. Army Corps of Engineers (ACE), the Bureau of Reclamation and the Soil Conservation Services [of the USDA], to explore the opportunity to develop a comprehensive water management plan for the Little Colorado River valley, including flood control, off-stream diversion and storage for multiple beneficial uses, and needs of the local community for a bridge across the river.

Indeed, what stood out in DNR's accounts were astute partnerships. The division was engaged in ongoing environmental management with the U.S. Department of Energy.[9] Along with the Navajo Nation Department of Justice, staff worked to "clarify and strengthen controls over livestock buying, and to develop an agreement with the Arizona, New Mexico, and Colorado Livestock Boards." The DNR had broad skills for identifying and acting upon shared interests.

D. THE DIVISION OF PUBLIC SAFETY (DPS)

In July 1993, DPS faced more challenges than DNR—most notably, its detention facilities needed massive improvements in order to reach basic standards for housing prisoners. But DPS was at work addressing these problems.

Diagnosing. The division was actively diagnosing many challenges. Planning staff, having identified highest priorities for action, were now drafting "budgets for renovation, personnel, and food." More broadly, DPS was working on diagnosing the best approaches to lean budgets:

> The Division is in the process of prioritizing services to be provided that are considered top priority, based on the severity and emergency nature of the complaints or incidents as well as administrative services requested.

Anticipating. Furthermore, DPS saw this need as not just a one-time job, but also anticipated future consequences and prepared comprehensive plans for the next three fiscal years, "by preparing budgets from each district, program, and section," and also worked on "identifying minimum, medium, and maximum levels of services that are appropriate at each facility for additional personnel, equipment, vehicles, and operations." The division was able to see the need for contingency planning and to see how to act upon it.

Partnering. The division developed mutual aid agreements with other fire departments. With help from federal partners, the division was implementing an electronic incident tracking system. DPS won federal grants to expand the size of detention facilities, develop new operating procedures, and expand electronic records management.

Initiating. There were actions that weren't directly tied to partnerships, as well: the DPS was reorganizing to allow its Internal Affairs division greater autonomy and it had a new plan to expand emergency services and hazardous materials response.

E. THE DIVISION OF ECONOMIC DEVELOPMENT (DED)

What happened to the agency that operated with less federal assistance? Even though the Division of Economic Development reported accomplishments in July 1993, DED was the most constrained of the three agencies, and the effects showed.

Anticipating. Undergirding DED's performance was careful anticipation of the future. With two new development projects—a marina and a private housing development—the division identified in great detail the steps ahead and a timeline for completion. In another instance, personnel gathered information to anticipate the prospects of a furniture manufacturing plant and thus make a decision on whether to pursue it.

Diagnosing. The division engaged in a great deal of diagnosing. DED extended technical assistance, including "feasibility analysis" to one community that was developing an enterprise. It determined "site plans and necessary location of all utilities" for another. Additionally, the division turned its diagnostic abilities on its own operations, as it carried out an evaluation of its shopping center program.

There was a striking reliance, however, on contractors who conducted expertise-centered analysis in DED's stead. DED contracted out the planning for a tribal company, an assessment of prospects for economic development at one location, and "an acquisition strategy for the Navajo Nation to acquire the lands and facilities." Certain skills were not held in-house.

Partnering. Notable partnering involved federal agencies: the National Park Service was involved in new marina development; the BIA was funding a new tribal oil company. DED also persuaded the BIA to prioritize road construction that was essential to a particular project. Note than only one of these projects was a true economic development project. The other two hinged on persuading federal agencies in other policy domains (parks and roads) that their mission could intersect with economic development.

There were shortcomings in partnerships as well. The division was encountering delays in its plans for a vendor village where Navajo craftspeople could sell their goods to tourists. The division was coordinating with a local division of the tribal government, a local business association, and the tribe's Parks and Recreation Department. In spite of these efforts, it was still the case that "[l]and is a major problem."

Initiating. Like other tribal divisions, DED accomplished new initiatives. Two new tribal shopping centers had been completed and a new tenant had been secured for a tribal industrial park. Two new cooperatives were started in the eastern part of the reservation.

Yet the July 1993 report also described the failure of DED's Wool Marketing Program:

> No demand for wool and mohair products worldwide, therefore, price per pound is very low.... [C]onsultancy to plan an in-house grading program and to develop a spinning operation has been completed.... An audit was also done by the Navajo Nation Auditor General's office. The recommendations from this audit are being applied to the program.

DED could see that the program needed to be fixed; it could also diagnose the root of the problem. But DED depended on others to devise a solution.

F. TALLIES OF EXPERTISE-CENTERED BEHAVIORS

I used quantitative analysis to cover a larger sampling frame. Specifically, I tallied expertise-centered behaviors in a total of seven reports, all from different years. Table 4.5 shows the results.[10]

TABLE 4.5

Expertise-Centered Behaviors within Three Departments in the Navajo Nation

	Economic Development: small budget	Public Safety: large budget	Natural Resources: large budget	Average for programs with large budgets	Difference between programs with large & small budgets
Expertise-Centered Analysis	1.84	2.55	3.68	3.12	1.27**
	(0.30)	(0.83)	(1.65)	(1.39)	(0.57)
Expertise-Centered Action	1.62	2.21	2.49	2.35	0.73
	(0.93)	(0.46)	(1.56)	(1.12)	(0.49)
Diagnosing	1.31	1.81	2.26	2.03	0.72
	(1.05)	(0.76)	(1.36)	(1.08)	(0.50)
Anticipating	0.53	0.74	1.42	1.08	0.55**
	(0.28)	(0.39)	(0.51)	(0.56)	(0.23)
Initiating	0.59	0.73	1.30	1.01	0.42
	(0.55)	(0.33)	(1.16)	(0.87)	(0.36)
Partnering	1.03	1.49	1.19	1.34	0.31
	(0.48)	(0.48)	(0.55)	(0.52)	(0.24)
Number of reports	7	7	7	14	

For differences, significance at the 1%, 5%, and 10% levels is indicated by ***, **, and *, respectively. Standard deviations in parentheses for agencies; standard errors in parentheses for differences. Expertise-centered analysis=diagnosing and anticipating. Expertise-centered action=initiating and partnering.
Average per page in reports.
Source: Quarterly Reports of the Navajo Nation.

The economic development office was notably different from the other two departments. The law enforcement and natural resources offices engaged in more expertise-centered analysis: the difference was significant at the 5% level. In particular, the extent of anticipating was significant at the 5% level. The differences for expertise-centered actions—initiating and partnering—were positive but fell short of statistical significance.

As we have seen in the other cases, the results from expertise-centered coding were consistent with advance expectations about differences among the three agencies. Throughout the analysis, the organizations with more means to support specialized skills tallied up more expertise-centered behaviors. In sum, they better understood their problems and they executed responses.

VIII. Conclusion

This chapter has examined levels of expertise in several contexts. It has compared two cases—Tribes A and C—with much in common but with key differences in underlying capacity for organizational expertise. It has examined a single tribe—Tribe F—that experienced change over time in its capacity for expertise. Finally, it has evaluated differences between units within one tribal government with varying resources to support expertise accumulation—the Navajo Nation Divisions of Natural Resources, Public Safety, and Economic Development. The three comparisons—between Tribes A and C, within F over time, and among agencies in the Navajo Nation—allowed for careful testing of the consequences of variation in expertise. As expected, this analysis found different levels of problem-solving skills among these tribal governments, skills that can be measured by looking to expertise-centered abilities to *diagnose, anticipate, initiate,* and *partner.* Put simply, there were three core results. First, better-endowed tribes displayed expertise-centered behaviors more frequently. Second, federal partnerships were a useful tool for achieving those behaviors. Third, even tribes in marginal circumstances displayed some expertise-centered behaviors; they were not wholly incapacitated. Across a wide range of circumstances, expertise could serve community needs.

The sources for each of the three comparisons addressed different audiences, yet for each, expertise-centered behaviors unfolded as expected. The results held even when the formats of records within a given comparison varied over time. Furthermore, for each of the three comparisons, I laid side-by-side tools of detailed description and of coding. The patterns for expertise-centered behaviors persisted:

meaningful differences in knowledgeable analysis and action emerged consistently when capacity-building resources were available.

More broadly, this chapter illustrated expertise's consequences for problem-solving. Specialized knowledge allows groups to better understand processes, to envision what the future will hold, to pinpoint allies, and to forge new approaches. Such skills have far-flung consequences. Subsequent chapters demonstrate their benefits in interactions with state and local governments.

5 Expertise and "Soft" Disempowerment
RACE, LAND, AND LOCAL POWER IN AMERICAN INDIAN POLITICS

I. Introduction

Earlier chapters explored the role of institutional niches in building expertise and the role of expertise in expanding tribal governments' problem-solving options. Here, I begin linking those findings to tribal governments' influence in regional politics. Tribes' relations with counties show that tribes use greater expertise to behave differently and more effectively in politics. First, they learn to pick their interactions with counties, avoiding the investment of energy into lost causes. Also, they learn how to be more persuasive, and as a consequence counties pursue courses of actions that are not taken otherwise.

To evaluate expertise's effects, I examine tribes with governments and economies that improve capacities to house, sustain, and reproduce expertise. I find that these tribes' political strategies hinge on expert calculations. An alternate hypothesis might suggest that all tribes know what they want from nearby governments and how to get it; but some lack tangible, traditional resources for realizing their aims. This chapter demonstrates that such an explanation is inadequate: expertise changes tribes' approach to regional politics. Specifically, when tribes have moderate capacities to house, sustain, and reproduce expertise, they are extremely selective about county relations and they pick the winning issues. Tribes with the greatest capacities figure out how to take on an ambitious agenda without overextending themselves.

There are, however, some sobering limits on these opportunities. Tribal-county relations are often grounded in broader Indian-white conflict. Pronounced hostility impedes tribes' successes, but tribes can still use expertise to figure out some creative coalitions and arguments. The situation worsens acutely, however, when Indian-white conflict generates specific and wide-ranging demands on tribes' expert capacities. Then, contestation depletes expert wherewithal. In other words, Indian-white conflict alone cannot foil creative strategizing, but exhaustion related to Indian-white conflict erodes vital expert resources.

In short, expertise has two sides. When tribes have governments and economies that make it easier to capitalize on expertise, their behavior reveals savvy assessments of policy and politics. Expertise also provides a point of vulnerability, however. Disempowerment and marginalization can result simply by draining expert capacity.

A. THE QUESTION

Tribes and neighboring governments, although distinct authorities, still affect each other. Granted, tribal sovereignty and federal policy constrain the ability of local governments to intervene in tribal affairs. The Constitution and 19th-century court decisions established Native American affairs as the domain of the federal government, a zone free from state and local government jurisdiction (Wilkins 1996, 1998; Cohen 1988; Harring 1994). Yet we know that localities and tribes have been brought into frequent contact in recent years.

Most importantly, some policy concerns—such as environmental management, transportation, law enforcement, and regional economic vitality—do not adhere neatly to jurisdictional lines, meaning that policy decisions made by neighboring authorities will have impacts beyond their borders (Lopach, Brown, and Clow 1998; Biolsi 2001). Conflicts between tribes and localities over law enforcement, business regulation, and fishing rights have been well documented (Ashley and Hubbard 2004, Bobo and Tuan 2006). Also, the federal government can expressly delegate its authority to states and localities, and indeed Congress has delegated important powers to state and local governments—casino regulation is the most high-profile arena of federal delegation today (Corntassel and Witmer 2008, Mason 2000). Also, as a joint task force on state-tribal relations by the National Congress of American Indians and the National Council of State Legislatures (Johnson et al. 2002, ix) noted:

As tribal governments continue to build their capabilities and exercise their powers of self-government, and as the federal government continues to devolve responsibilities to them, states and tribes must address policy questions that concern jurisdiction and shared governance.

In short, as tribes build independent expert organizations, they find their voice in local and state politics.

Finally, tribal governments often play key roles in defending the rights of American Indians to participate fully in state and local politics. Cohen (1988) noted that in the mid-20th century, many states still refused to recognize the rights of Indians to participate in state and local politics. From the 1940s to the 1970s, tribal members in a number of Western states mounted successful legal challenges to various state and local laws restricting their ability to participate in state and local public life (McCool 1985, Phelps 1991) and many of those fights continue today (McCool, Olson, and Robinson 2007).

There are many prospects for mutually beneficial interactions: joint efforts to address externalities across jurisdictional lines, coordinated service delivery to achieve economies of scale, and cooperative efforts to redesign and integrate programs that serve American Indians. But a great deal of the existing literature indicates that state and local governments approach tribal relations with hostility.[1] This chapter evaluates the forces behind tribal-county relations. I examine whether capacities to house and sustain expertise improved tribes' successes in county interactions. Most particularly, I investigate whether the details of tribes' behavior hinge on expertise.

II. Data and Methods

I examined tribal-county interactions for 12 tribes from 1990 to 2000.[2] To compile this dataset, I read all the minutes of the 12 County Boards of Supervisors/County Commissions/County Courts from 1990 to 2000 and identified all interactions with tribal governments in a sample of policy areas. This analysis focused on public safety, natural resources protection and management, business regulation and development (which included gaming), and elections. Initial fieldwork underscored the need for a focused search through non-indexed, meagerly organized county records.

The county journals that record county decision-making contained a wealth of information about local politics.[3] These journals included much more than just policy proposals and votes. They recorded commentary and discussion from board members, county bureaucrats, tribal officials, invited guests, businesses and organizations with particular interest in the day's agenda, and the general public.

A. MEASURING INTERACTIONS

The methods that I used to identify a tribal-county interaction were as follows. If anyone at the meeting identified a proposal as impacting or involving the tribe in the sample, it was included in this analysis. Also, any project within an Indian community on the reservation was included in the sample, even if no one ever spoke directly of the tribe. I did not limit the sample to highly formal proposals or to proposals where all the details had been elaborated. Vague or general proposals, along the lines of "the county should do more to help the tribe," or "the tribe should shoulder more of the costs for services in this community," were not included in the analysis. But if someone at the meeting remarked, for example, "the county should include reservation communities in its Economic Development District," and thereby offered a specific policy proposal which the board could act on or ignore, then it was included even if the proposer did not furnish any detail. In short, I cast a wide net for actions (or inaction) that could affect the reservation. I presume, however, that the dataset did not capture some county policies with diffuse or indirect effects on tribes.

Interactions were coded as favorable or unfavorable to the tribe, according to the position that tribal representatives took on the matter. In most cases, a tribal official provided some commentary, either by directly speaking at the meeting or by communicating with a county official who then relayed the conversation to the board. This coding task turned out to be quite straightforward—there were no instances where third parties debated what the tribal government's preference was, and there were no instances that indicated actors seeking to misrepresent the tribe's position. When no commentary was available, I considered an interaction favorable if it increased the power or resources accorded to tribal governments.

I took a conservative approach to labeling an interaction as successful for the tribe. If a specific favorable proposal was mentioned in the minutes, but no follow-up action was ever reported, the interaction was treated as if the proposal failed. If a proposal included multiple components to address tribal concerns but the county only enacted some of those components, I considered the interaction failed.

I have collected local newspapers—some serving largely white audiences, some serving largely Indian audiences—for certain time periods for a few of the cases, to see if other actors characterized interactions differently. I found no instances where news coverage characterized a measure as impacting tribes while the county minutes did not; nor did the newspaper coverage identify tribal preferences on a given issue differently than the county minutes did. I did find, however, that the minutes captured many more interactions than newspapers. This finding fits with existing literature, which has found that tribes' concern receive limited coverage in local news. Existing work has also documented that when local papers do cover tribes' relations with other authorities, coverage can be dominated by frames that cast tribes as uncooperative or intrusive (Miller 1993, Sayer 1997, Bobo and Tuan 2006).

The dataset identifies each time a decision was made that might impact tribes. In other words, a series of decisions about one policy would result in multiple interactions and multiple observations in the dataset. For example, when local authorities were considering developing a regional waste management facility in one county, they faced a series of decisions over time: whether to form a planning committee, whether to fund a feasibility study, and where to locate the facility (by the time the sample ended, actors had failed to agree on a location). Because various decisions on the same topic may involve different constraints and different leadership due to the passage of time, each decision was treated as an individual observation. As a result, a successful long-term project could generate a number of positive interactions. In the statistical analysis, I introduced controls to account for this pattern in the data.

B. KEY VARIABLES

1. Government Institutionalization and Economic Development

Chapter 2 provides detail on the 12 tribes in the sample and on sampling procedures. First, I test whether well-established *government institutionalization* matters. Here, I hypothesize that tribal governments with greater in-house specialization have greater capacities to acquire, retain, and reproduce expertise and thus have better tools for achieving broader influence. More precisely, I look to tribal governments that have achieved greater functional specialization, which we can also think of as greater differentiation of the tribal government. They stand in contrast to tribes where officials function as generalists and operate in less routine ways.

Additionally, I evaluate whether well-established *economic development* matters. Here, my hypothesis is that a certain infusion of funds makes it easier to build and sustain expertise, by allowing tribes to bring in additional staff or build new programs. Essentially, independent funds give tribes better means to support their independent expert organizations.

I want to evaluate whether there were differences in behavior across the conditions of government institutionalization and economic development that reflected greater expertise and information, rather than just differences due to greater, more general resource accumulation (votes, dollars, or other fairly tangible means for realizing their ends). If these hypotheses are right, better-endowed tribes would cultivate expertise more extensively, and these tribes would then see their environment differently and alter their approaches accordingly.

More precisely, expertise should relate to success in several ways. First, more expert actors are better at issue selection: they pick winning issues, winning frames, and winning coalitions. Second, more expert actors are better at persuasion: they make a better case in their interactions. Henceforth, I measure whether better-endowed tribes channeled their capacities into expertise-centered pathways, and if it made a difference to do so.

2. Indian-White Conflict

I also want to consider the ways that racial conflict may or may not shape tribal-county interactions and, most particularly, work against the gains from expertise. Indian-white conflict wouldn't undo expertise, but it could overshadow its impact.

To measure Indian-white conflict, there is good reason to give special attention to one classic source of conflict: the extent to which land within reservation boundaries is "checkerboarded." In some regions, federal policy in the late 19th century resulted in private ownership by non-tribal members of land tracts within reservation boundaries. Such entanglement of interests has fueled political, economic, and social conflict, as Biolsi (2001) documented. See chapter 2 for more discussion of checkerboarding.

There is compelling evidence that entangled land doesn't just lead to principled debate between governments; it's an angry, bitter, and fearful clash between communities. For starters, Bobo and Tuan (2006) find such patterns in Indian-white conflict over fishing rights on the Great Lakes. Checkerboarding is rarer in the Southwest and Pacific Northwest—it was present on only one of the eight reservations in the sample—but more commonplace in the Upper Plains—where three of the four reservations were checkerboarded. It is difficult to measure whether race relations are worse or better in the Upper Plans than in the other regions in this sample: there are no nationwide data that speak to this particular question.

Yet there is some evidence suggesting that Upper Plains politics are poisoned by negative attitudes and stereotypes about American Indians as a people. There was one survey of racial attitudes in the Upper Plains in the mid-1980s (Peterson 1987). On key questions, typically one-fifth to one-quarter of respondents expressed negative attitudes about American Indians.[4] There are other indicators of racial hostility in the Upper Plains as well. In coverage in the 1990s by a newspaper based in a largely white community within the boundaries of one reservation in the sample, a county official wrote a letter opposing candidates for state and local office with ties to tribal government because they would show "bias" and calling for "representatives who will protect the constitutional rights of all parties concerned, *not those who will help strip those rights away from the citizens.*" (Emphasis added.) Of course, tribal members are as much citizens as anybody else. On another occasion, when one U.S. senator visited, some white locals described disputes with tribal government as "'explosive' and 'about ready to blow.'" The senator responded, "I get a feeling you're almost being driven out." Soon thereafter, the paper published a guest column calling on the community "to finally set aside our jealousies, gossip, envies, distrust, and assumptions so we can hash out our land disputes, our jurisdictional concerns and our sovereignty issues."

There are other contemporaneous, well-publicized examples from various parts of the Upper Plains. Perhaps most notably, a county official at a public meeting in the early 1990s described American Indian culture as "mongrelized," "primitive," and "a culture of hopelessness, godlessness, joblessness and lawlessness" (*Argus Leader* 1990).[5]

Again, this should not suggest that racial tensions were absent in other regions. County records elsewhere make clear that hostility toward tribal governments and American Indians afflicted tribal-county interactions. In one example from the Southwest, a newspaper ran the following coverage of tribal-local relations. In a first article, the county sheriff announced that he was cutting off law enforcement and emergency response to the reservation to "hold out for compensation for his department's services." The newspaper editor's column the next day did not raise concerns about the potential public safety consequences of such political brinksmanship. Rather, the column attacked the tribe for its recent position in water use negotiations. The tribe was developing some new businesses and wanted to secure more access to water. As the newspaper's editor saw those negotiations, the tribe had decided to "hold hostage" the wider community: "In other words, the [tribal] negotiators are saying 'You give us exactly what we are asking for in order for us to destroy your business community' … [Tribal officials], true to form, are refusing to return phone calls…"

In a case from the Pacific Northwest, in a discussion of a tribe's new casino, a county commissioner remarked caustically:

I don't think it's right that a so called sovereign nation can open up a casino and do damn well what it wants to do and totally unregulated by the feds and the State.... It's not fair that a sovereign nation that you can't sue that you can't do anything about operates gambling and can dictate to you the payoffs and not pay a dime to the counties and not pay a dime to the state unless they are compact[ed] and we are looking into [what] the compact between the state and the [tribe] has provided for.

The commissioner's statement contains a raft of factual errors, beyond his reference to "so called" sovereign nations. Tribal casinos are subject to regulations and taxes—although clearly not the kind of regulations and taxes that this county commissioner would prefer. As tribes managed interactions with counties, non-Indian officials that they faced did not simply have different preferences or priorities. Some officials and community leaders held pronounced hostility toward the very enterprise of tribal government.

In short, I am not suggesting that the absence of checkerboarding meant racial conflict was at zero. In the analysis that follows, I considered checkerboarding to be one important dynamic—and an element that can be measured reliably—that increased Indian-white conflict. By measuring the potent and easily quantified patterns of checkerboarding, I can examine whether Indian-white conflict could overshadow the benefits from expertise. To assess the extent of checkerboarding for the four counties where it exists, I measured the percent of the county population that is non-Indian living within the reservation boundaries.[6]

3. Exhaustion Elsewhere

I also wanted to measure variation in the energy that tribes expend in response to racial tensions. Here, I distinguish an overall environment of conflict from the effort expended at a particular moment in response to conflict. My theory is that baseline racial conflict overshadows the benefits of expertise, whereas effort expended in response to conflict saps the very tools needed for expert behavior. In short, we should still see expert behavior when racial conflict is present, but expert behavior should dissipate at specific moments of exhaustion.

I wanted to identify activities with the following characteristics: (a) they demanded significant time and energy; (b) the skills that they generated were not highly portable to county legislative interactions; (c) their frequency varied over time; (d) that variation was due in part to exogenous forces, so that tribes would have difficulty predicting or controlling the exact timing of demands; and (e) tribes couldn't necessarily adjust their involvement quickly and easily.

Here, I turned to the extent to which the tribe was involved in legal disputes—appeals cases in particular—as an indicator of varying exhaustion. At moments when there were more suits, I expect that tribal capacities would be stretched thin. I am not at all suggesting that lawsuits are a less desirable means of conflict resolution. Lawsuits offer unique benefits; they also impose particular costs. Lawsuits are a way of forcing accommodations from highly intransigent adversaries, and they set precedents that can preclude or minimize potential future disputes. Lawsuits consume enormous government resources, however, as many tribal leaders would attest: lawyers are expensive, and lawsuits can take a great deal of time to reach resolution. Furthermore, the skills generated in winning legal battles can be quite venue-specific. Indeed, while McCool, Olson, and Robinson provided excellent documentation of the accomplishments that Voting Rights Act litigation has achieved for American Indian voters, they also noted (2007, 89), "[l]itigation, however, is complex, time-consuming, and heavily dependent on access to sophisticated counsel."

Also, I looked to lawsuits—appeals in particular—because their timing is not entirely under the control of the parties involved. Neither party determines when exactly cases are heard. Additionally, either party may feel compelled to continue in an appeals process, even if the nature of the initial context changes over time, because of the precedent at stake. As a result, it can be difficult—or simply impracticable—for a tribe to back out of a suit at moments when they are stretched particularly thin.

It is reasonable to ask whether this variable really preponderantly reflects other dynamics. A natural question is whether it simply measures baseline conflict. Fortunately, the data allowed me to test these two hypotheses in the regressions that follow. If it were the case that the number of suits in a narrow time period was just another measure of baseline conflict, then we would expect that the number of suits and persistent Indian-white conflict would produce similar and interchangeable effects. In fact, as I show in the data analysis that follows, I found differing effects, and that the effects were stable when one variable was omitted from the model. In short, increased lawsuits involved dynamics that were distinct from baseline conflict.

It is equally reasonable to ask whether the number of lawsuits at one moment reflects variation in overall tensions, not a change in exhaustion. If this were the case—in other words, that more disputes in appeals courts were associated with momentarily greater pessimism or disinterest about county relations—we would expect to see the number of legislative interactions fall off notably when legal appeals were high. If the variable simply captured a spirit of noncooperation, why wouldn't tribes and counties just retreat into separate corners in that moment? Such a pattern did not appear in the data, as analysis below will show.

I argue that a peak in lawsuits represents something beyond long-standing grudges. Because tribes must expend considerable effort on lawsuits, suits are a reliable indicator of some unique consequences. When more capacities are directed to suits, it means less strategizing and diagnosing are directed to relations with county commissions.

I measured the number of legal disputes with states and localities that were in the appeals process, and whether the tribe (a) was arguing an appeal in a given time period, (b) had an appeal that was upcoming, and (c) was currently between appeals on a case.[7] To control for noise in this measure, I generated a dichotomous threshold for whether the number of suits at a given moment was especially high.

III. Findings: Summary Statistics

The sample included 529 county-tribal interactions. The types of interactions can be grouped into several categories. The first two categories were what I considered to be "easier" interactions, as they involved relatively minor commitments by tribes and counties. These included (1) instances where the county was considering a small-scale subsidy or support to the tribe and (2) cases where the tribe asked the county to endorse an initiative it was undertaking in another sphere, such as seeking a federal grant. Easier issues were 33% of the sample.

The next set of interactions was what I would term "harder" interactions, in that they entailed greater commitments of dollars, time, or obligation. These included (3) decisions that would affect tribal representation in the decision-making bodies of the county, (4) decisions about larger-scale delivery of goods or services from the county to tribe (or vice versa), and (5) regional initiatives or authorities, where tribes and counties were considering jointly designing and implementing programs. Harder issues comprised 52% of the sample.

Finally, the last category included negative externalities from either the county's or the tribal government's actions. This was the only category where there were always explicit tradeoffs between tribal and county interests: these issues arose because one set of actors felt they were harmed by actual actions or could be harmed by potential actions of the other. Negative externalities were 15% of the sample.

Table 5.1 breaks down other features of the data. First, note the regional divide.[8] The tribal governments in the Upper Plains were consistently less successful. Upper Plains tribes succeeded in 62% of the interactions they started, versus a 78% success rate for the Southwest and Pacific Northwest. On interactions started by counties, the disparities were even starker. Tribes won in 48% of county-initiated interactions in the Upper Plains, versus a 72% success rate in the other regions. There were differences in support and opposition, too. In 83% of interactions in the Southwest and Northwest, someone else came forward to endorse the tribe's position, versus 49% for the Upper Plains.

Yet to a great degree, tribal governments in all regions set the agenda of which issues came up for consideration. About half of all the interactions began solely at tribes' instigation. Another one-sixth of these interactions were begun by the counties but required tribal participation before they could be resolved. For example, if a county wanted to start a joint initiative, the tribe was in a position to end or table consideration of the issue quickly, easily, and completely. In around one-third of interactions, it was possible for counties to begin and resolve a matter unilaterally, but often tribes did speak up in these decision-making processes.

As noted before, checkerboarding is rare in the Southwest and Pacific Northwest but commonplace in the Upper Plains. Among the four checkerboarded counties in the sample, there was substantial variation in the percent of the county population that was non-Indians living within the reservation boundaries. The average for this measure was 19% and the upper bound was around 40%.

The statistical analysis pulls in additional variables to account for other potential dynamics in tribal-county relations.

Access to a closely related venue—specifically, whether the city or town that was adjacent to the reservation was incorporated. Here, I considered whether portable expertise trumped potential exhaustion. If flexible expertise dominated, then tribal governments should have benefited from facing another local legislative authority. Skills built in municipal legislative negotiations should be quite portable to county legislative interactions.[9] If more layers of local government helped tribes, while more lawsuits hurt them, then it would appear that problems of exhaustion faded where knowledge was transferrable.[10] If expertise wasn't important, however, having another set of local government interactions should increase tribes' exhaustion.

Interactions over zoning in growth-management states. Some states—Oregon and Washington most notably—have imposed extensive growth planning requirements on county government. Counties in these states took up a substantial task that might otherwise be dispersed across various local governments or might have failed to come onto the agenda at all. Growth management could generate a large volume of county business.

Other recent interactions and success in those interactions. I considered whether tribes had a track record on an issue and whether that track record was positive or negative. In most cases, there were two measures that must be interpreted jointly.

TABLE 5.1

Descriptive Statistics on County Interactions

	All Regions	Northwest and Southwest					Upper Plains				
	All	All	Institutionalized government	Developed economy	Institutionalized government, developed economy	Institutionalized government, less developed economy	All	Institutionalized government	Institutionalized Developed economy	Institutionalized government, developed economy	Institutionalized government, less developed economy
Number of observations	529	271	64	40	107	60	258	89	31	118	20
Success rate	70%	78%	81%	83%	82%	63%	62%	56%	71%	67%	50%
Tribe had visible supporters	66%	83%	89%	83%	86%	72%	49%	45%	26%	64%	10%
Tribe had visible opponents	39%	43%	47%	53%	35%	47%	35%	40%	29%	31%	45%
Agenda-setting: Tribe initiated the interaction	51%	46%	25%	63%	47%	58%	56%	62%	74%	49%	45%

Agenda-setting: interaction initiated jointly	17%	17%	22%	3%	20%	18%	17%	6%	13%	22%	40%
Agenda-setting: County initiated interaction	32%	37%	53%	34%	33%	24%	17%	32%	13%	29%	15%
Checkerboarded reservations	4	1					3				
Indian–white conflict		19%		up to around 40% across all three regions							
Exhaustion elsewhere	1.07	1.07		from 0 to 6 for the two regions		1.07	from 0 to 8 for the region				

Indian–white conflict= If checkerboard reservation, percent of county population that was non-Indians living within reservation bounds per year.
Exhaustion elsewhere= Number of ongoing legal disputes with states and/or localities in appeals process per year.

The first variable assessed the consequence of recent interactions that had been negative; the combined effect of the first and second variable assessed the consequence of recent interactions that had been positive.

Policy area. I controlled for whether an interaction was about business regulation or development, natural resource management, public safety, or elections. Also, since land control may be at the base of many tribal-county interactions, I distinguished interactions that related most directly to zoning and land management.

Stages in participation. I controlled for the average number of stages in decision-making in tribal-county interactions for each county. In some places, a greater proportion of intermediate decisions were made in closed proceedings or by the county bureaucracy, and County Commission hearings were more apt to be reserved for final, up-or-down decisions. In other places, more decision-making was vested in the County Commission rather than in the county bureaucracy

Urbanized areas. I controlled for whether a reservation was near or within an urbanized area, as defined for Census 2000. I suspect that in urbanized areas, tribal-county interactions would be less pressing and of lower stakes. In cities, where knowledge-based jobs played a bigger role, the control over particular pieces of land ought not be quite so important. Outside of urbanized areas—where land-based economies of agriculture or natural resources management mattered more—land control had greater importance.

IV. Determinants of Interactions

There are many elements that are possibly at play in tribes' relations with counties, of course. In the analysis that follows, I attempt to account for the varying contributions of multiple forces. I employ multivariate regression analysis, which allows me to assess both the magnitude of many different effects and also the likelihood that a particular result reflects random chance rather than any true effects.

Readers who are uninterested in the details of the statistical analysis may want to skip ahead to the presentation of predicted probabilities in section D. Below, I conduct two kinds of multivariate regression analysis. To begin, I use a negative binomial count model to estimate the effects of various forces on the number of interactions between a tribe and county. Then, I employ logistic regression to evaluate what drives tribes' successes in interactions. With all the calculations, I want to consider whether the results reflect random variation rather than any real patterns. Therefore, for each estimated effect, I calculate a standard deviation and I estimate the probability that a result is due to random variation. If there is a less than 10% chance that a result is due to random variation, I deem the effect to be statistically significant.

With the models that are presented here, keep in mind that—unlike ordinary least squares regression—the magnitude of the effects cannot be directly interpreted from the tables, even though the direction and statistical significance of effects can be read straight from the table. Consequently, I conclude the statistical analysis by converting some of the estimates into predicted probabilities. There is one exception to the rule about direct interpretation. For dichotomous variables that comprise subcategories of a broader set, the magnitude of effects can be compared directly to one another. For example, it is possible to make a direct comparison among the measures of whether or not a tribal government is less endowed, moderately endowed, or most endowed.

A. NUMBER OF INTERACTIONS

The analysis presented in table 5.2 examined all 12 tribes and predicted the number of interactions for each tribe for each quarter of the year. One very clear pattern from the examination of all 12 tribes was the role of Indian-white conflict—measured by checkboarded land—in explaining unique features of the Upper Plains. At first, it would appear that being from the Upper Plains increased interactions on its own; the effect is positive and statistically significant. But when Indian-white conflict was added to the model, it swamped the effect from the Upper Plains. Conflict increased interactions and the effect was statistically significant; the effect for the Upper Plains became negative and insignificant. In other words, while at first the Upper Plains looked fairly unique, its distinctiveness was in driven by Indian-white conflict and not some intangible features of the region.

In a parallel way, the Pacific Northwest may have at first seemed distinctive. There were more interactions in the Northwest and the effect was statistically significant. But in fact, the uniqueness was driven by state mandates for growth management, which produced a statistically significant increase in interactions. The effects from state mandates for growth management overwhelmed the importance of being from the Northwest; the effect from the region became negative and insignificant. In short, state growth management requirements increased interactions, not some diffuse features of the Northwest.[11]

The most-endowed tribal governments—governments with economic development *and* institutionalized governments—interacted more and the effect was statistically significant. Tribes with a developed economy but without an institutionalized government interacted less; the effect was statistically significant in two of the three models.

TABLE 5.2

Negative Binomial Regression Predicting Number of Interactions in a Quarter

Independent Variable		Coefficient	Coefficient	Coefficient
Tribal traits	Tribe with institutionalized government only	0.02 (0.47)	0.02 (0.30)	−0.10 (0.36)
	Tribe with developed economy only	−0.19 (0.16)	−0.18 * (0.10)	−0.21 * (0.12)
	Tribe with institutionalized government and developed economy	0.62 * (0.36)	0.57 ** (0.24)	0.51 * (0.27)
Regional climate	Exhaustion elsewhere	0.25 (0.17)	0.17 (0.16)	0.25 (0.17)
	Indian-white conflict		4.46 ** (2.17)	2.49 *** (0.90)
	Interactions over zoning in growth management states		1.10 *** (0.08)	1.07 *** (0.08)
	Tribe is in the Upper Plains	0.68 *** (0.26)	−0.62 (0.50)	
	Tribe is in the Pacific Northwest	0.41*** (0.10)	−0.05 (0.08)	
	Access to closely related venue	0.25 (0.23)	−0.04 (0.16)	0.14 (0.17)
	In an urbanized area	−1.48 *** (0.47)	−2.09 *** (0.37)	−2.04 *** (0.44)
	Near an urbanized area	0.85 (0.86)	−0.57 (0.50)	0.13 (0.55)
Recent past	Agenda setting: tribe active in starting at least one interaction	0.83 *** (0.22)	0.70 *** (0.23)	0.74 *** (0.22)
	Tribe had at least one interaction with the county	−0.65 *** (0.24)	−0.57 ** (0.22)	−0.58 ** (0.23)
	At least one "hard" interaction	0.36 *** (0.12)	0.31 ** (0.13)	0.28 ** (0.13)
	At least one "easy" interaction	0.11 (0.20)	0.15 (0.18)	0.15 (0.18)
	At least one interaction about negative externalities	−0.01 (0.09)	−0.05 (0.11)	−0.06 (0.11)

Other	County has more stages in decision-making	−0.25 ** (0.12)	0.41 * (0.27)	0.08 (0.09)
Constant		−0.69 *** (0.21)	−1.56 *** (0.43)	−1.08 *** (0.20)
Alpha		0.00 (0.00)	0.00 (0.00)	0.00 (0.00)
Log likelihood		−577.63	−558.36	−558.93
Number of observations		480	480	480

Robust standard errors are below the coefficients in parentheses and are adjusted for clustering by tribe. Significance at the 1%, 5%, and 10% levels is indicated by ***, **, and *, respectively.
Exhaustion elsewhere=At least three ongoing legal disputes with states and/or localities in appeals process per year. Indian-white conflict=If checkerboard reservation, percent of county population that was non-Indians living within reservation bounds per year. Access to closely related venue=Reservation was adjacent to incorporated city or town. Number of observations=quarters *tribes, omitting first four quarters for lags.

It would appear that having an institutionalized government but a less developed economy did not influence the number of interactions. Also, it would appear that exhaustion elsewhere—measured by the number of lawsuits—had no influence. As the analysis in table 5.2 will show, however, these two seeming noneffects were due to countervailing regional forces that muddled the results in the analysis of all 12 tribes.

I also considered the influence of the recent past: Did a tribe have any interactions at all in the previous four quarters? Did a tribe initiate any of those interactions? These coefficients need to be interpreted jointly. I found that if a tribe had at least one interaction in the previous 12 months but was not involved in getting the interaction underway, the likelihood of future interactions was lower and the effect was statistically significant. If the tribe had interactions but was involved in starting at least some of those interactions, there was no effect on future interactions: the two variables' effects were of similar magnitudes but opposite signs; to a large degree they canceled each other out if both conditions were true. I take this as further evidence that tribes were the central actors driving interactions. When tribes were having interactions and initiating interactions, this was a normal state of affairs that provided no new information about what the near future would be like. When tribes were only having interactions that counties led, however, that was a more unusual course of events. The expectation, then, is that such interactions were an aberration of the moment and were unlikely to reoccur in the near future.

Note that the types of interactions in the recent past mattered as well. Tribes with recent experience with at least one interaction in a "hard" policy area—pursuing

TABLE 5.3

Negative Binomial Regression Predicting Number of Interactions in a Quarter

Independent Variable	Northwest and Southwest Coefficient	Upper Plains Coefficient	Upper Plains Coefficient
Tribal traits			
Tribe with institutionalized government only	-0.45 *** (0.07)	1.46 *** (0.26)	
Tribe with developed economy only	-0.33 *** (0.06)	0.26 (0.21)	
Tribe with institutionalized government and developed economy	0.56 *** (0.15)	1.71 *** (0.25)	
Regional climate			
Exhaustion elsewhere	0.17 (0.23)	-0.17 *** (0.01)	-0.25 *** (0.05)
Indian–white conflict			4.37 *** (0.41)
Interactions over zoning in growth management states	1.15 *** (0.07)		
Access to closely related venue	0.05 (0.04)		
In an urbanized area	-1.62 *** (0.33)		

	(1)	(2)	(3)
Recent past			
Agenda setting; tribe active in starting at least one interaction	0.80 ***	−0.02	0.19
	(0.28)	(0.07)	(0.17)
Tribe had at least one interaction with the county	−0.67 **	−0.61 **	−0.80 ***
	(0.32)	(0.30)	(0.07)
At least one "hard" interaction	0.36 **	0.23	0.23
	(0.17)	(0.23)	(0.15)
At least one "easy" interaction	0.10	0.41	0.55
	(0.19)	(0.58)	(0.52)
At least one interaction about negative externalities	0.02	−0.10 ***	−0.10 **
	(0.21)	(0.02)	(0.05)
Other traits			
County has more stages in decision-making	0.22 ***		
	(0.04)		
Constant	−1.24 ***	−0.61 ***	−0.54 ***
	(0.12)	(0.07)	(0.22)
Alpha	0.00	0.00	0.00
	(0.00)	(0.00)	(0.00)
Log likelihood	−335	−214.8	−218.82
Number of observations	320	160	160

Robust standard errors are below the coefficients in parentheses and are adjusted for clustering by tribe. Significance at the 1%, 5%, and 10% levels is indicated by ***, **, and *, respectively.

Exhaustion elsewhere=At least three ongoing legal disputes with states and/or localities in appeals process per year. Indian–white conflict=If checkerboard reservation. Percent of county population that was non-Indians living within reservation bounds per year. Access to closely related venue=Reservation was adjacent to incorporated city or town Number of observations=quarters*tribes, omitting first four quarters for lags.

more representation, large-scale services, or joint initiatives—had more interactions with a statistically significant effect. Interactions over negative externalities or over "easy" issues—small services or endorsements—had no statistically significant effect. This difference may reflect the particular abilities needed in, and generated by, harder interactions. More complex issues required higher skill levels, and tribes that built such capacities were well-positioned to take on a greater number of interactions. An alternate hypothesis might point to an effect in the opposite direction: harder interactions would exhaust limited resources and leave a tribe less capable of such interactions in the near future. I argue that exhaustion appeared only in circumstances where it was difficult to apply lessons learned across two very different contexts. In contrast, interactions from the recent past provided tribes with clear, portable insight for subsequent interactions.[12]

I also examined whether a tribe had access to a closely related venue—whether a tribe was adjacent to an incorporated town or city. I expected a positive result, but this variable had a statistically insignificant effect. In an urbanized area, however, there were fewer interactions and the effect was statistically significant. This result fits with my expectation that stakes were lower for tribal-county relations in urbanized areas.

Clearer patterns emerged when the Upper Plains was separated out, as table 5.3 shows.[13] For the Northwest and Southwest, the key finding was that moderately endowed tribes—tribes with institutionalized governments *or* constrained economies—were more selective about their interactions. These tribes engaged in fewer overall interactions, and this effect was statistically significant. In sum, moderately endowed tribes were pickier about interactions. This behavior could lay the groundwork for future success: if tribes knew enough about issues, outside interests, and their own capacities, then they could make savvy choices about where to invest their scarce capacities. This hypothesis requires further testing; analysis in tables 5.4 and 5.5 examines if these tribes were adept at making the right picks about allocating their limited energy.

Additionally in the Southwest and Pacific Northwest, tribes with both institutionalized governments *and* developed economies had more interactions than less-endowed tribes, and this effect was statistically significant. Of course, these most-endowed tribes—with impressive governmental and economic means—did not face the same capacity constraints as other tribes. Possibly, this behavior laid the foundation for expansive successes. If these tribes knew enough about issues, outside interests, and their own capacity, they could take on a big agenda without overextending themselves. All the other significant effects from the overall model persisted for the Southwest and Pacific Northwest.

For the Upper Plains, the differences were pronounced. It first appeared that government institutionalization was what matters for the rate of interaction. Yet this effect was eclipsed by Indian-white conflict, which increased interactions to a much larger degree and was highly statistically significant.[14] Where entangled Indian and white interests generated intense conflict, in essence there was no possibility for tribes and counties to retreat to their separate corners and engage in a kind of détente without surrendering powers. Instead, there were more interactions. Finally, when Upper Plains tribes faced more exhaustion elsewhere, they engaged in fewer interactions, although the magnitude of this effect was slight. If my hypotheses are correct, this result bodes trouble for tribes. I expect that exhaustion elsewhere is depleting, since it demands significant resources but does not generate portable knowledge. To invest more elsewhere without substantially adjusting behavior seems like a recipe for overexertion.

There were other statistically significant effects that dampened the number of interactions in the Upper Plains. Lots of interactions in the recent past drove down interactions, and whether or not tribes started those earlier interactions didn't seem to matter. Also, interactions over negative externalities drove down subsequent interactions.

C. SUCCESS IN INTERACTIONS

Tables 5.4 and 5.5 present analyses of tribes' successes in interactions. I begin by discussing outcomes for all 12 cases, shown in table 5.4. First, the overall models show that all three types of tribes with some sort of endowment—and institutionalized government and/or a developed economy—were more successful than the less-endowed tribes; the effects were statistically significant. Here, though, there were no clear distinctions betwixt the three kinds of tribes with some sort of endowment. Second, where racial conflict was higher, performance suffered. Also, when exhaustion elsewhere was higher, tribes' performance dipped. Both effects were statistically significant. Additionally, Indian-white conflict explained why tribes in the Upper Plains generally fared so much worse: once again, when both variables were included in the same model, racial conflict eclipsed the effect for the region.[15]

These results revealed further evidence of the benefits of learning. Agenda-setting mattered: tribes did better on the interactions that were started jointly, as compared to interactions that the county initiated solely. Of course, if tribes had a say in which interactions to have, they could specify times and topics that fit with their capacities. There was a weak indication that portable learning matters. In two of the specifications, access to a closely related venue improved performance, although the effect was statistically significant in only one of the models.

TABLE 5.4

Logistic Regression Predicting Tribal Success in Interactions, for All Tribes

Independent Variable	Northwest and Southwest Coefficient	Upper Plains Coefficient	Upper Plains Coefficient
Tribal traits			
Tribe with institutionalized government only	1.65 *** (0.50)	1.51 *** (0.40)	1.15 *** (0.37)
Tribe with developed economy only	1.24 *** (0.21)	1.30 *** (0.16)	1.20 *** (0.20)
Tribe with institutionalized government and developed economy	1.28 ** (0.53)	1.27 ** (0.36)	0.79 ** (0.39)
Regional climate			
Exhaustion elsewhere	-0.91 *** (0.18)	-0.69 ** (0.30)	-0.82 *** (0.16)
Indian-white conflict		-8.12 ** (3.62)	-4.25 *** (0.54)
Interactions over zoning in growth management states		-0.80 (0.57)	-0.53 (0.49)
Tribes is in the Upper Plains	-1.16 *** (0.28)	1.09 (1.02)	
Tribe is in the Pacific Northwest	0.21 (0.30)	0.64 ** (0.31)	
Access to closely related venue	-0.25 (0.37)	0.53 (0.56)	0.58 *** (0.20)
In an urbanized area	1.41 *** (0.82)	1.76 *** (0.57)	2.36 *** (0.90)
Near an urbanized area	-1.25 (1.27)	1.19 (1.59)	1.27 (0.91)
Traits of interaction			
Agenda Setting: Tribe initiated interaction solely	0.29 (0.25)	0.33 (0.25)	0.31 (0.25)
Agenda Setting: interaction initiated jointly	1.21 *** (0.39)	1.30 *** (0.39)	1.29 *** (0.38)
Involved a negative externality	-0.36 (0.41)	0.25 (0.45)	-0.27 (0.45)
Involved an "easy" issue	0.48 (0.30)	0.48 (0.33)	0.47 (0.32)

Previous interaction on this issue	0.02	−0.09	−0.08
	(0.29)	(0.26)	(0.26)
Tribe's success rate in previous interactions	0.77**	0.80**	0.83**
	(0.36)	(0.36)	(0.35)
Tribe had visible supporters	1.57***	1.63***	1.58***
	(0.28)	(0.29)	(0.28)
Tribe had visible opponents	−2.12***	−2.06***	−2.07***
	(0.50)	(0.53)	(0.52)
Tribe had both supporters and opponents	−0.59	−0.63	−0.60
	(0.42)	(0.47)	(0.46)
County has more stages in decision-making	0.31	−0.82	−0.40**
	(0.23)	(0.67)	(0.16)
Policy area			
Business not about zoning or land	−0.46	−0.51	−0.53
	(0.45)	(0.47)	(0.47)
Business about zoning or land	0.09	0.13	0.12
	(0.26)	(0.29)	(0.28)
Natural resources not about zoning or land	−0.25	−0.40	−0.34
	(0.44)	(0.52)	(0.50)
Natural resources about zoning or land	0.29	0.53	0.45
	(0.49)	(0.44)	(0.47)
Public safety about zoning or land	−0.02	0.00	0.00
	(0.60)	(0.66)	(0.63)
Elections	0.79**	0.79*	0.77**
	(0.35)	(0.41)	(0.37)
Constant	−0.36	1.12	0.68
	(0.66)	(1.12)	(0.57)
Log likelihood	−217.43	−213.69	−214.23
Number of observations	529	527	527

Robust standard errors are below the coefficients in parentheses and are adjusted for clustering by tribe. Significance at the 1%, 5%, and 10% levels is indicated by ***, **, and *, respectively.

Exhaustion elsewhere=At least three ongoing legal disputes with states and/or localities in appeals process per year. Indian–white conflict=If checkerboard reservation, percent of county population that was non-Indians living within reservation bounds per year. Access to closely related venue=Reservation was adjacent to incorporated city or town.

TABLE 5.5

Logistic Regression Predicting Tribal Success in Interactions

Independent Variable		Northwest and Southwest	Upper Plains	Upper Plains
		Coefficient	Coefficient	Coefficient
Tribal traits	Tribe with institutionalized government only	2.15 *** (0.38)		1.04 *** (0.27)
	Tribe with developed economy only	2.40 *** (0.37)		1.15 *** (0.29)
	Tribe with institutionalized government and developed economy	1.20 *** (0.42)		0.52 * (0.29)
Regional climate	Exhaustion elsewhere	-0.83 ** (0.37)	-0.71 *** (0.21)	-1.10 *** (0.14)
	Indian-white conflict		-0.59 (1.24)	
	Interactions over zoning in growth management states	-1.27 (0.97)		
	Access to closely related venue	1.14 *** (0.27)		
	In an urbanized area	2.81 (1.81)		
Traits of interaction	Agenda Setting: Tribe initiated interaction solely	0.63 (0.40)	0.13 (0.27)	0.11 (0.28)
	Agenda Setting: interaction initiated jointly	0.81 (0.79)	1.33 *** (0.47)	1.56 *** (0.59)
	Involved a negative externality	-0.73 (0.47)	0.08 (0.75)	0.06 (0.75)
	Involved an "easy" issue	0.93 ** (0.45)	0.61 (0.40)	0.63 * (0.38)
	Previous interaction on issue	0.39 (0.28)	0.06 (0.38)	0.10 (0.48)
	Tribe's success rate in previous interactions	-0.05 (0.72)	0.81 (0.59)	0.74 (0.75)

Tribe had visible supporters	2.63***	1.07***	1.05***
	(0.87)	(0.27)	(0.28)
Tribe had visible opponents	−3.90***	−1.64***	−1.63***
	(1.21)	(0.49)	(0.47)
Tribe had both supporters and opponents	−0.25	−0.51	−0.51
	(1.03)	(0.62)	(0.68)
County has more stages in decision-making	0.69		
	(0.58)		
Policy area			
Business not about zoning or land	1.20	−0.84**	−0.99**
	(1.60)	(0.44)	(0.41)
Business about zoning or land	1.71***	−0.39*	−0.34**
	(0.60)	(0.42)	(0.17)
Natural resources not about zoning or land	0.09	−0.65	−0.66
	(0.55)	(0.43)	(0.54)
Natural resources about zoning or land	1.52***	0.84	0.88
	(0.35)	(0.67)	(0.66)
Public safety about zoning or land	0.29	0.10	0.13
	(1.26)	(0.64)	(0.68)
Elections	0.76	0.68	0.75
	(0.74)	(0.46)	(0.54)
Constant	−2.38**	0.37	−0.47*
	(1.17)	(0.54)	(0.26)
Log likelihood	−78.17	−127.41	−125.73
Number of observations	271	258	258

Robust standard errors are below the coefficients in parentheses and are adjusted for clustering by tribe.

Significance at the 1%, 5%, and 10% levels is indicated by ***, **, and *, respectively.

Exhaustion elsewhere=At least three ongoing legal disputes with states and/or localities in appeals process per year. Indian-white conflict= If checkerboard reservation, percent of county population that was non-Indians living within reservation bounds per year. Access to closely related venue=Reservation was adjacent to incorporated city or town.

There were two notable effects that, in the overall model at least, ran against the theory of the importance of expertise. Table 5.5 will consider if these patterns were true across all the regions. I would expect that all previous interactions on an issue would enable learning and breed future success. Instead, the results showed only the past successes had enduring consequences.[16]

Other effects were not terribly surprising. Tribes in urbanized areas did better in county interactions. As I hypothesized, the lesser importance of land-based economies in urban areas would lessen tensions between tribes and counties. Also, it helped to have supporters; it hurt to have opponents. These two variables helped control for important dynamics in the process. Tribes' successes weren't explained away by the prospect that someone else was doing the heavy lifting for them.

Of course, the question lingers which effects persisted across regions. Table 5.5 separated out the Upper Plains. The importance of expertise was more pronounced in the model that focused on the Southwest and Northwest. Tribes with developed economies *or* institutionalized governments had the greatest rates of success, which were statistically significant. Tribes with both developed economies *and* institutionalized governments, however, clearly had more success than the less-endowed tribes; the effect was statistically significant. But the most-endowed tribes had less success than the moderately endowed tribes.

At first blush, this result might seem counterintuitive, but it makes sense when considered alongside the earlier results for number of interactions. In the Northwest and Southwest, tribes in moderate circumstances focused on a limited set of interactions. In essence, they deployed their scarce resources in selective and savvy ways. Tribes that were the most-endowed, in contrast, took a modest hit and didn't succeed quite as frequently as their moderately endowed counterparts. Of course, we know from tables 5.2 and 5.3 that the most-endowed tribes embraced a more ambitious agenda and took on many more interactions. Thus, while the most-endowed tribes didn't succeed quite as frequently as moderately endowed tribes, they won a greater number of successes in the end. Finally, tribes with the least capacity to build expertise engaged in very inefficient behavior: they interacted lots and failed frequently. Without much expertise about which interactions they could win, they threw a lot of darts at the board, with scattered outcomes.

Effort expended on racial conflict lowered success in the Southwest and Northwest, with statistically significant effects. Also, when tribes experienced exhaustion elsewhere, they performed poorly before the county legislature, with statistically significant effects. Note that, in contrast, investments in a closely related venue did *not* lead to exhaustion. Instead, success rates in county interactions climbed significantly when there was a closely related venue. When tribes could apply learning from one arena to another, their performance improved, in spite of the fact that an additional layer of political arenas added complexity to the political environment.[17]

In sum, theory of expertise held up in the Northwest and Southwest findings. The most constrained tribes interacted frequently but at relatively low success rates; tribes in mixed circumstances interacted far less but with great success; the most advantaged tribes had a high number of interactions and accepted a modest hit to their success rates in the pursuit of a more ambitious agenda. Also, the data indicated that tribes benefited when they had opportunities to learn from another legislative arena.

In the Upper Plains, tribal traits affected success in comparable ways and the results were statistically significant. Tribes with economic development *or* government institutionalization were the most successful. Tribes with both traits had slightly lower rates of success than their moderately endowed peers. Tribal governments with neither endowment fared the worst. It was somewhat surprising that the pattern from tribal traits persisted here, given that tribes in the Upper Plains didn't control their number of interactions in the way that their peers in the Northwest and Southwest did. However, expertise ought to have consequences through two pathways. It should improve abilities to select winning issues and avoid more challenging questions—an avenue that was largely closed for tribes in the Upper Plains, since the number of interactions wasn't driven most powerfully by tribal traits. Expertise should also, however, improve abilities to present a persuasive proposal once an interaction is underway. This second pathway was still possible for Upper Plains tribes and it appeared to make a difference. The next confirmation that expertise still mattered in the Upper Plains: agenda-setting improved success significantly. In short, it helped to be the one who first framed the conversation. Also, Indian-white conflict didn't explain away the variation in success rates within the Upper Plains: the effect from conflict was insignificant. Exhaustion elsewhere was an important factor—it depressed success rates and the effect was statistically significant—but not the only factor. In sum, while baseline levels of success were much lower in the Upper Plains, the more- and most-endowed Upper Plains tribes still managed to shape their fates and avoid some of the pitfalls of the less-endowed tribes.

D. THE RESULTS THUS FAR: PREDICTED PROBABILITIES

Figures 5.1 and 5.2 graph predicted probabilities from the models in tables 5.2 through 5.5. The figures illustrate the magnitude of the effects from the regression models.[18]

First note that, as figure 5.1 shows, exhaustion elsewhere didn't substantially change the number of interactions. When exhaustion was higher, the number of

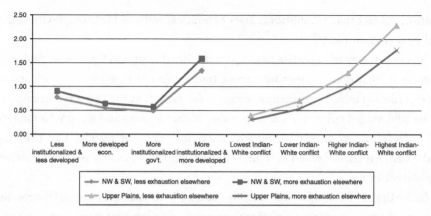

FIGURE 5.1 Predicted Probabilites for Number of Interactions per Quarter of Year
Lowest Indian-White Conflict: No checkerboarding. Lower Indian-White Conflict: 13% of county was non-Indians within reservation. Higher Indian-White Conflict: 27% of county was non-Indians within reservation. Highest Indian-White Conflict: 40% of county was non-Indians within reservation. Exhaustion elsewhere= At least 3 ongoing legal disputes with states and/or localities in appeals process per year

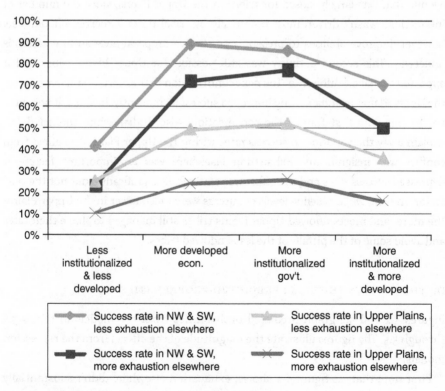

FIGURE 5.2 Predicted Probabilities for Success Rate in Interactions

interactions ranged from 0.94 to 0.77 of the number of interactions from when exhaustion was absent.[19] Here, we see confirmation that when tribes faced exhaustion in another arena, they were unwilling or unable to scale back their county interactions substantially. This is bad news: when resources are taxed in another, very different setting, tribes ought to be reallocating their energies or they will find themselves overextended. As predicted, exhaustion elsewhere did hurt success rates substantially and the gaps were largest across the Upper Plains. As figure 5.2 shows, when exhaustion was higher, success rates fell 15 to 26 percentage points in the Upper Plains and 9 to 20 percentage points in the Southwest and Northwest.[20] In short, exhaustion meant that tribes stumbled in politics more frequently.

Next, there were some region-specific effects. In figure 5.2, we see higher success rates for all Northwest and Southwest tribes with government institutionalization and/or economic development. Figures 5.1 and 5.2 show that more-endowed tribes interacted the most selectively and the most successfully, with predicted success rates above 70%. The most-endowed interacted a good deal more, as figure 5.1 illustrates, with well more than twice the interactions of moderately endowed neighbor tribes. Furthermore, the most-endowed tribes' predicted success rates were all above 50% and were notably higher than less-endowed tribes' success rates.

In short, the expertise associated with government institutionalization and economic development mattered in the Northwest and Southwest. The most-endowed tribes could take on a wide-ranging agenda while still achieving impressive successes. They figured out how to use their resources expansively without overextending themselves. The moderately endowed tribes used expertise to husband their limited means. They invested their energies selectively, with enough foresight to pick winning issues. These successes contrasted sharply with the outcomes for less-endowed tribes.

In the Upper Plains, as shown in figure 5.1, the number of interactions was driven by Indian-white conflict. Where conflict was heightened, Upper Plains tribes and counties had vastly more interactions—2.29 interactions per quarter. In contrast, where conflict was lowest in the Upper Plains, the volume of interactions was 0.4 a quarter and in fact was lower than for any cases in the Northwest and Southwest. Figure 5.2 illustrates that interactions in the Upper Plains were far less successful that in the Northwest and Southwest. Success rates in the Upper Plains ran from 25% to 52% when exhaustion elsewhere was low. Success rates fell even further when tribes may have been too exhausted to present coherent arguments: success rates were from 10% to 26%. It's a glum story, but there was one encouraging point from tribal governments' perspective. Upper Plains tribes appeared to have enough expertise to marshal their resources to a degree. More-endowed tribes were the most successful, succeeding 24% to 52% of the time. The most-endowed tribes had lower success rates, succeeding 16% to 36% of the time. The less-endowed tribes succeeded 10% to 25% of the time. None of the Upper Plains tribes erased the disadvantages in the region: but as in the Northwest and Southwest, expertise still made some difference.

E. FURTHER TESTS OF EXPERTISE

In results above, it seemed that tribes with some capacities figured out how to make sounder arguments, while tribes with the most capacities were still relatively persuasive but not quite as cautious. In contrast, tribes in the worst circumstances were prone to stumbling. These implications can be investigated further by delving in specific ways into the dynamics within an interaction.

Figure 5.3 shows the results of an investigation into two of the implications. First, we should see more strategic mishaps among the less-endowed tribes and where external circumstances were more trying. Second, the most-endowed tribes should have a unique capacity to pursue an ambitious agenda. Figure 5.3 presents descriptive data on which tribes made strategic miscalculations and which tribes pursued a more ambitious political agenda. To begin, I examined mishaps—specifically, whether tribes presented incomplete or inconsistent proposals in a given interaction. Indeed, the less-endowed tribes were most apt to present incomplete or contradictory arguments. They did so 13% of the time, while all other kinds of tribes did so 3% of the time, and the pattern was consistent across all three regions. Furthermore, in general these slip-ups were more common among the Upper Plains tribes, where they happened 6% of the time, versus 3% for the Northwest and Southwest.

Second, scope of agenda. To identify cautious agendas, I calculated the extent to which tribes within each region concentrated interactions in a just a couple of policy areas, in just a couple of kinds of interactions,[21] or in topics where they'd had prior interactions. Tribes with institutionalized governments *and* developed economies pursued the least cautious agenda in five of the nine measures included: for two of the three measures in the Northwest and Upper Plains each, and for one of the three of the measures in the Southwest. This frequency was more than one would expect by chance. It's clever, really—when actors have more resources at their disposal, it's rational to sometimes reach beyond the sure-fire winners and branch out into issues where the odds are good but not great.

Next, I considered whether the three types of tribes with at least some endowment made more effective arguments than their less-endowed peers. Specifically,

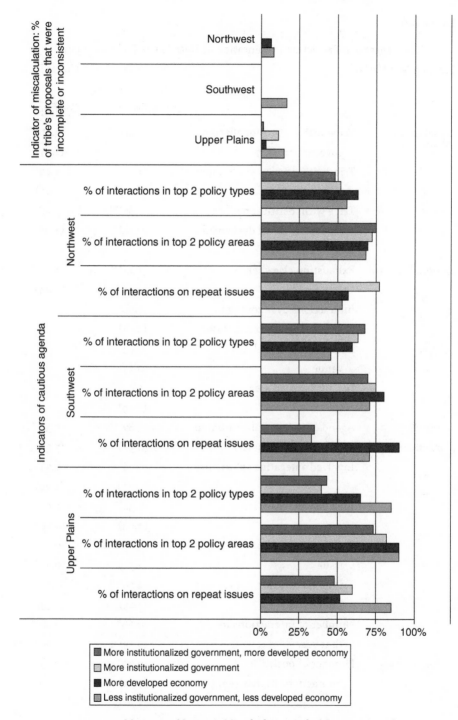

FIGURE 5.3 Measures of Strategic Miscalculation and of Cautious Agendas

TABLE 5.6

Logistic Regression Predicting Presentation of Detailed or Technical Plan

Independent Variable		Northwest and Southwest	Upper Plains
		Coefficient	*Coefficient*
Tribal traits	Tribe with institutionalized government only	2.40*** (0.75)	3.98*** (1.07)
	Tribe with developed economy only	1.92*** (0.37)	1.42** (0.66)
	Tribe with institutionalized government and developed economy	1.61*** (0.54)	3.98*** (1.08)
Regional climate	Exhaustion elsewhere	1.24*** (0.40)	−1.66*** (0.44)
	Interactions over zoning in growth management states	1.86* (1.01)	
	Access to closely related venue	0.93 (0.79)	
	In an urbanized area	−3.99*** (1.49)	
Traits of interaction	Agenda Setting: Tribe initiated the interaction solely	3.87*** (0.94)	5.31*** (1.36)
	Involved a negative externality	0.50 (1.80)	−0.22 (1.42)
	Involved an "easy" issue	1.52** (0.64)	−1.07 (0.78)
	Previous interactions on issue	3.48*** (1.30)	−0.11 (0.80)
	Tribe's success rate in previous interactions	−2.26* (1.29)	0.92 (1.33)
	Number of interactions in that year	0.68* (0.35)	0.18 (0.20)
	Number of positive interactions in that year	−0.99* (0.51)	−0.35 (0.30)

Policy area	Business not about zoning or land	−0.87*	−0.59
		(0.47)	(1.57)
	Business about zoning or land	−1.50*	4.15***
		(0.91)	(1.15)
	Natural resources not about zoning or land	−2.28***	2.61*
		(0.47)	(1.40)
	Natural resources about zoning or land	−1.56	0.78
		(1.01)	(1.54)
	Public safety about zoning or land		1.79***
			(0.69)
	Elections	−0.51	0.00
		(0.54)	(0.13)
Constant		−4.18***	−6.71***
		(1.23)	(1.83)
Log likelihood		−63.01	−58.41
Number of observations		171	187

Robust standard errors are below the coefficients in parentheses and are adjusted for clustering by tribe.
Significance at the 1%, 5%, and 10% levels is indicated by ***, ** and *, respectively.
Analysis excludes interactions that counties initiated solely, since tribes rarely present plans in those cases.
Exhaustion elsewhere=At least three ongoing legal disputes with states and/or localities in appeals process per year. Access to closely related venue=Reservation was adjacent to incorporated city or town.

table 5.6 considered who presented a detailed or technical plan when interacting. The answer was that moderately and more-endowed tribes were more likely to do this. The effects were statistically significant. Also, there was evidence that agenda-setting was tied to the ability to make better arguments. Tribes were much more likely to present plans when the choice of time and topic was exclusively theirs; the effect was significant.

There were interesting, statistically significant effects for moments of greater exhaustion. In the Upper Plains, underlying conflict was high to begin with, and more exhaustion elsewhere depressed detailed arguments. In the Northwest and Southwest, however, where baseline conflict was lower, tribes seemed to be able to redouble their efforts and presented more detailed arguments when they faced more challenges in other, distinct arenas.

Lastly, there was some evidence that tribes figured out where detailed arguments would matter more. In the Northwest and Southwest, tribes presented detailed or technical plans more frequently when fighting uphill political battles;

all these effects were statistically significant. Specifically, tribes presented plans more frequently when they had lots of previous interaction on an issue but low success rates on that issue, and when they had lots of interactions happening in the present time but few of them yielded success.[22]

Tribes in the Upper Plains didn't appear to adjust with the same sensitivity to political context. They did react in the big ways—more plans when they had some endowments, fewer plans when they were more exhausted—with statistically significant effects. Also, Upper Plains tribes focused on presenting plans for policy areas where county hostility was more likely. For all policy areas that related most closely to entangled land claims, the Upper Plains tribes were more likely to present detailed or technical plans. The effect was positive for all three variables and significant for two of the three variables.[23] Upper Plains tribes didn't seem quite as subtle in their assessment of where a detailed plan could yield the greatest return, but their choice of when to expend such efforts wasn't random, either.

V. A Closer Look at the Minutes

By turning to analysis of particular cases, I offer some more insight into precise mechanisms in tribal-county relations. Several findings came through in a careful read of county minutes. First, tribes with basic levels of government institutionalization or economic development possessed clear expertise. Also, they avoided a series of mistakes that the most constrained tribe made. In addition, there were a number of indications that interactions were a learning process, for both tribes and counties. With repetition, interactions became both easier and more extensive. Frequently, initial interactions were marked by confusion and caution on both sides, but both tendencies subsided quickly with early success. Finally, there was evidence that networks facilitated this learning process, and the absence of networks impeded it.

The capacities of the most-endowed tribes were extremely impressive. The Navajo Nation participated in some very technical debates with county officials and it launched some very sophisticated proposals. In the late 1990s, the tribe was at work organizing a project to tap new sources of water in the region. The tribe asked various other authorities, who were quite enthusiastic about the idea, to help finance the endeavor, but the initial planning and scientific work were all done by the tribe. Another well-endowed tribe got a regional enterprise zone organized, of benefit to the tribe and neighboring communities. Also, this tribe was well equipped to debate the particulars of county environmental impact findings for various proposed developments, and it did so regularly.

Tribes with either economic development or government institutionalization also exhibited a great deal of knowledge. One tribe housed expansive expertise about area water quality, and the county frequently sought tribal input in deciding the specifics of growth management and water quality protection. Officials from another tribe displayed their knowledge in the area they knew best, economic development. Their major series of interactions with the county involved redesigning the regional transportation system, to improve access to the tribe's enterprises and to eliminate bottlenecks resulting from new development. The tribe joined existing county initiatives in this area, but it also made unique and substantial contributions to the effort. Specifically, the tribe identified and won new sources of funding for the projects and it brought in new regional partners to share the burdens.

County governments regularly displayed their appreciation for tribal expertise. They appointed tribal officials to boards that drafted legislation or carried out other technical tasks, and they contracted with tribes to deliver certain county services. For example, officials from one institutionalized tribal government helped write the county gravel mining regulations and helped supervise the county elections department. Officials from a local intertribal organization helped design county programs aimed at reducing DWI offenses. By the mid 1990s, another county had contracted out with the nearby economically developed tribe for the delivery of certain juvenile crime prevention programs.

These tendencies were in marked contrast to the circumstances of the tribes with neither economic development nor government institutionalization. Although these tribes succeeded in many of their interactions, what sticks in the memory is failure to win the simplest of requests: small grants, a few speed bumps, a stop sign, a new sidewalk. Often, the less-endowed tribes learned from failure but not always. When one less-endowed tribe failed to win a small grant from the county's tourism development fund, the commission making the determination noted shortcomings in their application: the application was incomplete in places and the commission was confused about how the tribe's project related to the stated goals of the fund. When the tribe applied to the same fund a second time, for the same project, they avoided these pitfalls and won the award. Relatively speaking, this instance involved fairly simple problems to fix; with harder problems, constrained tribes did not always figure out new approaches.

The county records showed a range of examples of how learning shaped these interactions. Often, early interactions in a given area were quite tentative, on the part of both tribes and counties. Early proposals were frequently small in scope yet still provoked hesitation and confusion. With practice, however, the hesitation faded and the scope expanded.

We can take as an example the case where an economically developed tribe and the nearby county considered a contract whereby the county would provide building inspection services for tribal enterprises. At first, the actors involved struggled with uncertainty about how the arrangement should be structured, the exact obligations the county should hold, and precedents that would be set. Yet when the agreement was renewed in subsequent years, such concerns were absent. In fact, the renewals only showed up on the county consent agenda, a procedure whereby county boards approve agreements that simply require formal ratification without debate. Similar patterns appeared where a consortium of tribes and counties worked to develop a regional landfill. One of the counties involved had limited familiarity with tribal interactions, was nervous about how legal obligations would play out, and was hesitant to sign on. Two other counties, with more experience, displayed no such hesitation. They tried to reassure officials in the other county, and one specifically vouched for the reliability of its neighboring tribe.

Finally, we can sense this trepidation in the incremental approach that many tribes and counties took in their interactions. At first, when one county contracted with an institutionalized tribal government to deliver substance abuse prevention services, the contract was for a trifling sum and covered a very narrow range of services. Year by year, the dollar amount and the scope of the contract expanded.

Signs of the learning process were clearest for the most constrained tribes, probably because they had the most learning to do. Two of the less-endowed tribes increased their specialized skills as a result of county interactions. One got experience participating in a drug education program with the county and eventually it branched out to running a drug education program on its own. After the second tribe collaborated with the county in providing services to reduce juvenile delinquency, it also successfully pursued funds to support the development of its own staff in this area. Because both tribes learned more about working in these particular policy areas, they developed capacities to do more in these areas.

Finally, preexisting networks eased the learning process. Appreciation of networks may explain the popularity of regional intergovernmental councils in so many of these places. These councils lacked precise mandates, other than to meet regularly. Whether these councils actually built meaningful networks is difficult to say, but it is clear that many actors valued the effort at improving communication. We can also observe the effects of networks more directly. For one of the less-endowed tribes, their main series of interactions with the county in these data— a range of programs to combat juvenile crime—got underway at the instigation of a county official who previously worked for the tribe. That relationship provided a starting point for extensive coordination. In the case of the Navajo Nation, a county commissioner who was also a tribal member served as an important conduit. Simply, when the county acted on a matter of concern to the Navajo Nation, there was always someone prepared to speak for the tribe, and the tribe never appeared unready to put forward a position on the issue at hand.

In contrast, the absence of networks linking one highly endowed tribe and its nearby county was a source of repeated frustration and confusion. County officials frequently noted issues where they really ought to coordinate with the tribe, but they were unclear about how to carry out that coordination or even whom to call in the tribe to begin the process. In some cases, the county surmounted those obstacles and joint efforts got underway. Most commonly, however, the recognition by the county that cooperation was desirable failed to translate into even basic communication. The county and the tribe had some genuine disputes with one another, and networks would not eliminate conflicting interests. But to make matters worse, the county was ill-equipped to identify where commonalities lay and how to build upon them. One can only imagine what more might be accomplished in that region if county and tribal officials knew each other's processes, priorities, and phone numbers.

VI. Alternate Hypotheses

A. CHAOS AND CO-OPTATION

These findings speak to alternate hypotheses. One might hypothesize that greater government institutionalization can result in excessive complexity, chaos, and thus less effective advocacy. In fact, the more institutionalized governments were more likely to avoid such behavior, while less institutionalized governments did encounter this pitfall.

These data discredited another alternate hypothesis as well. I did not observe indications that tribes had been co-opted or shackled by outside actors. The tribes in this sample were hardly placid or compliant. They disputed county decisions and they pushed a tribal agenda, aggressively. For example, the Navajo Nation objected repeatedly and vociferously to the county's initial redistricting plan after the 1990 Census. Another highly endowed tribe frequently protested county zoning permits. Over several years, one institutionalized tribal government fought hard against county plans to allow greater growth in the area around the reservation. These tribal officials weren't shy about challenging county decisions.

B. PATH DEPENDENCE

It is natural to wonder whether tribes' strategies are wholly path-dependent processes. My findings indicate, however, that tribes weren't as locked in to a particular path as we might naturally suspect. For one, even a brief reprieve from lawsuits produced different outcomes. For example, for one tribe, lawsuits were particularly high in 1990 and 1992, but not in 1991. Lawsuits were also particularly high in 1999, but not in 1998 or 2000.[24] The first question is whether this tribe's behavior in 1990, 1992, and 1999 differed from 1991, 1998, and 2000. The answer is yes. The next question is whether the change in behavior looked like savvy agenda-setting or calculated deployment. The answer is no.

In years like 1990, 1992, and 1999—when lawsuits were particularly high—this tribe was less selective and less successful. High levels of appeals cases and successes with county legislation were correlated at −0.20. High levels of appeals cases and incomplete or inconsistent proposals from the tribe were correlated at 0.27. In 1990, 1992, and 1999, a variety of the tribe's initiatives failed: coordination on animal control, policing, ambulance services, 911 services, and a rodeo. The tribe couldn't even persuade the county to write a letter supporting a federal declaration of a natural disaster emergency. In 1991, 1998, and 2000, the patterns differed. Coordination on 911, telephone services, and traffic safety moved forward. The county provided a letter supporting the tribe's opposition to a federal declaration of an endangered species.

Models based wholly on path dependence ought not to predict such fluctuation; we should expect more "sticky" behavior. Fortunately, other sources offered insights into the mechanisms at hand. Tribal officials were stretched across lawsuits and legislative interactions with counties. For example, the proceedings of one tribal council revealed that program staff assisted with a brief in one lawsuit and compiled "statistics on land holdings, land losses, and land acquisition." Thus, the staff redirected time away from other endeavors. If the statistics were portable to county interactions, we might expect them to show up in county interactions over land issues. That didn't happen.

On another occasion, a tribal chair instructed fish and wildlife program staff on tactics that would help with a lawsuit. For the sake of the lawsuit, the tribal chair wanted game wardens who look authoritative, and he wanted more equipment purchased to that end, but he didn't want wardens to actually make any arrests of fishermen or hunters who trespassed onto tribal land. Again, the staff expended energy that may have helped with lawsuits but diverted away from other activities. In general, it was remarkable how much time this tribal council devoted to discussing lawsuit status and strategies. County legislation scarcely made it into the discussion. One might mistakenly presume, from reading the tribal council minutes, that the tribe hardly ever dealt with the county commission. In fact, county-tribal interactions happened frequently, just not necessarily with a lot of forethought.

Indeed, tribal leaders acknowledged routinely the exhausting nature of lawsuits. They made these acknowledgements to both internal and external audiences. There were comments made within tribal council proceedings and comments that appeared in local newspapers. A tribal attorney made similar remarks at a conference on tribal government concerns.

C. HISTORY

All the same, there are serious reasons to think that American Indian tribal governments' travails in the Upper Plains are due to internal problems with deep historical roots. There is much concern that some Upper Plains tribes face deep, long-standing governance challenges and divisive conflict, and perhaps some tribal officials are consumed by patronage priorities and give little attention to public affairs. When the federal government pushed a particular type of constitution for tribal governments in the 1930s, it chose a government structure that was particularly ill-suited to tribal culture in the Upper Plains (see, for example, Biolsi 1992 and Cornell and Kalt 1992). Given the mismatch between formal institutions and social practices, the argument goes, tribal governments descended quickly into deep troubles. No one would argue that these tendencies are uniform: to their great credit, some Upper Plains tribes have initiated a number of effective programs. For example, a number of units in tribal governments have been awarded the prestigious Honoring Nations Awards from the Harvard Project on American Indian Economic Development for their accomplishments (2007). But if their environment weren't so grim, perhaps they could achieve much more. There is no doubt that history and the resulting internal dysfunctions matter. I am arguing, however, that we should add another pressing problem to that list.

D. STATE AND COUNTY MOTIVES

What do we know about the motives of state and local officials engaged in lawsuits against tribes? The information at hand doesn't provide a definitive answer. Perhaps some state and local officials were aware of the payoffs from tribal exhaustion, but presumably there were other motives at play. Perhaps state and county officials faced particularly hostile tribal governments and therefore felt they have no choice but to pursue courtroom strategies. Perhaps they were committed ideologically to giving no ground and as a result used the courts to try to extinguish tribal claims. Probably all these things were true; governments contain multiple officials with varying perspectives and goals. The question remains whether legal strategies were at least in part chosen where states and localities had the most to gain from tribal exhaustion. After all, exhaustion from lawsuits was widely acknowledged; it was no secret that lawsuits brought troublesome consequences for tribes. In an additional, suggestive investigation, racial conflict remains a factor in the choices of non-Indian governments. All the same, it remains difficult to distinguish between ideological responses to racial conflict and strategic responses to conflict.

I examined minutes from meetings of the Montana Association of Reservation Counties, to see how varying county circumstances mattered for how county representatives behaved. I have at hand the minutes from 13 meetings of the association between 1993 and 1998. The minutes included meetings of the overall body and of the association's leadership. The minutes included the names and counties of all of the association's leaders. Also, for 9 of the meetings, there was a roster of all attendees. I tallied which counties sent representatives to meetings, which representatives voiced support for courtroom strategies to interact with tribal governments, and which representatives voiced support for other tactics.[25] The correlations were telling, as table 5.7 shows. When counties had larger American Indian populations, they were much more likely to participate in the association and to advocate for strategies outside the courts: legislative, bureaucratic, or nongovernmental approaches. The correlations were .77 and .63, respectively. When counties had more checkerboarded land, however, they were much more likely to advocate courtroom strategies; the features were correlated at .60.

Also, I considered tribal traits as described in Lopach, Brown, and Clow's (1998) detailed analysis of Montana tribal governments. I identified the tribes that they

TABLE 5.7

Correlates of County Behavior, Meetings of Montana Association of Reservation Counties, 1993–98

	Present at meeting	Support for courtroom strategy	Support for other strategies
Percent of county population that was American Indian	.77	.21	.63
Extent of checkerboarding	.15	.60	−.02
Tribe's reputation of confrontation	.33	.34	−.23
Tribe's reputation of cooperation	−.02	.12	.31

Extent of checkerboarding=percent of residents in the county within reservation boundaries who were non-Indian.

described as having a history of cooperation or confrontation with state and local governments. As would be expected, histories of confrontation made litigation more likely. Histories of cooperation made non-litigious strategies more likely. These weren't the most powerful correlates, however. Support for lawsuits and reputedly confrontational tribes were correlated at .34. Support for non-ligitious strategies and reputedly cooperative tribes were correlated at .31.

In the end, it appeared that potential influence in county affairs—when tribal members were a larger part of the citizenry—prompted county engagement outside of the courts. The most ominous source of Indian-white conflict— entangled lands—prompted county lawsuits. In short, where threat was most pressing, lawsuits appeared most popular. The effects from racial conflict over-shadowed the effects of tribes' reputation for cooperative relations. This fits with the patterns of racial conflict associated with checkerboarding that was seen in the exploration of Upper Plains politics discussed in section I.B. The evidence at hand didn't get inside the heads of state and local officials, but it shows coincidence bet-ween an aggressive legal strategy that could exhaust tribal capacity and circum-stances where local officials stood to gain from the disempowering effects on tribes from exhaustion.

VII. Conclusion

In the end, marginalized groups have certain capacities to change their circum-stances via expert decision-making. Many conditions are set by exogenous forces, of course. But groups can learn, and knowledge about politics and policy can change outcomes. Groups can learn how better to choose issues, to craft proposals, and to shepherd their measures through the legislative process.

The American Indian tribal governments with even limited resources appeared to be channeling their resources into expertise cultivation, because they behaved in ways that relied on a good deal of information-gathering and processing. Tribes with government institutionalization *or* economic development selected issues carefully: they identified correctly the places where they could win and they brought detailed and technical proposals to the table. Tribes that were better endowed did most of these things as well, but they also worked to build a more ambitious, wide-ranging menu of interactions. Furthermore, regardless of under-lying capacities, all tribes did better when they'd had highly relevant learning opportunities. In the Northwest and Southwest, and to a degree in the Upper Plains, American Indian tribal governments won meaningful successes through their deployment of expertise.

There were important limitations, however, that stemmed from intense Indian-white competition. Under these circumstances, tribal governments didn't exhibit as many of the expertise-centered behaviors seen in the other cases. Instead, interactions climbed, success rates fell, and careful and calculated interactions dipped. Hostility was exhausting and marginalized actors ended up depleted from the process.

In the end, in this setting, no one had to bother with classic tools of disempowerment—like legal disenfranchisement, daunting barriers to the formation of organizations, and massive obstacles to the articulation of interests. When tribal governments were spent, they were oftentimes incoherent. Such soft, indirect disempowerment often goes undetected. When we do notice its effects, the causes are easily misattributed to the organization itself. It's easy to mislabel exhaustion as failed leadership and to miss the vital influence of expertise's presence and absence.

6   Channels of Access, Frames for Persuasion
THE INFLUENCE OF TRIBAL GOVERNMENTS IN STATE POLITICS

I. Introduction

This chapter explores tribal governments' use of expertise in relations with state governments. Here, I show that expertise and outside aid shape these relations, even when more thoroughly controlling for other forces, such as differences across policy areas and the broader political environment.

This evaluation of state-tribal relations revealed the following evidence. First, I can link improved outcomes directly to federal support. When tribal governments had more help from the federal government for cultivating skills in a given policy area or for governance structures, they did better in state interactions. Furthermore, tribal advocates within state legislatures served tribal interests in ways that were based on accumulating expertise. The impact of tribal advocates came not from indiscriminate boosterism of tribal issues but from careful selection of which issues to put forward. Finally, I present evidence that learning over time mattered as well. Tribes did better at issues where they have experience interacting.

Yet context had important effects. Some Upper Plains states considered a strikingly small amount of legislation that addressed American Indian concerns. Furthermore, rates of enactment were especially poor in South Dakota. In the end, both skill and context had impacts. Expert tribes chose interactions selectively and made efficient use of whatever political capital they had. But in places where the potential for Indian-white conflict was greater, tribal advocates could not completely undo the marked neglect—be it benign or malign—of their concerns.

II. Overview of State Legislation Affecting Tribes

A. DATA COLLECTION AND CODING

I explored tribal interactions in eight states—Arizona, New Mexico, Oregon, Washington, Montana, North Dakota, South Dakota, and Nebraska—from 1990 to 2000. I selected two states from the Southwest and two states from the Pacific Northwest. Since state legislatures in the Upper Plains tend to have shorter sessions and generally consider less legislation each year, I included four states from that region in my analysis.[1]

The LexisNexis State Capital database provides bill synopses and bill histories for proposed state legislation in this time period. I used this database to identify bills in these eight states affecting American Indians and tribal governments.[2]

To gauge how these bills might impact Native Americans, I distinguished between pro-tribal, anti-tribal, and ambiguous legislation.[3] I treated legislation as pro-tribal if the state attempted to enhance the powers that tribal governments exercised; to improve state recognition of powers that tribes held; or to provide goods, services, or funding to tribal governments or American Indians. Examples of pro-tribal legislation included:

- Montana's 1991 House Bill 57: "Exempts tribal building inspections from state building inspections."
- Arizona's 1991 House Bill 2243: "Provides that Indian tribes could apply for and receive loans from the State Wastewater Treatment Revolving Fund; provides that tribal security for a loan could not be construed as requiring a tribe to waive any claim of sovereign immunity 'provided that adequate security is otherwise provided.'"

Legislation was designated anti-tribal if the state challenged tribal government powers; protested powers that tribes held; or rescinded goods, services, or funding that were once available to tribal government or American Indians. Examples included:

- Washington's 1990 House Bill 3010: "Directs the Attorney General to assert all possible defenses to Indian treaty claims to shellfish harvesting rights."

- Nebraska's 1995 Bill 798: Among other items, "[E]liminates the Commission on Indian Affairs, the commission on Mexican-Americans, and the Nebraska Commission on the Status of Women."

Finally, legislation was coded as ambiguous if the title and synopsis did not offer enough information to judge a measure's impact on tribal government, or if the content of the item was clear but the measure had no clear-cut effect of increasing or decreasing power. Most commonly, ambiguous items set long-term structures for tribal-state interactions. These structures could favor one actor in some circumstances and another actor in other circumstances. Examples included:

- Oregon's 1993 Senate Bill 781: "Requires the Department of Transportation, the State Board of Forestry and the Land Conservation and Development Commission, in consultation with the State Historic Preservation Officer and the Commission on Indian Services, to develop rules and guidelines concerning archeological sites and cultural resources; requires State Historic Preservation Officer and Commission on Indian Services to notify certain state agencies upon discovery of sites and resources."
- South Dakota's 1993 Senate Bill 220: "Pertains to continuing the cooperative state tribal tax collection agreement with the Cheyenne River Sioux tribe."

I also wanted to consider whether interactions varied by policy area. Accordingly, I sorted measures by their policy area. The policy areas in these data were as follows:

Economic development issues, including gaming (27% of sample). Example:
- Nebraska 1993 Bill 725, "Relates to enterprise zones. Names the Enterprise Zone Act. Changes the application procedures. Authorizes designations within tribal governments. Changes tax credits."

Education (14% of sample). Example:
- North Dakota 1993 Senate Bill 2170, "Provides financial assistance to tribally controlled community colleges; provides an appropriation."

Natural resources (13% of sample). Example:
- South Dakota 1994 House Bill 1122, "Increases the maximum duration of municipal agreements with other political subdivisions and persons regarding solid waste management. Allows the governing body of the municipality to enter into agreements with a county or counties, with 1 or more municipalities, with a regional recycling and waste management district, with Indian tribes, with private persons, corporations, or trusts to

provide or operate a solid waste collection and disposal system or site for such a system for up to 35 years in duration."

Governance and procedures for tribal-state interactions (12% of sample). Example:

- New Mexico 1999 Senate Bill 98, "Relates to joint powers agreements; includes as public agencies certain subdivisions of Indian nations, tribes, or pueblos"

Social services and employment (10% of sample). Example:

- Washington 1997 House Bill 2094, "Provides a cooperative agreement for child support between the Department of Social and Health Services and Indian Tribes."

Public safety (9% of sample). Example:

- Oregon 1999 House Bill 3080, "Includes tribal police officer within definition of police officer for purposes of Oregon Vehicle Code."

Health (5% of sample). Example:

- Montana 1997 House Bill 228, "Provides appropriations to the Department of Public Health and Human Services for distribution to Indian health clinics."

Awareness and recognition. These included acknowledgement both of the accomplishments of Native Americans and of the challenges they face (5% of sample). Example:

- South Dakota 2000 Senate Bill 203, "Provides for highway signs denominating South Dakota as the Home of the Lakota Sioux Nations"

Housing and community development (3% of sample). Example:

- Washington 2000 House Bill 2347, "Extends the housing authority tax exemption to Indian housing authorities."

Land issues and land control, including matters of which lands are included under tribal government authority (3% of sample). Example:

- Oregon 1993 House Bill 3287, "Requires City to transfer Title of cemetery property to Tribal Council free of encumbrances whenever such transfer is made; extinguishes liens, assessments and other encumbrances on such property that was transferred prior to effective date of this Act; provides that this Act is repealed on 1/1/94."

Transportation (2% of sample). Example:

- Arizona 1992 House Bill 1070, "States that a rural county receiving money from state highway-related taxes would have to spend a specified minimum amount for streets and roads on any Indian reservations in the county."

Most legislation was sorted into only one category, but there was one set of bills where I thought an exception to that rule was appropriate. In the Pacific Northwest, there were a number of bills about tribal fishing operations. This issue has been of great relevance in the Northwest for both environmental management and tribal economic development, and so I included it in both categories. Due to this double-counting, the percentages added up to more than 100%.

B. STATE PROFILES

All eight states have at least a few reservations within their borders, but they vary on multiple dimensions. Tables 6.1 and 6.2 summarize some of the key differences among the states. Variables in the tables are as follows.

I tallied the number of reservations, for a sense of the geographic concentration of reservation populations. I included American Indian share in the state population. I would expect that larger Indian populations make tribal-state relations a more pressing issue. These larger populations could result in greater power for American Indians, but they could also result in backlash from non-Indians in the state.

As indicator of potential anti-Indian politics, I examined entangled Indian and non-Indian lands, typically referred to as checkerboarding. Chapter 5 provided detailed discussion of the Indian-white conflict that can arise from checkerboarding. I included two measures of entangled lands: both the absolute number and population share of non-Indians living within reservations' outer boundaries.[4]

Another indicator of potential anti-Indian backlash is the extent to which Indian political power is concentrated by political geography and thus may be considered politically threatening to non-Indians. I tallied the number of counties that are more than 40% American Indian, using Key's (1949) threshold for when racial threat is likely to emerge.

It is not entirely clear what consequences emerged from the growth of Indian casinos. For the reader's reference, I tracked the development of the casino industry in each state. I included a tally of the number of gambling machines and bingo hall seats in each state in 1995 (Mason and Mason).

I tracked political procedures in the states. Some states have introduced standing committees on Indian affairs into their state legislatures. I expect that these committees would provide a forum for tribal advocates. I also examined whether states have affirmed a government-to-government relationship between tribes and states. This official recognition of tribal sovereignty is a formal step by states toward a more hospitable framework for tribes.

TABLE 6.1

Select Features of State Demographics and Economics

	New Mexico	Arizona	Oregon	Washington	Montana	South Dakota	North Dakota	Nebraska
Number of reservations	22	21	9	29	7	9	5	7
Percent American Indian, 1990	8.9%	5.6%	1.4%	1.7%	6.0%	7.3%	4.1%	1.3%
Percent American Indian, 2000	9.5%	5.0%	1.3%	1.6%	6.2%	8.3%	4.9%	0.9%
Number of non-Indians living within reservations, 1990	34,413	15,191	1,950	74,682	24,515	21,172	14,727	6,192
Percent of population that is non-Indians living within reservations, 1990	2.3%	0.4%	0.0%	1.5%	3.1%	3.0%	2.3%	0.4%
Number of counties where percent Indian more than 40%, 1990	1	2	0	0	3	9	2	1

Number of counties	33	15	36	39	57	66	53	93
Video gambling machines 1995	1,720	3,930	1,730	1,075	174	1,278	1,554	1,114
Bingo hall seats 1995	1,900	4,750	1,650	5,687	530	1,350	900	220

Sources: Demographics: U.S. Census Bureau (1992a, 2002b) and Tiller (1996, 2005). *Casinos:* Mason and Mason (1995). *Legislative Committees:* LexisNexis State Capital Database. *Government-to-Government Relations:* Websites of the Arizona Commission on Indian Affairs, New Mexico Indian Affairs Department, Oregon Legislative Commission on Indian Services, Washington Governor's Office of Indian Affairs, Montana Office of Indian Affairs, South Dakota Tribal Government Relations Office, North Dakota Indian Affairs Commission, and Nebraska Commission on Indian Affairs. Also, Wilkins (2002); Harvard Project on American Indian Economic Development (2008). *Lawsuits:* McCool, Olson, and Robinson (2007).

TABLE 6.2

Select Features of State-Tribal Political Relationships

	New Mexico	Arizona	Oregon	Washington	Montana	South Dakota	North Dakota	Nebraska
Standing committees on Indian affairs in legislature	Upper chamber 1990–2000	Lower chamber 1995–2000						
Affirmation of government-to-government relationship	Accord signed in 1996	Declaration by governor in 2006	Declaration by governor in 1996	Accord signed in 1989	Declaration by governor in 2003			In mission state office of Indian affairs
Years of lawsuits about representation & voting	1976, 1979 1982, 1984 1985, 1986 1988, 1993 1998, 2001	1965, 1966 1973, 1974 1977, 1981 1988, 1994 2002, 2006			1976, 1983 1996, 1999 2000, 2002	1974, 1978 1979, 1980 1984, 1986 1999, 2000 2001, 2002 2003, 2004 2005	1992, 1996 2000	1978, 1993
Years of lawsuits about Indian vote dilution & districting (subset of total)	1979, 1984 1985, 1986 1988, 2001	1965, 1973 1981, 1988			1983, 1996 1999, 2000 2002	2000, 2001 2002, 2003 2004, 2005	1992, 1996 2000	1978, 1993

For South Dakota and North Dakota, there is no mention of a government-to-government relationship on the websites of the state commissions of Indian affairs.

Finally, I drew on McCool, Olson, and Robinson's (2007) data on lawsuits over voting rights. I am curious about (a) any serious contentions over Indian voting rights, (b) legal battles waged in earlier decades, and (c) intense legal battles over voting rights in the 1990s. I am particularly interested in suits that allege Indian vote dilution, which would be a particularly strong indicator of anti-Indian political practices.

New Mexico

New Mexico has the largest American Indian population share among all the states, and there are not strong indicators of Indian-white conflict. Chapter 5 showed that intermingled land can be a foundation for conflict, but intermingled land was not very common in New Mexico: the number of non-Indians living within reservation boundaries was less than one-fourth the number of Indians in the state. Also, the degree of political concentration does not seem as intense as in other places. Only one of New Mexico's counties was more than 40% American Indian in 1990 and the state is home to 22 separate reservations.

Other features of New Mexico politics suggest that, relative to the other states with large Indian populations, conflict was lower. The upper chamber of the New Mexico legislature had a standing committee on Indian affairs throughout the 1990s. The state's governor signed an accord in the mid-1990s affirming a government-to-government relationship with tribes. Finally, although there was a strong history of legal battles by Native people to protect voting rights in New Mexico, much of that fight was waged and settled in earlier decades.

Arizona

As with New Mexico, some—but not all—indicators of Indian-white conflict were absent in Arizona. American Indians in Arizona are a large share of the population, but intermingled land was rare: the population of non-Indians living within reservation boundaries was less than a tenth the size of the Indian population in the state. American Indian political concentration was mixed: there were two counties that were more than 40% American Indian in 1990, but Indian lands spread across 21 different reservations.

The lower chamber of Arizona's legislature created a standing committee on Indian affairs in 1995. Like New Mexico, a large portion of the legal battle to protect Indian voting rights had been waged and won before the 1990s began. Arizona was slow to officially recognize the government-to-government relationship, however; an official declaration did not come until the mid-2000s.

Montana

Montana is another state with a large American Indian population (6.0% in 1990), but the political landscape appeared notably less hospitable for Indian advocacy than in the Southwest. Intermingled land was common in Montana; 3% of the state population was non-Indians living within the boundaries of reservations. This is large relative to the percent American Indian in Montana and it has potential to serve as the foundation for anti-tribal politics. Montana was second—although a distant second—in the number of counties that were at least 40% American Indian in 1990, with three such counties. Also, reservation populations are relatively concentrated in Montana; there are just seven reservations in the state. Montana did not arrive at affirmation of a government-to-government relationship until 2003. Furthermore, legal battles to protect American Indian voting rights were scarce in earlier decades and at a heated pitch in the 1990s.

North Dakota

North Dakota seems fairly similar to Montana. Intermingled land was relatively extensive in North Dakota. The state population in 1990 was 4.1% American Indian and 2.3% non-Indians living within reservation boundaries. The state had two counties with Indian populations above 40%. The reservation population was fairly concentrated, spanning just five reservations. I found no indication that North Dakota has acknowledged or affirmed a government-to-government relationship between tribes and states. McCool, Olson, and Robinson's (2007) indicate that legal battles to protect Indian voting rights were absent from North Dakota in earlier decades but were underway in the 1990s.

South Dakota

In these data, South Dakota looks the most vulnerable to Indian-white conflict. Intermingled lands were relatively extensive: 3% of the state population in 1990 was non-Indians living within reservation boundaries; 7.3% of the population was American Indian. South Dakota had an extraordinary degree of political concentration of its American Indian population—nine counties were at least 40% Indian. Reservation boundaries contributed to political concentration; the state has only nine reservations. Despite South Dakota's large American Indian population, there is no standing committee in the state legislature to address Indian affairs, and I found no indication that the state has ever officially acknowledged or affirmed the government-to-government relationship. Finally, legal battles over Indian voting rights in South Dakota have shown no sign of lessening over time and continue actively into the present day.

Washington

In Washington, the indicators suggest that American Indians were generally not a highly salient political group. Washington had a far smaller American Indian population share: 1.7% of the population was American Indian in 1990. While intermingled lands were not high in absolute terms, they were very high relative to the size of the state's American Indian population. In 1990, 1.5% of Washingtonians were non-Indians living within reservation boundaries. Washington was a front-runner among states, however, in signing an accord affirming government-to-government relations in 1989. There is no history of legal battles over voting rights, which seems consistent with the state's small American Indian population share. Vote dilution is only an issue when the electorate is large enough to be diluted, after all.

Oregon

Oregon also had a limited American Indian presence, in both demographics and politics. Oregon had a very small American Indian population—1.4% of the state in 1990—and virtually no non-Indians living within reservation boundaries. The governor did declare, in 1996, that the state-tribal relationship was a government-to-government relationship.

Nebraska

Nebraska looked quite comparable to Oregon. Nebraska had a very small American Indian population share—1.3% in 1990. The intermingling of land was moderate, relative to the size of the Indian population: 0.4% of Nebraskans were non-Indians living within reservation boundaries. Today, the state office of Indian affairs affirms a government-to-government relationship in its mission; it is unclear how long this has been official language. Although American Indians are a sliver of the Nebraska electorate, some legal battles over voting rights occurred in the 1970s and the 1990s.

American Indian State Legislators

The presence and absence of American Indians in state legislatures correlated with other state characteristics. I attempted to identify legislators with self-identified American Indian ancestry and a tribal affiliation, although available information was not always consistent or thorough over the course of the 1990s.[5] I found in places where American Indian political incorporation was greater, American Indian legislators were more common. In places where American Indians were at the periphery of state politics, there were fewer American Indian legislators.

New Mexico and Arizona each had American Indian legislators in both legislative chambers throughout the 1990s. Numbers fluctuated, but at the peak, there were seven American Indians in the New Mexico legislature and four American Indians in the Arizona legislature.

North Dakota, Montana, and South Dakota all had notable American Indian populations, but for each legislative session in the 1990s, each state had only one American Indian legislator in the entire body. It is especially notable that Montana and South Dakota had larger American Indian shares in their population than did Arizona, but representation in Montana and South Dakota lagged markedly behind Arizona. Oregon, Washington, and Nebraska all had small American Indian population and no American Indians in their legislatures.

Hall's (1996) model of legislator behavior offers tools for thinking about the role that American Indian legislators would play. Since most legislators do not participate on most issues, policymaking tends to rest with the small number of legislators who are particularly interested in an issue. In short, a small number of American Indian legislators could have a big impact by making a big investment of time and effort into legislation affecting American Indians. In a hospitable environment, that investment could result in lots of new legislation. In a less hospitable environment, legislators might invest in building coalitions behind a few bills. At a conference in 1992, South Dakota State Senator Paul Valandra, member of the Rosebud Sioux Tribe, described his role in softening up the legislative process. Valandra said that he did not try to introduce a lot of bills; instead, he focused on long-run efforts to persuade other legislators that their interests fit with the priorities of his constituents.

Overview of the States

In sum, certain general categories seem to emerge. First, there are the states with large American Indian populations: New Mexico, Arizona, Montana, North Dakota, and South Dakota. Among those, New Mexico and Arizona have fewer of the classic ingredients or indicators of intense Indian-white conflict. South Dakota has perhaps the strongest warning signs of combative relations. North Dakota and Montana fall somewhere in between.

Next, there are the states with small American Indian populations: Washington, Oregon, and Nebraska. Among these states, Oregon is notable for its virtual absence of intermingled lands and Washington for its proportionately extensive intermingled lands. Nebraska falls somewhere in between.

C. SUMMARY STATISTICS ON STATE LEGISLATION AFFECTING TRIBES

I examined 673 bills affecting American Indians that were introduced in the Arizona, New Mexico, Oregon, Washington, Montana, North Dakota, South Dakota, and Nebraska legislatures from 1990 to 2000. Table 6.3 offers some basic descriptive information on this legislation.

In brief, Arizona and New Mexico considered the greatest volume of legislation affecting American Indians—177 and 201 bills, respectively. Washington and Montana filled a second tier, with 91 and 78 bills, respectively. The four remaining states—Oregon, Nebraska, North Dakota, and South Dakota—considered very little legislation affecting tribes: over the 11-year period examined, each considered 41 or fewer bills. For legislation passed, three states—Arizona, New Mexico, and Montana—stand out for their higher volumes. 45 bills passed in Arizona, 27 in New Mexico, and 41 in Montana.

Two-thirds of bills were pro-tribal, around one-tenth were anti-tribal, and one-fifth were ambiguous. In all, only 22 anti-tribal bills were enacted in 11 years in these eight states. Washington considered the greatest volume of anti-tribal bills among the bunch—28 bills total—although in the end, it only enacted 3 of these bills. It would appear that active hostility to tribal interests was not terribly common in these state legislatures. Instead, the problem of malign neglect was the bigger issue: even though many of these states have large American Indian populations, many rarely took up issues that related specifically to Indian concerns.

The variation among states in American Indian population goes a good ways in explaining state differences. For example, Oregon and Nebraska have relatively small Indian populations and they considered relatively few bills relating to American Indians. Washington is in similar circumstances. While a relatively large number of tribal bills were introduced in Washington, very few bills passed.

Arizona, New Mexico, and Montana have relatively large Indian populations and they also took up relatively high volumes of Indian legislation. The odd cases, however, are the Dakotas. Despite a notable American Indian presence in the states, Dakota legislatures considered few tribal issues and enacted even fewer.

III. Volume of Interactions

A basic negative binomial count model, in table 6.4, went remarkably far in explaining variation in the number of bills in a session. Chapter 5, section IV offered more

TABLE 6.3

Summary Statistics on State Legislation Affecting Tribes

	Bills Introduced				Bills Signed			
	Total	Pro-tribal	Unclear	Anti-tribal	Total	Pro-tribal	Unclear	Anti-tribal
Arizona	177	125 71%	34 19%	18 10%	45	30 67%	8 18%	7 16%
New Mexico	201	157 78%	34 17%	10 5%	27	19 70%	7 26%	1 4%
Oregon	34	17 50%	12 35%	5 15%	17	11 65%	4 24%	2 12%
Washington	91	43 47%	20 22%	28 31%	14	7 50%	4 29%	3 21%
Montana	78	51 65%	13 17%	14 18%	41	29 71%	7 17%	5 12%
Nebraska	20	8 40%	9 45%	3 15%	9	3 33%	5 56%	1 11%
South Dakota	41	31 76%	9 22%	1 2%	15	12 80%	2 13%	1 7%
North Dakota	31	20 65%	10 32%	1 3%	18	9 50%	8 44%	1 6%
Total	673	456 67%	143 21%	81 12%	186	124 65%	47 24%	22 11%

discussion of the statistical methods used here. Readers who wish to skip the details of the statistical analysis may want to move ahead to the discussion of predicted probabilities in section III.D of this chapter. Table 6.4 models the number of bills at key stages throughout the legislative process: introduction, passing the first chamber, passing the second chamber, and signed into law. Keep in mind that these are not conditional models: as the legislative process unfolded, I considered the accumulated effect from the entire legislative process.[6]

A. NEW VARIABLES

In addition to the variables described in earlier tables, I included a small number of additional variables that might predict the number of interactions. Since the dataset only included 70 state-years, I had to be very selective about which variables to include.[7] My choices were as follows.

First, I evaluated federal support for building tribes' expert capacity. To measure this effect, I looked to the Bureau of Indian Affairs' annual Tribal Priority Allocations, which distributed funds directly to tribes from the BIA's Self-Determination programs and were the main source of funding from the BIA for tribal capacity-building (Bureau of Indian Affairs 1992–1999, 2000). Tribes that had accessed this federal support would have been able to gain experience managing budgets, personnel, and tradeoffs. Presumably, those experiences would generate skills that could carry into multiple arenas, including state politics. I included a measure of BIA *"self-government" support* for all the tribal governments in the state—specifically, support from the Consolidated Tribal Government Program and the Self-Government Program. These were grants with special features designed to enhance tribes' governing autonomy. The grants ought to have particular effects on strategic capacity. I also included *overall BIA support for tribal government* operations in a state. To allow for the possibility that this effect was not linear—that effects waned at the far end of the distribution—I included the square of this coefficient as well.

Next, I measured *whether gaming had emerged as an issue in a state* and whether gaming had been an issue in state-tribal relations for at least five years. I used the first year that legislation on gaming was introduced as the indicator of whether tribes and states had begun interacting over gaming. Perhaps the earlier arrival of gaming in some states altered relations in subsequent years.

I also included a measure of *tribes' campaign contributions*. I included here a measure of tribes' federal campaign contributions, drawing on the database of the Center for Responsive Politics at opensecrets.org.[8] I used federal donations as an indicator of tribes' potential to make donations in state politics. This particular

TABLE 6.4

Negative Binomial Count Model of Volume of Legislation per Year Affecting Tribes

		Introduced	Passed 1st house	Passed 2nd house	Signed by governor
State where measure was introduced	Arizona	0.42 (0.89)	2.39* (1.44)	3.80* (2.02)	3.25 (2.20)
	New Mexico	1.41** (0.71)	1.92** (0.97)	1.49 (1.23)	0.40 (1.31)
	Oregon	-0.95* (0.55)	-1.34 (0.83)	-1.87* (1.11)	-1.57 (1.21)
	Washington	0.86 (0.69)	0.66 (0.94)	-0.17 (1.18)	-1.64 (1.20)
	Nebraska	-2.26*** (0.69)	-2.00** (1.01)	-2.37* (1.29)	-1.88 (1.36)
	South Dakota	-0.97*** (0.24)	-0.90*** (0.31)	-1.17*** (0.39)	-1.43*** (0.40)
	North Dakota	-1.35*** (0.38)	-1.25** (0.53)	-1.46** (0.68)	-1.09 (0.71)
Features of legislative session	Have begun interacting over gaming	0.26* (0.15)	0.05 (0.19)	0.19 (0.24)	-0.11 (0.23)
	Interacting over gaming for at least 5 years	0.44*** (0.16)	0.17 (0.22)	-0.11 (0.29)	-0.17 (0.29)

	(1)	(2)	(3)	(4)
Campaign contributions by tribes in state	0.002 *	0.0008	0.0003	-0.002
	(0.001)	(0.002)	(0.0026)	(0.0026)
Volume of all legislation	0.0002 **	0.0004 ***	0.0005 **	0.0005 *
	(0.0001)	(0.0002)	(0.00002)	(0.0003)
Rate of being signed into law, all legislation	3.12 **	3.75 **	2.76	2.141
	(1.36)	(1.84)	(2.31)	(2.419)
BIA self-government support	-0.04 **	-0.04	-0.03	0.00003
	(0.02)	(0.03)	(0.04)	(0.00004)
All other BIA support	-0.07 *	-0.04	-0.05	0.003
	(0.04)	(0.06)	(0.08)	(0.0008)
All other BIA support, squared	0.0008 **	0.00003	-0.0003	-0.000001
	(0.0004)	(0.0006)	(0.0007)	(0.0000007)
Constant	1.77 *	0.65	1.33	0.712
	(1.07)	(1.56)	(2.00)	(2.095)
N	69	69	69	69
Log likelihood	-166.5	-136.3	-129.4	-116.1
Pseudo R-Squared	0.26	0.22	0.17	0.21

Significance at the 1%, 5%, and 10% levels is indicated by *** , ** , and * , respectively. All dollar values are in thousands.

variable measures both tribes' ability and proclivity to make political donations. The correlation between federal contributions and being at least five years into state-tribal gaming interactions was 0.51. This relationship is as expected: presumably, contributions would go up once tribes had a few years to begin amassing gaming profits.

Finally, I controlled for the *total volume of all legislation* for each session in these states and the *enactment rates for all legislation* in that session. Some states considered more bills than others; some states rejected a far greater portion of proposed legislation.

B. RESULTS

The state patterns that appeared in the descriptive statistics endured and dominated in the regression analysis. Oregon and Nebraska considered less tribal legislation and the effect was statistically significant for most of the models. The result is hardly surprising given that both states have small American Indian populations. The Dakotas remained unique as well. Even though both states have relatively large American Indian populations, they considered far less Indian legislation, and the effect was statistically significant for most of the models. Finally, as seen before, Arizona and New Mexico were more likely to pursue legislation addressing American Indians, and the effects were significant in two of the four models for each tribe.

The results from other variables were as follows. First, once gaming and gaming revenues appeared, the volume of introduced legislation affecting Indians increased. This change, however, may have entailed bills that died a quick death—by the end of the legislative process, the effects were negative but insignificant. I saw this pattern for gaming itself and for the presumably related pattern of tribal campaign contributions. When the ability and inclination to make campaign contributions grew, the volume of introduced legislation increased, but the effects did not carry through the legislative process.

The results also showed that when tribes in a state had more BIA support for building expertise, less tribal legislation was introduced in the state legislature. The pattern was true both for overall support and for self-government support. It appeared that the change in volume considered didn't change the volume enacted in the end: while the effects were negative and significant for bill introduction, they were positive and insignificant for bill enactment.

These patterns of lower introductions suggest some potential benefits of selectivity that will be tested further in subsequent models. If tribes with more federal support persuaded their legislative advocates to introduce fewer bills but achieved the same success rates in the end, it would suggest these tribes made effective, strategic selections of issues to pursue. There would appear to be an opposite effect for gaming and campaign dollars; advocates pushed more at the beginning of the process, but they didn't improve their yield as a result.

In sum, the most remarkable pattern was that basic state differences in the volume of interactions were not explained away by other variables. The enduring puzzle was that of the Dakotas. Even in the face of statistical controls, they considered remarkably few pieces of American Indian legislation, which was surprising in light of the large numbers of American Indians living in the two states.

IV. Analyzing Differences in Legislative Successes

To examine in more detail how tribal legislation fared, I turned to logistic regression analysis of the odds of success for legislation. I hypothesized that when tribes cultivate political and policy expertise, they are more successful before the state legislature. Expertise should have visible impacts on several dimensions of tribal-state interactions.

A. VARIABLES IN MODEL

1) *BIA support for expertise.* I used three sets of variables to test my hypotheses about the impacts of outside support. See chapter 2 and section III.A of this chapter for details about the sources of these data. First, I identified *policy areas with greater federal support for tribes.* I hypothesized that when tribes had more BIA assistance with building expertise in a particular policy area, they would develop a portable expertise on that topic.[9] For example, knowledge about water quality or social services delivery could be built or buttressed with federal support.

Just as some federal funds focused on particular subject areas, other funds targeted *support for self-governing management skills.* Such dollars came primarily through contracting and compacting funds. These programs sought not just to fund programs in tribal government; they also sought to build tribal autonomy, by targeting help at management tasks and by giving tribes discretion that allowed them to exercise more managerial decision-making. Self-government funding grew rapidly over the sample period. Thus, I controlled for year in my analysis of this funding. I wanted to consider whether even the smaller dollar amounts in the early years had positive impacts. I also wanted to be sure that the measure wasn't just capturing other over-time trends.

Thirdly, I included *all BIA support to tribes* other than self-government funds. Here, I wanted to be sure to account for generalized effects of federal support. I wanted to distinguish the effects of targeted BIA help from trends in overall BIA assistance.

The distribution of annual policy-area spending was fairly "chunky" and not very continuous, so I split the spending into two categories of analysis: state-year policy areas where (a) federal support was high (above the median support level) and (b) federal support was very high (about the 90% percentile of federal support). High support meant that all tribes in a state were receiving at least $3 million combined in federal aid for governance in that policy area. Very high support means that all tribes in a state were receiving at least $20 million combined in federal aid for that policy area—an unusually large amount of support.

In sum, I used multiple measures of federal support, so that I might capture different mechanisms through which outside assistance with capacity-building affected performance in state politics.

2) *Sent to Indian Affairs committee in 1st house.* I identified whether a given piece of legislation was sent to a standing committee on Indian affairs in the house where it was introduced. Such committees existed in New Mexico's upper house throughout the sample period and in Arizona's lower house from 1995 on. This variable explores how Indian Affairs committees dealt differently with tribal legislation early in the legislative process. I expect that these committees served as important points for accumulating expertise about how to promote tribal priorities in a given legislature.

4) *History of tribal legislation in previous session.* I used experiences in the preceding legislative session to evaluate learning opportunities for tribal advocates. I examined the volume of tribal legislation in the previous year for a proposal's policy area, the volume of tribal legislation in the previous year for a proposal's type of legislation action, and the overall volume of tribal legislation from the year before. My expectation was that more bills led to more opportunities to learn and thus improved outcomes for tribes in subsequent sessions.

5) *State where the measure was introduced.* Descriptive statistics above led to strong expectations about states: Arizona and New Mexico should be more amenable to Indian interests; South Dakota, North Dakota, and Washington should be more resistant; Oregon and Nebraska should fall somewhere in between. In the regressions, I used Montana as the comparison state. I want to evaluate whether the state-specific effects can be explained away by other trends in the data.

I expected other factors to matter, of course, and so I included a number of control variables. I wanted to evaluate whether the variables of interest still had effects even when competing explanations were considered. The control variables in this analysis were the following:

6) *Features of individual legislation Anti-tribal item.* Legislation was coded 1 if it decreased or challenged tribal government powers, 0 if it increased tribal government powers or was ambiguous. I would expect that if legislatures were actively hostile to tribal interests, the small number of anti-tribal actions would be more likely to pass.

Small-scale item. I classified legislation as small-scale if it involved an especially limited grant of power, goods, services, or funding. I would expect that small-scale items were more likely to pass.

Items affecting good/services/funding. Perhaps states may be particularly averse to spending money on tribal interests, although they could be more willing to acknowledge powers or share powers.

7) *Features of the legislative session Gaming.* I constructed three measures of the stage of state-tribal interactions over gaming, all of which were also included in the analysis of the volume of legislation in section III. First, I identified the first year when gaming legislation appeared in a state. Second, I identified the point at which states and tribes had been interacting over gaming for at least five years. Third, I identified federal campaign contributions made by tribes in each state in each year, to proxy for tribe's capacity and proclivity to make campaign contributions at the state level. Gaming might increase tensions, although those tensions might also decline with time. All the same, savvy tribal advocates ought to adjust their behavior to match these differing conditions.

Overall features of legislating. I also included controls for the nature of the law-making in a given state in a given year. I included the volume of bills introduced and percentage of bills that were eventually signed into law.[10]

B. OVERALL RESULTS

Table 6.5 examines factors shaping the success of tribal legislation at different stages in the legislative process.[11] The most notable findings were as follows.

First, where tribes had more federal support, proposals went further in the legislative process. Effects were significant all the way through to bill enactment for two measures of targeted federal support measures: tribes in a state with very high (90th percentile) federal support in that policy area and tribes in a state with support specifically designed to bolster tribal self-government. Effects from high policy area support and from overall support were positive throughout the process and significant for the first chamber in the process. In short, it helped to have aid with building expertise. Help with internal capacity-building translated into greater successes in state capitals.

Referral to an Indian Affairs committee had intriguing effects. First, referral to such a committee had a negative, statistically significant effect on passing the first house; yet it had positive, significant effects on a bill's odds of enactment. Clearly,

TABLE 6.5

Logistic Regression Analysis of Features Shaping Legislative Outcomes

		Passed 1st house	Passed 2nd house	Signed by governor
Federal support for tribes in a state	Policy area with high funding	0.24 ** (0.11)	0.14 (0.13)	0.06 (0.26)
	Policy area with very high funding	0.35 * (0.21)	0.80 *** (0.16)	0.91 *** (0.15)
	BIA self-government support, controlling for year	0.63 *** (0.24)	0.86 *** (0.32)	1.16 *** (0.42)
	All other BIA support	0.07 *** (0.02)	0.08 (0.06)	0.11 (0.08)
	All other BIA support, squared	-0.000001 *** (0.0000002)	-0.000001 *** (0.0000004)	-0.000002 *** (0.0000005)
Behavior of tribal advocates	Sent to Indian Affairs committee	-0.62 * (0.33)	0.02 (0.07)	0.45 *** (0.18)
Tribal legislation in previous session	How many times this issue came up	0.07 ** (0.03)	0.06 ** (0.02)	0.09 *** (0.02)
	How many times this kind of action came up	0.06 (0.04)	0.08 ** (0.04)	0.04 (0.03)
	Total number of Indian-related proposals	-0.02 ** (0.01)	-0.02 (0.01)	-0.003 (0.01)
Features of individual legislation	Anti-tribal	-0.32 (0.21)	-0.13 (0.33)	-0.29 (0.43)
	Small-scale	0.50 *** (0.17)	0.10 (0.28)	0.06 (0.44)
	Affects goods/services/funding	-0.61 (0.44)	-0.82 ** (0.42)	-0.65 * (0.34)
State	Arizona	1.76 ** (0.81)	1.68 (1.64)	1.88 (2.35)
	New Mexico	0.65	-0.50	-0.95

	(1)	(2)	(3)
	(0.47)	(0.81)	(1.42)
Oregon	0.44 (0.75)	-0.07 (1.17)	0.96 (0.94)
Washington	-1.58 * (0.87)	-3.41 *** (1.22)	-3.80 ** (1.65)
Nebraska	1.53 *** (0.57)	1.92 (1.2)	2.96 *** (1.07)
South Dakota	-0.16 (0.31)	-1.19 *** (0.45)	-1.19 ** (0.6)
North Dakota	1.12 *** (0.13)	1.10 ** (0.53)	1.68 * (0.9)
Features of the legislative session			
Have begun interacting over gaming	0.15 (0.4)	0.19 (0.43)	-0.07 (0.44)
Interacting over gaming for at least 5 years	-0.19 (0.13)	-0.61 *** (0.19)	-0.10 (0.18)
Log of campaign contributions by tribes in state	-0.08 *** (0.02)	-0.03 (0.04)	-0.06 ** (0.03)
Volume of all bills	0.0003 ** (0.0001)	0.0005 *** (0.0002)	0.0006 *** (0.0001)
Rate of being signed into law, all bills	1.62 (1.45)	2.22 (2.38)	3.95 * (2.12)
Constant	-2.26 ** (1.1)	-3.16 * (1.91)	-5.13 *** (1.29)
N	590	590	585
Log likelihood	-371.1	-327.9	-289.3

Standard errors, clustered by state, are below the coefficients
Significance at the 1%, 5%, and 10% levels is indicated by ***, **, and *, respectively. All dollar values are in thousands.

Indian Affairs committees were not indiscriminate advocates, pushing through as many measures as possible. Rather, they were selective about what they reported out, even more selective than other committees in the body. Outcomes in later stages of decision-making indicated that this early selectivity paid off down the road. The bills that survived Indian Affairs committees became *more* likely to become law. Interestingly, it appears that Indian Affairs committees served tribal interests early in the legislative process by killing tribal bills, and by killing pro-tribal bills. Of course, for such later effects to pan out, the decisions about which legislation to dump early had to be well-informed choices, based on accurate calculations about where tribes stood a better chance of winning. The other implication is that tribal advocates knew that they couldn't pull off an ambitious agenda. Either they didn't have the wherewithal or they didn't face a sufficiently receptive environment.

The result persisted even when I conducted robustness checks for whether legislation was sent to any committee at all and for the number of committees to which the legislation was sent. Alternate specifications showed that Indian Affairs committees killed pro-tribal bills more frequently than they killed ambiguous bills. In the legislatures that have Indian Affairs committees, anti-tribal bills were rare; these committees didn't have to bother with axing those proposals.

Learning from prior legislation mattered as well. Furthermore, learning had contingent impacts that were consistent with expertise-centered behavior. By itself, a high volume of tribal legislation in the previous year made it harder to move tribal legislation forward in the current year: the effect was negative throughout the process and statistically significant for passing the first house. But if legislation in the recent past was concentrated in particular policy areas or in particular types, the effect turned around. Most notably, the effect of experience in that policy area was positive and statistically significant throughout the legislative process. Experience in a particular kind of action was significant in one phase and positive throughout.

I offer the following interpretation of these results: a large volume of legislation spread out across a range of topics may have stretched tribal advocates too thinly and did not offer many opportunities for tribal advocates to learn much in particular. But if a large volume of legislation was concentrated in a specific domain, then opportunities for learning emerged. Of course, if tribal advocates, and Indian Affairs committees in particular, noticed these patterns, it might help explain some of their apparent selectivity about the sorts of issues to advance. Overall, the data indicate that careful selection was worthwhile because it could reap results in the end. This is also another indicator that tribal advocates couldn't pursue an ambitious agenda. Instead, they targeted their energies.

Other variables in this analysis controlled for different dynamics. Anti-tribal measures tended to do worse in the legislative process, although the effect was not significant. Small-scale items seemed to do better earlier, as the effect was positive and statistically significant at first. Allocations of goods/services/funding ran into greater trouble at various stages in the legislative process. Interestingly, gaming and potential campaign contributions had insignificant effects in the process. It seems implausible that political climates were unaffected by these new dynamics. The more compelling explanation is that tribal advocates adjusted their strategies to these settings—they changed the bills that they proposed and the arguments that they made—to offset conflicts related to gaming.

The state controls revealed several patterns. In short, the basket of features in each state continued to have impacts. Nebraska and North Dakota seemed apt to pass the small amounts of tribal legislation that they encountered: there were positive and significant effects for both states. South Dakota had an especially inhospitable environment. As we saw before, the state has a high percent of American Indians yet considered very little tribal legislation. Table 6.5 shows that the few tribal bills making it before the South Dakota legislature faced poor prospects throughout the lawmaking process; the effects are statistically significant at every stage. Finally, as the descriptive statistics indicated, Washington was very unlikely to pass tribal legislation: effects were negative and significant throughout the process. The descriptive statistics showed that Washington was unusually likely to see anti-tribal bills introduced. The finding here is that bills introduced were not a good indicator of laws passed; most of those anti-tribal bills were killed.

In sum, the findings are partly heartening and partly troubling, from tribes' perspectives. First, the greatest harm to tribes in the state legislatures came from neglect—either benign or malign—rather than from active hostility. Some states spent very little time on American Indian legislation. Mostly, these states were the ones with fewer American Indians, but the Dakotas also followed the pattern of few Indian bills. Yet the findings in table 6.5 show that tribes were not simply at the mercy of their environment. Tribes didn't have means to advance a wide set of initiatives, but their skills and strategies still mattered. When tribes had more outside support for building expertise, where committee structures allowed tribal advocates to house legislative expertise, and when tribes had experience on an issue, they improved their fate in state politics.

C. ALTERNATE SPECIFICATIONS

The tables that follow evaluated subsets of these data, to see if the trends differed for particular types of bills. As a first test, I excluded bills about economic development from the sample. Perhaps bills over gaming, commercial fishing, mining, and other key elements in people's livelihoods generated a different legislative dynamic. In large part, results from the original model persist. Table 6.6

TABLE 6.6

Logistic Regression Analysis of Features Shaping Legislative Outcomes, Excluding Bills about Economic Development

		Passed 1st house	Passed 2nd house	Signed by governor
Federal support for tribes in a state	Policy area with high funding	0.33*	0.41*	0.36*
		(0.18)	(0.24)	(0.2)
	Policy area with very high funding	0.70***	0.93***	0.91***
		(0.1)	(0.28)	(0.33)
	BIA self-government support, controlling for year	0.06	0.43	0.71
		(0.28)	(0.34)	(0.51)
	All other BIA support	0.09***	0.11**	0.19***
		(0.03)	(0.05)	(0.06)
	All other BIA support, squared	-0.000001***	-0.000002***	-0.000003***
		(0.0000002)	(0.0000004)	(0.0000005)
Behavior of tribal advocates	Sent to Indian Affairs committee	-0.94***	-0.34***	-0.01
		(0.1)	(0.03)	(0.28)
Tribal legislation in previous session	How many times this issue came up	0.11**	0.02	0.01
		(0.05)	(0.05)	(0.06)
	How many times this kind of action came up	0.04	0.06	-0.05
		(0.04)	(0.05)	(0.03)
	Total number of Indian-related proposals	-0.06**	-0.04**	-0.04
		(0.02)	(0.02)	(0.02)
Features of individual legislation	Anti-tribal	-0.69*	-0.34	-0.41
		(0.4)	(0.41)	(0.52)
	Small-scale	0.69***	0.29	0.08
		(0.24)	(0.24)	(0.49)
	Affects goods/services/funding	-0.83*	-0.90*	-0.61**
		(0.44)	(0.46)	(0.29)
State	Arizona	0.54	0.95	2.69
		(1.83)	(1.84)	(2.65)
	New Mexico	1.09	-0.78	-0.90
		(0.96)	(1.15)	(1.42)

	(1)	(2)	(3)
Oregon	0.91	-0.20	0.45
	(1.32)	(1.65)	(1.49)
Washington	-0.28	-2.80*	-3.14
	(1.49)	(1.7)	(2.01)
Nebraska	0.82	1.17	3.37**
	(0.65)	(1.43)	(1.38)
South Dakota	0.1	-1.22**	-1.07
	(0.5)	(0.51)	(0.74)
North Dakota	0.45	0.52	1.50**
	(0.4)	(0.52)	(0.77)
Features of the legislative session			
Have begun interacting over gaming	0.60	0.51	0.40
	(0.57)	(0.56)	(0.62)
Interacting over gaming for at least 5 years	0.08	-0.60**	0.03
	(0.27)	(0.23)	(0.03)
Log of campaign contributions by tribes in state	-0.07**	0.01	-0.06
	(0.03)	(0.05)	(0.05)
Volume of all bills	0.0001	0.0005*	0.0010***
	(0.0004)	(0.0003)	(0.0004)
Rate of being signed into law, all bills	1.70	1.62	4.33
	(1.78)	(3.81)	(3.67)
Constant	-2.05	-2.87	-6.71***
	(1.28)	(2.57)	(2.5)
N	416	416	413
Log likelihood	-247.97	-222.71	-189.81

Standard errors, clustered by state, are below the coefficients
Significance at the 1%, 5%, and 10% levels is indicated by ***, ** , and * , respectively. All dollar values are in thousands.

displays the details. Note that the sample size declined from 590 to 416, so by itself, the fact that a given variable may lapse out of significance is not entirely noteworthy. When datasets are smaller, meaningful dynamics are more likely to appear to be due to random chance.

Some results did change. All kinds of federal support were positive both in the presence and absence of economic development. The statistical significance of federal support fluctuated once economic development was excluded, however. Specifically, effects from high levels of policy-specific BIA support—in addition to very high levels—became statistically significant in all three models. Also, overall BIA support to a tribe became statistically significant throughout the process. All the effects became statistically insignificant from BIA support targeted at self-government capacity. Again, given the large reduction in sample size, it is difficult to draw any conclusions from variables lapsing out of significance. It is possible that aid with management and planning skills was more meaningful for the trickier economic issues. In contrast, policy-specific knowledge and general expertise added less value to economic debates.

The consistently negative effect from considering a large number of bills dispersed across policies and actions now became statistically significant. Also, Indian Affairs committees were still very critical and killed lots of bills, but in the final analysis, those bills didn't necessarily do better than ones that went through other committees. Apparently, Indian Affairs committees' greatest impact may have come on the tricky issues of economic development.

Finally, there were weak indications that bills that weren't about gaming became more successful in gaming's presence. The arrival of gaming brought consistently positive, but still insignificant, effects. After gaming has been around at least five years, there were largely positive but insignificant effects.

The upshot is that most results persisted when bills on economic development were absent. Statistical significance fluctuated for some variables, but nearly all positive effects remained positive.

Table 6.7 considers another subset of the data: when analysis was limited to bills that are pro-tribal—bills that are an unqualified boon for tribes—did the process differ? The results for this subset were remarkably similar to the original model. Again, any interpretation of changes in statistical significance must be couched in the fact that the sample size dropped considerably, from 590 to 388, thus making it harder to distinguish true effects from random chance.

The most distinct finding was that the effects of federal aid persisted. There were just a few changes in the results. The introduction of gaming had a consistently negative effect that was statistically significant in two models, although as before, gaming's influence became insignificant with time. Also, Indian Affairs committees were just as choosy and critical as before. The end consequence of their actions was positive, although now it lapsed into statistical insignificance. Finally, the effect from previous experience on a given issue was positive as always, but now it was significant throughout the process. The bottom line was that most results were stable when the analysis was restricted to pro-tribal bills.

D. PREDICTED PROBABILITIES

Table 6.8 translates the regression analysis into predicted probabilities of success. It provides a useful context for interpreting all these findings. The first big lesson related to pro-tribal bills: they were much, much more likely to make it through the process. 83% became law—an extraordinary success rate—as compared to an enactment rate of 52% for all bills. Of course, as with all other effects, this outcome was predicated on a bill being introduced in the first place. Tribes didn't win a lot of victories, but they didn't waste energy on losing issues. Apparently, tribal advocates made the right assessments about which pro-tribal bills would be winners.

Also, when bills about economic development were excluded, the end success rates were no different from that of the overall sample. Whatever unique complexities are involved in negotiations over economic development, it appears that tribal advocates in the legislature managed them and generated comparable success rates.

Table 6.8 also examined the ways that success rates varied in the overall sample. Federal support for building expertise had impressive effects. Enactment rates rose 21 percentage points when tribes had very high levels of federal funding in a policy area. Interestingly, the value added from this kind of federal support didn't appear in the early stage of the legislative process. It would seem that tribes with more help building subject-specific skills did especially well as bills moved into a broader and increasingly complex legislative environment. In a parallel fashion, tribes with federal help building government capacities saw similar improvements to enactment success. When federal help targeted for building self-government was high, enactment rates increased 25 percentage points. These effects also grew as legislation progressed.

The behavior of Indian Affairs committees came through sharply. Bills that went to these committees were 15 percentage points less likely to make it out of the first house. In the end, the bills that these committees handled were 11 percentage points more likely to see enactment. A lot of bills saw their doom inside these committees, but the ones that made it out thrived. The committees were picky, but they had the foresight to calculate effective choices.

Past experience had a notable impact. If a bill took on both an entirely new issue and a new action, enactment rates were 12 percentage points below the baseline.

TABLE 6.7

Logistic Regression Analysis of Features Shaping Legislative Outcomes, Pro-Tribal Bills Only

		Passed 1st house	Passed 2nd house	Signed by governor
Federal support for tribes in a state	Policy area with high funding	-.28**	0.05	-0.32
		(0.11)	(0.17)	(0.39)
	Policy area with very high funding	0.26	0.91***	0.82***
		(0.3)	(0.23)	(0.21)
	BIA self-government support, controlling for year	0.55	1.31***	1.34**
		(0.36)	(0.51)	(0.52)
	All other BIA support	0.14*	0.07	0.08
		(0.08)	(0.1)	(0.13)
	All other BIA support, squared	-0.000002***	-0.000001	-0.000002
		(0.0000006)	(0.0000008)	(0.0000010)
Behavior of tribal advocates	Sent to Indian Affairs committee	-1.00***	-0.29***	0.20
		(0.35)	(0.04)	(0.16)
Tribal legislation in previous session	How many times this issue came up	0.08***	0.09***	0.13***
		(0.03)	(0.02)	(0.04)
	How many times this kind of action came up	0.12**	0.15***	0.09*
		(0.06)	(0.05)	(0.05)
	Total number of Indian-related proposals	-0.06**	-0.05*	-0.04
		(0.03)	(0.03)	(0.03)
Feature of individual legislation	Anti-tribal	0.44*	-0.17	-0.47
		(0.23)	(0.29)	(0.48)
	Small-scale	-1.22**	-1.36	-0.93*
		(0.61)	(0.5)	(0.48)
	Affects goods/services/funding	-0.75	0.35	1.25
		(1.54)	(2.08)	(2.38)

		(1)	(2)	(3)
State	Arizona	-1.04	-1.46	-2.55
		(0.94)	(1.59)	(2.15)
	New Mexico	1.13	-0.35	-0.72
		(1.34)	(1.35)	(1.82)
	Oregon	-3.08*	-6.60***	-7.02***
		(1.62)	(1.85)	(2.07)
	Washington	0.62	0.32	-0.57
		(1.62)	(1.35)	(1.77)
	Nebraska	-1.04**	-2.06***	-1.93***
		(0.52)	(0.69)	(0.7)
	South Dakota	0.92	0.18	0.03
		(0.72)	(1.03)	(1.46)
	North Dakota	-0.66**	-0.82	-1.15**
		(0.33)	(0.66)	(0.54)
Features of the legislative session	Have begun interacting over gaming	0.02	-0.47	-0.37
		(0.4)	(0.36)	(0.42)
	Interacting over gaming for at least 5 years	-0.06**	0.01	-0.01
		(0.03)	(0.06)	(0.05)
	Log of campaign contributions by tribes in state	0.00	0.00	0.00
		(0.0001)	(0.0003)	(0.0003)
	Volume of all bills	-2.10	0.54	-0.33
		(2.91)	(3.75)	(4.61)
	Rate of being signed into law, all bills	0.40	-0.24	0.29
		(2.9)	(2.22)	(2.45)
Constant		388.00	388.00	384.00
		(-233.08)	(-201.81)	(-176.29)
N		416	416	413
Log likelihood		-247.97	-222.71	-189.81

Standard errors, clustered by state, are below the coefficients.
Significance at the 1%, 5% and 10% levels is indicated by ***, **, and *, respectively. All dollar values are in thousands.

TABLE 6.8

Predicted Probabilities, Features Shaping Legislative Outcomes

		Passed 1st house	Passed 2nd houses	Signed by governor
	Baseline	59%	66%	52%
	Pro-tribal bills only	90%	87%	83%
	Excluding bills about economic development	60%	74%	51%
Federal support for a tribes in a state	Policy area with low funding	53%	63%	50%
	Policy area with very high funding	62%	81%	73%
	High BIA self-government support	73%	82%	77%
	Low BIA self-government support	44%	46%	23%
Behavior of tribal advocates	Sent to Indian Affairs committee	44%	66%	63%
Tribal legislation in previous session	Issue never came up	54%	62%	44%
	This kind of action never came up	52%	57%	47%
	Neither this issue nor this kind came up	47%	53%	40%
Features of the legislative session	Have not yet begun interacting over gaming	55%	62%	52%
	Interacting over gaming for at least 5 years	54%	51%	49%
	Small campaign contributions by tribes in state	68%	69%	59%
	No campaign contributions by tribes in state	71%	70%	62%

Low and high defined as 1 standard deviation increases and decreases.

When tribes departed from the issues where they had experience with policy and politics, they had more trouble advancing their agenda.

Effects from gaming ran from none to slight—at most, final enactment rates changed 3 percentage points. Before, we saw that gaming's effects were statistically insignificant; here, we see they were substantively unimpressive. As noted before, it is hard to imagine that gaming didn't affect state legislative politics. A more plausible explanation is that tribal governments adapted their political strategies so as to offset conflicts and tensions surrounding gaming.

Campaign contributions had negative effects throughout the process—when tribes were either completely unable or disinclined to make contributions, enactment rates were up to 10 percentage points higher. It raises the question of what overall circumstances generated tribes that were willing and able to make campaign contributions. Gaming didn't change things, but inclinations to campaign contributions emerged in different circumstances.

V. Conclusion

This analysis showed that overall context mattered for tribal-state relations, but tribal capacities made a difference as well. To be sure, relations were shaped by general, relatively stable features of state politics and history. Yet where tribes had more outside support for their capacity-building, tribal legislation did better. Where tribal advocates had an institutional space in the statehouse to corral and pool their strategic recourses, they succeeded more. Where tribal advocates had more opportunities to learn a policymaking environment, their proposals did better. These findings help us better appreciate the wide-ranging and subtle consequences of expertise. For example, once built, a skilled staff of environmental scientists, budget analysts, or transportation planners that knows their external environment can speak effectively for tribal needs in many different arenas. For example, when a group of seasoned tribal advocates has the opportunity to review and deliberate on bills affecting tribes, they are unsparingly critical and choose their issues very carefully.

Many of the state legislatures in the sample usually ignored tribes' concerns. These data show clearly that New Mexico and Arizona tended more toward the political incorporation of American Indians while the Dakotas tended toward the neglect and exclusion of American Indians. Furthermore, in states where American Indian populations were especially small, tribal concerns just didn't get a lot of attention. But not every context had a dramatic, unmitigated impact. For example the arrival of gaming—with all the new and uncertain dynamics that it generated—didn't erase successes for tribal governments. Rather, Indian leaders adapted their strategies to their new context and forged forward.

Hyneman (1938, 22) once remarked about state legislators that:

Effective representation, when groups are in conflict, depends upon a flair for reading, in what men ask, just what they will take; capacity for gauging the rigidity of prejudices and the intensity of convictions; canniness in distinguishing the forthright from the sly among allies and opponents; confidence in measuring the pillars of popular approval upon which oneself, a friend, or an opponent stands; sureness in judging just how high up the tree one may climb without being left out on a limb.

It appears that Indian leaders have internalized Hyneman's lessons.

7   Forging the Future

The American Indian tribal governments in this study have learned a great deal about policy problems and political environments. They have come to understand the needs and preferences of actors in external settings, they can develop sophisticated proposals for action, and they have figured out how to effectively pitch those proposals. Furthermore, tribal governments have maintained supportive relationships with outside actors that provide key subsidies for cultivating capacities. Expertise—and specifically, independent expert organizations—open up new political opportunities.

Tribal governments have managed federal institutional niches, used them to accrue expert resources, and nudged those niches toward even more hospitable frameworks. Indian leaders haven't shied away from high-profile fights, but they've had a backup plan as well. Through institutional niches, outside actors subsidize tribes' capacity-building by helping with developing technical policy expertise and other specialized knowledge, providing opportunities to get to know the external environment, and offering exposure to a variety of strategies and organizational forms. Such relationships support better understandings of specific problems and policies, of outside interests and potential collaborators, and of both program and process design. To maintain this support, tribes seek gradual adjustments in programs over time that can secure the relationship. Specifically, tribes seek modest yet serial adjustments in their access to federal officials, in overall policy frameworks, and in specific procedures. Combined, those approaches enable tribes to build sympathies, finesse susceptibilities, and smooth obstacles. In the end, tribal leaders play a small number of federal actors against each other, corral them toward their own stated missions, and act upon their need to demonstrate their own efficacy and thus reap the rewards that follow.

American Indian tribal governments use outside support to develop expertise-centered behaviors, which enable tribes to better envision and implement new courses of action. With expertise, tribal governments better analyze their circumstances by diagnosing and anticipating more. Then, they pursue new courses of action by partnering and initiating more.

As a result, tribal advocates approach state and local politics with the knowledge needed to craft arguments and to identify issues that are winnable. Tribal leaders cannot make vanish the bitter political legacy of entangled Indian-white lands and American Indian political exclusion. They can, however, spot the windows that emerge amidst sometimes hostile, sometimes indifferent forces. When tribes house independent expert organizations and when they have federal aid to build those organizations, they succeed more in state and local politics. In particular, when tribal advocates have more knowledge of policy and politics, they pursue strategies for state and local relations that rely on the skillful allocation of their time and energy.

Surely we all expect expertise to matter, but there is certainly reason to be skeptical that expertise makes a genuine difference for groups on the fringes. The experiences of tribal governments run against those skepticisms. I find that marginalized actors may push for particular, unexpected, and unobtrusive political gains. Those gains look unimpressive until we fully trace out their consequences by looking across time and across venues. Then, the unremarkable adds up to something bigger. American Indian advocates become better problem-solvers, more productive partners, and quick-witted adversaries. They can build political opportunities, both inside tribal government and on the outside as well.

These moments of success suggest a new framework for understanding how marginalized groups—and marginalized governments—can approach the political arena. In the end, marginalized actors don't make their marginalization disappear, but they can maneuver in insightful ways that maximize opportunities. To a notable degree, tribes manage more powerful partners, a task that seems intrinsically impossible.

II. Broader Implications

The strategies of American Indian tribal governments contain a string of surprises. The findings here tell us new things about historical forces, about institutions, about marginalized groups, about strategic capacity, and about state and local politics within a system of federalism.

First, the analysis unveils strategies that are deeply historical. It is surprising the extent to which advocacy groups can carry with them a strategic legacy from their elders, even when those who came before faced strikingly different contexts and employed different organizational forms. There are advantages to strategies that are grounded in accumulated experience and learning. Where there is little room to maneuver, groups must strike a delicate balance between adapting to the outside environment and staying true to their values and mission. Wisdom from earlier generations can inform authentic adaptation.

Second, the analysis shows how advocates' specific strategic constraints and opportunities shape the institutions within which they operate. This analysis demonstrates that there is much to be revealed through a nuanced examination of actors at the center of institutional change. Institutional change comes from someone pushing on the system, even if the outcomes are not quite what the instigator expected. In particular, it is surprising that the story behind policy success and institutional change may be about constancy. A key strategic element is to *not* adapt to changing circumstances. In fact, innovation is a perilous move. It is surprising that slow dribs and drabs merit serious attention, that they can be at the root of important policy change.

Third, the analysis offers a new lens on what it means to be at the periphery of power and the options for maneuvering in a narrow space. It is surprising that tribes have found a space between trivial and co-optive outside involvement. Tribal governments have set their sights on both broad goals and small, discrete, attainable steps. Small wins have to fit with a larger picture, and vice versa. Furthermore, both partners and adversaries are treated with wariness; the end objective is as much about self-sufficiency as about political integration and access. If you'll never fully control the levers of outside power, you need to develop another set of levers within your own control. In other words, the strategy is filled with contingencies allowing that peripheral power will not vanish any time soon and that outside sympathies may be fragile. With that awareness, weaker actors who are commonly losers in politics can devise strategies to manage more powerful partners.

Fourth, the analysis reveals the processes of building and deploying strategic capacity. It is surprising how much expertise can change from within, transforming environments from mystifying to maneuverable. A series of minor investments, of the right kind, can nourish such capacity. As expertise grows, tribal governments see their problems in new ways; they spot more of the forces at play and act upon those insights. Even in remarkably hostile environments, creativity and insight enable some victories. In supportive environments, creativity and insight can support the flourishing of collaboration and joint problem-solving.

Finally, the analysis situates state and local politics within the federalist context. It is surprising that expertise has consequences even when other actors are hostile to the very enterprise of tribal government. The findings illustrate the deep interconnections within federalism, and the ways that one set of interactions provokes changes on any number of dimensions. State, local, and federal governments affect each other directly, but they also affect the advocates who pursue their objectives across the layered powers in a federalist system. There are Indian leaders who want to move tribal governments beyond having problems and into a position where they have answers, too. Leaders with energy, commitment, and foresight use seemingly slight federal resources to build the expertise needed to become meaningful, independent, problem-solving governments. When they succeed, a once-silenced voice has the skills to reenter regional decision-making.

III. Further Work

These lessons change how we look at politics in multiple ways. In short, these findings give us tools to think differently about disadvantage and about innovation in political life. They redirect our attention to lower-profile arenas, with the realization that certain actors have compelling reasons to focus their efforts in those arenas. Disadvantaged actors can sometimes find and develop political opportunities because of the smaller political spheres that institutional variation provides. The findings spotlight the influence of variegated institutional environments, not simply as settings of multiple veto opportunities but also as venues for nuanced positive action. They open up further investigation into the ultimate consequences of the small actions of government.

These findings demand that we understand activism and advocacy by looking at interconnections between the internal dynamics of advocates' organizations and the external institutional contexts within which those organizations are situated. This book makes the case for more actor-centered institutionalism: to think more about agency in agenda-setting. When attention turns more centrally to actors, we can start to flesh out the ways that advocates' specific features affect institutional trajectories. American Indian tribal governments chose pathways of policy change that were grounded in their specific endowments and deficits.

The lessons learned from tribal governments also make the case for further assessments of strategic capacity and of the malleability of political resources. Know-how matters, but there's much more to be said about various pathways for acquiring cleverness and the dynamics that lead to those paths. Maybe, in the end, strategic capacity is the most important political resource of all. If so, there is much to learn from a fuller, richer account of its origins. After all, other political resources won't have much impact if leaders don't realize how to knit them together and apply them to the appropriate contexts. When studies focus on powerful interests—and just examine which powerful actor won in a given moment and which one didn't—we can under-appreciate the role that capacity-building plays in politics at the periphery.

Finally, tribal governments' experiences give a new perspective on state, local, and federal policy. When governments negotiate with one another—as when tribes, states, and locals engage with one another—they bring with them the experiences, injuries, and resources from their interactions elsewhere. This finding raises further questions about both the scope and sequencing of interactions. To understand outcomes at any one level of government we need to understand pathways generated by the traits and timing of relationships at other levels.

IV. Policy Implications

For American Indians, federal policy has always had tremendous impacts, and it is hardly surprising that as America's first nations sought to reshape their fate, much attention and energy was focused on altering federal actions. To reclaim self-determination, they had to confront federal usurpation and redirect federal power. For other communities, differing institutional contexts and paths could easily lead to other sources of relations that are potentially supportive, in other parts of government or even outside of government. Tribes' organizational setting is a critical, case-specific ingredient. Tribal governments solve the collective action problem for many Indian communities, and the creation of national Indian organizations mid-century facilitated much coordinated strategy and pooled information. Their status as governments gives tribes a framework for pressing claims, as they can push other governments to bring their day-to-day actions in line with their overarching legal commitments. Native nations were the first Americans who saw European governments and then the United States overlook principles on paper for the sake of ignoble motives, but they are not the last. This is not to understate the unique status and experiences of American Indian tribal governments. Yet for other groups, the broader pattern may remain applicable.

These findings also offer cogent advice to policymakers, both in government and in public organizations outside of government. Simply, outside help matters, if recipients are able to shape it to their needs. Aid with capacity-building is meaningful. It is tempting, at this point, to embark on a laundry list of what government and nonprofits could do differently, but policy changes must be built first on political circumstances that make change feasible and durable. In that light, the most realistic prescription is a remarkably straightforward one: do everything possible to help marginalized groups build autonomous resources, so that they are positioned to design solutions and win changes that meet their needs. In short, support independent expert organizations. Applied more generally, the suggestion is that stable, supportive relationships of various kinds offer great potential when they are built as meaningful partnerships. When this lesson is applied to federal Indian policy in particular, the resulting counsel is to support tribal capacity-building and self-determination.

When this lesson is applied to state and local policymaking, the counsel is to forge genuine government-to-government relations. Many reservations are found in areas with struggling economies. Both Indians and whites face problems that need creative solutions. Everyone's resources are scarce. The need is for serious conversations about regional partnering and about what various governments can contribute, not for festering slights and fragmented policy.

V. Reflections on Gaming and Sovereignty

Debates about federal Indian policy almost always turn to Indian gaming at some point. This book profiles a decade that began when Indian casinos were uncommon and that ended with the proliferation of Indian casinos. Many fears—that tribes would never truly control their casinos, that they would be victim to unscrupulous outside manipulations—have not been realized in most cases. No doubt, there have been problems: there are plenty of would-be manipulators, some of whom who are quite successful at their trade. Some tribes entered the gaming era with weak governments; fights over the control of new wealth exacerbated weaknesses and split communities. At the same time, there are tribal governments that have used gaming dollars to build their own capacities and to solve their own problems. They have invested in "mainstream" enterprises. They have infused rural areas with new prosperity, and through their payments to state and local governments negotiated through state-tribal compacts, enriched the revenues of neighboring authorities. There are both Indians and non-Indians who have secure casino jobs. There are elders with safe housing and students with college scholarships.

Tribal managers, like all entrepreneurs, must seek out a comparative advantage if their investments are to succeed. It doesn't make sense to invest scarce resources into sectors of comparative disadvantage, where inexperienced tribes must somehow keep apace of well-established firms. The realms where tribal businesses can achieve equal footing with outside businesses are scarce, given the host of social, economic, and infrastructure problems that plague reservation communities. As a result, tribal governments will always encounter comparative advantages in sectors that are constrained elsewhere by state and local regulations. Many Americans have chosen to banish cheap cigarettes and slot machines from their neighborhoods, but they have chosen those steps precisely because many of their neighbors dearly enjoy those things. We can hardly be surprised when tribes choose business investments among the slim portfolio where their prospects for returns are stronger.

For those who find tribes' business choices unsavory, there are two options. First, bar those activities and overlook the abrogation of sovereignty and the deliberate devastation of Indian economies. Second, provide meaningful support that helps tribal firms develop and compete directly and vigorously in existing sectors. Of course, this second approach would require accepting that some non-Indian firms could lose profits and customers, as is the nature of meaningful competition. Certainly there are established economic interests that have no desire for more competitors. These would be very real costs. The casino experience gives good cause to hope, fortunately, that in the long run greater regional economic vitality can boost a wider business community. Chapter 4 captured the especially meager federal support for Indian economic development and the barriers to economic development that result. It is ironic that the federal government is more willing to invest in patching up poverty's various harms than in programs that can solve poverty most directly.

I have often heard some non-Indians casually dismiss the importance of sovereignty but accept casinos as "payback" for past injuries. The disturbing implication is that a time will arrive when the past is somehow repaid and tribal governments and enterprises will no longer be justified. There is no repayment for the near-total devastation of a society. There is no point at which we can just stop talking about it, when it is somehow unfair or ill-mannered to bring up the subject. Furthermore, sovereign nationhood is not a special favor bestowed and then retracted if poverty and social ills are resolved. Prosperity does not and cannot obviate self-determination.

We should always remember that, for all its flaws, the treaty system was embraced by the United States government and was not an act of charity. Americans preferred not to behave like a people who completely ignored the rule of law; if we had, we could carry a very dangerous precedent today. Also, to put it crassly in order to make the point more sharply, total annihilation is hard work. It would have required a lot of time, money, and lost soldiers. Treaties didn't just save Indian lives; they saved the lives of U.S. soldiers, too. We carry forward the legacy of treaties in the descendants of soldiers from all sides, some of whom are in our own lineages and others in the lineages of our fellow citizens.

Respect for sovereignty lies in our respect for laws and in our respect for all nations' rights—including the American nation—to set their path. Finally, sovereignty is not contingent on tribes acting in ways that outsiders approve. At the heart of sovereignty is the right to make choices that other people don't like. Self-determination isn't about the actions that would have happened anyhow.

VI. Seeing Success While Still Noticing Problems

We must keep in mind the challenges that American Indian tribes still face: high poverty and unemployment rates, low levels of education, high rates of violence, and poor health plaguing tribal populations. Yet is it equally important to remember the great strides that tribes have made in the past century, as they have challenged extreme forms of disadvantage and exclusion. I do not suggest that native peoples and native nations have solved all their challenges. Colonialism devastated culture, community, family, economy, natural resources, and sacred spaces. If the wounds are ever to be healed, the end is many generations away.

Here, I explored tribal leaders' success at winning outside political victories and building internal skills. In short, I measured political success but not necessarily policy desirability. The unanswered question is whether tribal leaders have sought the policy changes that best serve their communities. Do tribal leaders seek to accrue the most appropriate powers, and do the ends to which they apply these powers address the most urgent priorities of their communities? Do effective external relations fit into authentic internal governance? These questions still loom.

In the end, tribal governments can be both vibrant and deeply flawed all at once. Like all governments, they can do some things very well and some things very poorly. It is important to catalogue shortcomings; it is equally important to catalogue strengths. Furthermore, outsiders must be careful that they do not hold tribal governments to a sentimental ideal that their own governments could never meet. Politics is about imperfect humans coming together to decide thorny trade-offs. We need realistic expectations from that process. In this book, I have sought to put tribal leaders on the same plane with other politicians, assuming they have all the same human weaknesses and strengths. Given their extreme circumstances, their foibles are hardly surprising, but their successes are remarkable.

There is room and need for scholarship that explores the grave dysfunctions that may occur in some tribal governments. But there are dangers if the conversation centers exclusively on the great failings that tribal governments may experience. Forty years ago, Vine Deloria, Jr., (1969, 27) remarked with aplomb:

> Some years ago at a Congressional hearing someone asked Alex Chasing Hawk, a council member of the Cheyenne River Sioux for thirty years, "Just what do you Indians want?" Alex replied, "A leave-us-alone law!!"
>
> The primary goal and need of Indians today is not for someone to feel sorry for us and claim descent from Pocahontas to make us feel better. Nor do we need to be classified as semi-white and have programs and policies made to bleach us further. Nor do we need further studies to see if we are feasible. We need a new policy by Congress acknowledging our right to live in peace, free from arbitrary harassment. We need the public at large to drop the myths in which it has clothed us for so long. We need fewer and fewer "experts" on Indians.
>
> What we need is a cultural leave-us-alone agreement, in spirit and in fact.

Self-definition and self-determination writ broadly are at the center of hard-fought political contestations. We should always keep in mind that the administrators and supporters of the late-19th-century reservation system would scarcely comprehend the pathways that have emerged over time. Captain Richard C. Pratt, the founding superintendent of the Carlisle Indian Industrial School, remarked in 1892 (1973, 260–271), "A great general has once said that the only good Indian is a dead one.... In a sense, I agree with the sentiment, but only in this: that all the Indian there is in the race should be dead. Kill the Indian in him, and save the man." He continued:

> Inscrutable are the ways of Providence. Horrible as were the experiences of its introduction, and of slavery itself, there was concealed in them the greatest blessing that ever came to the Negro race,—seven millions of blacks from cannibalism in darkest Africa to citizenship in free and enlightened America; not full, not complete citizenship, but possible—probable—citizenship, and on the highway and near to it.
>
> There is a great lesson in this....
>
> It is a great mistake to think that the Indian is born an inevitable savage. He is born a blank, like all the rest of us. Left in the surroundings of savagery, he grows to possess a savage language, superstition, and life. We, left in the

surroundings of civilization, grow to possess a civilized language, life, and purpose. Transfer the infant white to the savage surroundings, he will grow to possess a savage language, superstition, and habit. Transfer the savage-born infant to the surroundings of civilization, and he will grow to possess a civilized language and habit....

The school at Carlisle is an attempt on the part of the government to do this. Carlisle has always planted treason to the tribe and loyalty to the nation at large.

The intent to obliterate native cultures failed. Sovereignty is no longer just a dusty legal concept. Tribal leaders today defend and exercise their sovereign powers. To a striking degree, the power structure was upended. To fixate on the shortcomings of tribal governments means that we miss out on this incredible story in American politics.

I come to this story as an outsider. I have no Indian heritage; as a child, the tales that made an impression upon me were of relations to John Jay and to Meriwether Lewis, of frontiersmen and Confederate veterans. I didn't think much about native people in the first couple decades of my life. My experiences shape the inferences that I am able and entitled to draw. If this book were intended as a soliloquy, I would be the wrong person to write it. My hope, however, is that it contributes to a conversation, in which more voices help build a more lively and boisterous discourse. We need more written about American Indians in present-tense verbs, writings that speak to contemporary and future experiences. To students who read this book and who are intrigued by parts, and undoubtedly aggravated by others: this book is for you. Now get to work, pick up a pen, and keep the conversation going.

Notes

CHAPTER 1

1. See Benally 2000; Beyal 2000; Shebala 1999, 2000; *The Navajo Times* 1999a, 1999b, Horn 2000, *The Navajo Times* 1999c, Giles 2000.

2. See Barfield 2001, Groark 2001, Sweeney 2001, Hansen 2002, McClure 2001, *The Spokesman-Review* 2000.

3. In this framework, business influence is predicated on mobility. As a result, we would not expect tribes, even those with substantial economic development, to have equivalent political power. Tribal control over such enterprises hinges, to a large degree, on their location on tribal lands, meaning these firms would lack the mobility that compels local officials to be so attentive to business needs.

4. Examples can be found in Bachrach and Baratz 1962, Burns 1994, Hirsch 1983, Jackson 1985, Schulman 1991, Stone 1989, Sugrue 1997, and Wood 1958.

5. As Stinchcombe (1990) noted, the problem is not just about generating innovations and insights. If innovations and insights are to have consequences, they need organizations that allow them to persist and diffuse.

6. See, for example, Lieberman's (1988) argument about the difficulties that marginalized groups face in decentralized political environments. See also Schulman (1994) and Lamb (2005).

7. See, for example, Skocpol 1979, Weir, Orloff, and Skocpol 1988, Skocpol 1992, and Campbell 2003. Gottschalk 2006, Keck 2004, and Dudziak 2000 described how frameworks created by one advocacy group were co-opted by subsequent competing advocacy groups.

8. Sayer 1997, Miller 1993, Berkhofer 1979, Deloria 2004, and Deloria 1969. Bobo and Tuan 2006 for further examples.

9. When Kingdon (1984) describes how big events can change power dynamics, change is predicated on a long process of "softening up" other political actors well in advance. Rare but powerful ruptures open windows only for actors who deployed stable, long-run advocacy. In Lawrence's (2000) analysis, the actors who can move quickest are the ones who capitalize on rare moments of upheaval. It is unusual for marginalized advocates to act fast enough to take charge of meaning-making after dramatic events; it is the exception that proves the rule. Pralle (2006) argues that dominant interests will have the upper hand when there is venue stability, but her model is predicated on the idea that venue-shopping is a viable strategy for their opponents. As I note, venue-shopping is often too costly for marginalized groups.

10. Sheingate (2000, 2003) makes the case for revisiting the roles of advocates, although he has focused on the influence of advocates that comes from their strategic adaptations over time. Miller (2008) also moves this discourse forward; she distinguishes between the prospects in local, state, and national politics for marginalized and mainstream anticrime and antiviolence groups.

11. Goss (2006) showed how gun-rights advocates used federal patronage to win big victories on the national stage and gun control groups didn't. And of course, the literature on the civil rights movement shows how cultivating capacity allowed big changes in federal policy (McAdam 1982, Morris 1984.)

12. Manna's (2006) study of "borrowing strength" focused on the behavior of political elites. Miller (2008) examined both marginalized and mainstream interest groups; she argued that marginalized groups routinely fail to capture federal attention. Pralle (2006) described mainstream environmental groups that faced defeats in low-profile, small-venue advocacy and succeeded in bigger venues. Warren (2001) analyzed marginalized groups at the state and local level; he focused on unique and impressive ways for building conventional political resources, such as becoming the electoral base for local officials and developing deep, broad coalitions through community building.

13. As in Manna (2006) and Lamb (2005). Also, Neidt and Weir (2010) show how "scalar repertoires" allow advocates to achieve federal and state restrictions on local legislation.

14. Kingdon (1984) continued the exploration of "puzzlement," documenting how problem definition and the quality of policy proposals matter for political outcomes.

15. See also McCarthy and Wolfson 1996, Jenkins 1983, and Jenkins and Eckert 1986.

16. Here, scholars do not use the term "indigenous" to refer to the politics of indigenous people; they refer broadly to leadership from within a marginalized community.

17. McCarthy and Wolfson (1996) noted that the National Highway Traffic Safety Administration distributed information and organized conferences for local Mothers Against Drunk Driving chapters. Payne's (1995, 103–130) study of the civil rights movement in Mississippi described how the Kennedy administration's policy shifts meant small amounts of federal funding were now available for voter registration drives; access to those funds shaped the organizational development of activism. Similarly, Andrews (2001) demonstrated variance in the effectiveness of the Mississippi civil rights movement that emerged as some local organizations better managed the federal Community Action Program. The same patterns appear in studies of the women's movement. Harrison (1988) and Duerst-Lahti (1989) both highlighted federal initiatives that cultivated women's organizations and supported their information-gathering and information-processing needs.

18. I am referring to Dillon's rule and the fact that state government can create and dissolve local governments as they wish. In short, municipalities are not sovereign. Tribal governments are sovereign, of course, but the reality on the ground has often radically diverged from the principles on paper.

CHAPTER 2

1. Those states are Alabama, Alaska, Arizona, California, Colorado, Connecticut, Florida, Idaho, Iowa, Kansas, Louisiana, Maine, Massachusetts, Michigan, Minnesota, Mississippi, Montana, Nebraska, Nevada, New Mexico, New York, North Carolina, North Dakota, Oklahoma, Oregon, Rhode Island, South Carolina, South Dakota, Texas, Utah, Washington, Wisconsin, and Wyoming.

2. Overviews of federal-tribal interactions can be found in the historical chapters in David Wilkins's *American Indians and the American Political System* (2002) and Sharon O'Brien's *American Indian Tribal Governments* (1989). For more detailed discussion, see Francis Paul Prucha's *The Great Father: The United States Government and the American Indians* (1984). Also, Stephen Cornell's *The Return of the Native* (1988) explores tribal political resources vis-à-vis the federal government over time, and George Pierre Castile's *To Show Heart: Native American Self-Determination and Federal Indian Policy, 1960–1975* (1998) focuses on a critical period of change in federal Indian policy.

3. See Cornell (1988) for a more detailed discussion of changes in Indian Country in this time frame.

4. David Lewis used the Office of Management and Budget's Program Assessment Rating Tool to evaluate the performance of federal programs. He noted that one of the lowest scoring programs was in the Bureau of Indian Affairs. In the overall assessment of nine BIA programs, the BIA scored 10 percentage points below the average federal program. In the most up-to-date scoring, four BIA programs are considered "Not Performing" by OMB. Only 20% of all federal programs have received such a poor rating.

5. Miller 1993, Berkhofer 1979, Deloria 2004, and Deloria 1969. Bobo and Tuan 2006 for further examples. This pattern fits with Lawrence's (2000) finding from other contexts.

6. See Handbook of North American Indians, Volumes 4 and 7–13 (1978–2001) for more background. Harmon (1998) provides more detail on the Pacific Northwest. Biolsi (1992) offers more detail on the Upper Plains. Wilkins (2002) describes further the differences among treaties.

7. Sources of the information that I used to select or pass over tribes included websites of tribal governments and organizations such as the Intertribal Council of Arizona, All Indian Pueblo Council, Eight Northern Indian Pueblos Council, Northwest Portland Area Indian Health Board, Northwest Indian Fisheries Commission, Columbia River Intertribal Fish Commission, Affiliated Tribes of Northwest Indians, Council of Energy Resource Tribes, and National Indian Gaming Association. Sources about various tribes in a region included the *Handbook of North American Indians* (1978–2001), Tiller (1996), Mason (2000), Ruby and Brown (1992), Wray (2002), Lopach, Brown, and Clow (1998). I referenced books, articles, and pamphlets about specific tribes. I reviewed documents produced by tribes and I spoke with tribal officials.

8. The more institutionalized tribes vary greatly in population; the smallest more institutionalized tribe has a smaller population than the largest less institutionalized tribe.

9. According to the Commission's website, the member tribes are Lummi, Nooksack, Swinomish, Upper Skagit, Sauk-Suiattle, Stillaguamish, Tulalip, Muckleshoot, Puyallup,

Nisqually, Squaxin Island, Skokomish, Suquamish, Port Gamble S'Klallam, Jamestown S'Klallam, Lower Elwha Klallam, Makah, Quileute, Quinault, and Hoh.

10. Member agencies in 2001 included the Acoma Tribal Police, Sandia Pueblo Police Department, and New Mexico State Police in New Mexico; the Ak-Chin Police Department, Salt River Tribal Police Department, and Yavapai-Prescott Tribal Police in Arizona; the Navajo Division of Public Safety in Arizona, New Mexico, and Utah; the Cabazon Indian Tribal Police Department in California; the Las Vegas Paiute Tribal Police in Nevada; the Keweenaw Bay Tribal Police in Wisconsin; the Mille Lacs Tribal Police Department in Minnesota; the Saginaw Chippewa Tribal Police in Michigan; the Mashantucket Pequot Tribal Police and the Mohegan Tribal Police Department in Connecticut; the Oneida Indian Nation Police in New York; the Chitimacha Tribal Police Department in Louisiana; the Miccosukee Police Department in Florida; the Poarch Creek Tribal Police Department in Alabama; the Osage Indian Nation Police in Oklahoma; the Sac and Fox Nation Police Department in Kansas and Nebraska; and the Potawatomi Tribal Police Department. The U.S Bureau of Indian Affairs, Department of Justice, Immigration and Naturalization Service, and National Park Service were also members.

CHAPTER 3

1. Much previous work has stressed the dangers of outside aid, with a dim view on strategies for managing those dangers. Fossett (1984) described how mayors eye federal grants with a certain suspicion because of the risks associated with accepting such help.

2. In systems where greater numbers of players must agree on action, the costs of policy change rise and policy monitoring rise. This argument is consistent with Tsebelis's (2002) claim, drawing on Franzese's (2002) work, that political systems with many veto points are more prone to generate pockets of discretion.

3. With records that are suited solely for qualitative analysis, I extracted certain examples that are particularly detailed or illustrative. I had to select some examples and exclude others. The criterion for selection was the amount of detail that each example provided. My intent was to best capture processes of decision-making and implementation. As it turned out, each data source provided multiple examples, but the inclusion of all the examples would have added massively to length of the text—and compromised the anonymity of some tribes by spelling out so many of their circumstances—without providing much additional insight into tribes' behaviors. In short, I did not cherry-pick examples that fit my hypotheses. Indeed, the analysis includes some examples that run counter to my hypotheses.

4. For Tribes F and G, I draw on records that are lengthy and not indexed. I did not analyze their behavior for all years. For each of the tribes, I tallied their strategies for one year in the early 1990s and another year at the far end of records that were available to me: a year in the mid-1990s for Tribe G and in the late 1990s for Tribe F. For each of the tribes, I then compared the tallies from the earlier year and the later year, to see if behavior had changed and if analysis of an additional, mid-point year was warranted. In each case, behavior was stable over time, so I limited the coding to those two years.

5. For Tribes H and J, I drew a sample of available records while I was in records repositories, due to limitations from time for access and the organization of materials. The tribes' newspapers and minutes exist across the 1990s; the contours of my sample were not set by those who housed the materials. My first priority was to capture one moderately lengthy time period, so that I could see how strategies unfolded month to month. My second priority was to draw samples from later years, which I was able to achieve for Tribe J. For Tribe

J, I accessed council minutes from 12 months in the early 1990s, 4 months from one year in the mid-1990's, 4 months from another year in the mid-1990s, and 4 months from one year in the late 1990s.

6. Zah Papers. "Exhibit A: Statement of Recommended Actions and Initiatives." 1992(?) Box 32, Folder 5.

7. Zah papers. Cover Letter from Peterson Zah to Tribal Leaders, dated 11/18/93, with attachment: *Base Closures, Acquisitions, and Tribal Issues*. Agenda for conference on Base Closures, Acquisitions, and Tribal Issues, dated 10/21/93, with attachment: *Procedures for Tribes to Obtain Excess Real Properties under the Base Closure and Realignment Act*. Box 38, Folders 1 & 2.

8. International Association of Chiefs of Police, http://www.theiacp.org/. Accessed 1/28/10.

9. American Indian Records Repository. *Organizational Reform, Revised Draft Task Force Report for Comments by Members*, 8/31/94. See table entitled "Status of Tribal/BIA Planning for Area Restructuring." Accession number 075 05 1981, Box number 522 05 1560, Series number 1213-P3. File name: Cherokee.

10. See pages 15, 16, 22, and 24 in particular.

11. Zah Papers. *Exhibit A: Statement of Recommended Actions and Initiatives*, 1992(?). Box 32, Folder 5.

12. Zah Papers. *Legislative Priorities of President Peterson Zah and the Navajo Nation, Prepared for the Honorable John McCain and the Honorable Bill Richardson, Southwest Legal Forum, Phoenix, Arizona*, 1/21/94. *Southwest Tribal Leaders Legislative Forum, Hosted by Senator John McCain, Vice Chairman, United States Senate Committee on Indian Affairs and Congressman Bill Richardson, Chairman, Subcommittee on Native American Affairs of the House Committee on Natural Resources*. Scottsdale Community Center, January 21, 1994. Box 39, Folder 12.

13. Zah Papers. Memorandum from Jack C. Jackson, Jr., Deputy Director, Navajo Nation Washington Office, *Re: Navajo Nation Legislative Agenda for the 104th Congress*, 11/21/94. Box 38, File 5.

14. Zah Papers. *Conference Call with Coordinating Committee*, 12/7/92. Box 35, Folder 2.

15. Participants included NCAI Executive Director Mike Anderson and Treasurer W. Ron Allen.

16. The letter also stated that the National Indian Economic Summit communicated these same goals in March 1993.

17. Zah Papers. Letter from gaiashkibospresident of NCAI, to President William J. Clinton, 12/14/94. Files on Federal Listening Conference.

18. American Indian Records Repository. *The Tribal Budget System, 1992 Progress Report and Development Plan to the Secretary of the Interior and the Appropriations Committees, Joint Tribal/BIA/DOI Advisory Task force on Bureau of Indian Affairs Reorganization*, February 1993. Memo from NCAI Welfare Reform Program Director Sarah Hicks to NCAI/BIA Data Management, Needs Assessment, and Auditing Workgroup, 6/19/00. Letter to Kevin Gover, BIA from Eddie Tullis, Jonathan Windy Boy, and Pamela Norris on behalf of NCAI, 3/28/00. Accession number 075 05 0576, Box number K00 04 00332, Series number 1213-P3. File: BIA Reorganization Files. See also *Data Management, Needs Assessment & Auditing Workgroup, Summary of Major Workgroup Decisions*, April 13–14, 2000 Meeting. No author stated, but notes, "NCAI staff Sarah Hicks and Heather Woods are contacts. *BIA/Tribal Workgroup on Tribal Needs Assessments, TPA Contract and Support Costs*. Labeled draft. 7/21–23/98, Arlington Hilton and Towers. Accession number 975-05-0576, Box Number K00-04-0032. File: TPA project meeting.

19. The letter was written on behalf of NCAI and on NCAI letterhead from three tribal leaders—Eddie Tullis, chairman of the Poarch Band of Creek Indians; Jonathan Windy Boy, councilmember of the Rocky Boy's Reservation; and Pamela Norris, self-government coordinator of Shoalwater Bay Indian Tribe—to the assistant secretary of Indian Affairs, Kevin Gover.

20. They wrote, "[S]ome of our workgroup members have suggested the participation of Terry Virden from the Office of Trust Responsibilities; Larry Blair from the Office of Tribal Services/Division of Social Services; and Jerry Fiely from the Office of Audit and Evaluation."

21. Member tribes today include the Hoh, Jamestown S'Klallam, Lower Elwha, Lummi, Makah, Muckleshoot, Nisqually, Nooksack, Port Gamble S'Klallam, Puyallup, Quileute, Quinault, Sauk-Suiattle, Skokomish, Squaxin Island, Stillaguamish, Suquamish, Swinomish, Tulalip, and Upper Skagit (Northwest Indian Fisheries Commission 2008).

22. *Northwest Indian Fisheries Commission News*, "Puget Sound Coho Escape ESA Listing," Summer 1995, 12.

23. *Northwest Indian Fisheries Commission News*, "Put Up or Shut Up," "Tribes Facing Massive Federal Funding Cuts," "For the Sake of the Salmon;" Summer 1995, 2–5.

24. *Northwest Indian Fisheries Commission News*. "TFW: Negotiations Could Result in Better Ecosystem Protection." Fall 1997, 8.

25. *Northwest Indian Fisheries Commission News*. "ESA: Are Tribal Fisheries At Risk From Weak Stocks and a Strong Law?" Winter 1997, 7 & 10.

26. *Northwest Indian Fisheries Commission News*. "Tribes Applaud ESA Secretarial Order," Spring 1997, 8.

27. *Northwest Indian Fisheries Commission News*. "Elwha River Restoration Funding Stalled," Fall 1998, 8.

28. *Northwest Indian Fisheries Commission News*. "Federal Government Buys Elwha Dams," Winter 1999/2000, 4.

29. Environmental Protection Agency, Radon Division, Office of Radiation Programs, 1991, 15.

30. American Indian Records Repository. FAX to Gary Rankel, BIA-Central, 7/10/98. FAX from Yakama Indian Nation Wildlife Resource Management to Gary Rankel, BIA, 7/16/98. *Testimony of the Yakama Indian Nation on HR3987, The "Deer and Elk Protection Act," Presented to the Resources Committee of the United States House of Representatives, 7/27/98. Testimony of Todd Wilbur, Chairman, Intertribal Wildlife Committee of the Northwest Indian Fisheries Commission on H.R. 3987, Deer and Elk Protection Act before the House Resources Committee, 7/28/98. Statement of Michael J. Anderson, Deputy Assistant Secretary for Indian Affairs, Department of the Interior, at the Hearing before the House Committee of Resources on H.R. 3987, A Bill to Protect and Conserve Deer and Elk and to Provide for Consistent and Equitable Hunting Laws in the State of Washington*, 7/28/98. Accession number 075 05 2081, Box number Koo 05 2503, Series number 1230-P3. File: Deer and Elk Hunting in Washington.

31. American Indian Records Repository. Collected comments on H.R. 128 and H.R. 277 from Area Offices, from 3/3/97 to 4/11/97. All are addressed to Director of Office of Congressional and Legislative Affairs, Bureau of Indian Affairs. Accession number 075 05 3081, Box number Koo 05 2503, Series number 1230-P3. File: State Authority over Water Rights.

32. American Indian Records Repository. *Department of Interior Legislative Plans for the 105th Congress*, undated. Memo from Director, Office of Congressional and Legislative Affairs, *Subject: Comments on Misc#6: DOI Legislative Plans for the 105th Congress*, 2/14/97. Memo from Portland Area Director, *Subject: Request for views [sic] on Proposed Draft Bill*, 1/24/97. Email from Larry Scrivner at officeoftrust [sic], *Subject: Comments MISC#6, DOI Legislative Plans*

105th, 1/29/97. Memo from Area Director, Aberdeen Area, *Subject: MISC#6, DOI Legislative Plans for 105 Congress [sic]*, 2/24/97. Accession number 075 05 3081, Box number K00 05 2503, Series number 1230-P3. Files: Deer and Elk Hunting in Washington, State Authority over Water Rights.

33. There were BIA bills to clarify tribes' water status, to give certain tribes more flexibility in their control of land and water, to allocate more funding for road projects on the Navajo Nation, and to create a more stable funding stream for reservation road maintenance. One Bureau of Land Management proposal exempted information about the location of Indian sacred sites from Freedom of Information Act requirements.

34. American Indian Records Repository. Letter from Navajo Nation President Albert Hale to Ada Deer, assistant secretary, Bureau of Indian Affairs, 6/10/96. Letter from Hilda Manuel, deputy commissioner of Indian Affairs, to Albert Hale, president, Navajo Nation, 7/1/96. Accession number 075 05 3081, Box number K00 05 2503, Series number 1230-P3. File: State Authority.

35. American Indian Records Repository. Letter from Cora Jones, area director, Bureau of Indian Affairs Aberdeen Area Office, to Senator Tom Daschle, 12/9/97. Letter from Senator Tom Daschle to Cora Jones, area director, Bureau of Indian Affairs Aberdeen Area Office, 12/19/97. Letter from Cora Jones, area director, to Senator Tom Daschle, 12/30/97. Accession number 075 05 3081, Box number K00 05 2503, Series number 1230-P3. File name: S. 1905, Equitable Compensation to the Cheyenne River Sioux Tribe.

36. Environmental Protection Agency, 1994.

37. Zah Papers. Written to the attorney general by Gerald Torres, of the Office of the Assistant Attorney General in the Environment and Natural Resources Division, which was passed by Torres' staffer Karen Skelton to Chairwoman Wilma Mankiller of the Cherokee Nation, who then passed the document to Peterson Zah of the Navajo Nation. *Memorandum to the Attorney General, From: Gerald Torres, Re: Project to Redefine the American Indian/Federal Relationship for the 21st Century*, 1/8/94. Files on Federal Listening Conference.

CHAPTER 4

1. Walsh (1995, 306–308), in his detailed review of the literature on organizational learning, observed that there was no single, standard approach for measuring either knowledge structures or their effects. See Rainey 1997, 131–134 for a similar discussion and also Fiol and Lyles (1985, 803, 811). More recently, Dekker and Hansen (2004, 212) highlighted "a striking lack of empirical studies in the field of organizational learning," and made the case for more empirical work and for setting aside fears about "the risk of ignoring theoretical nuances."

2. Scholars of organizational studies have proposed models of inventing, producing, and generating (Argyris and Schön 1978, 141); observing, reacting, judging, and intervening (Schein 1987, 64); scanning, interpreting, and acting (Daft and Wieck 1984); and filtering, interpreting, processing, and adapting (Dekker and Hansen 2004). Ganz (2000), as an analyst of social movements, presented a two-stage model of learning as well: in his model, effective problem-solving relied on the ability to understand one's environment ("salient knowledge") and to design innovations based on those understandings ("heuristic processes"). Scholars who focus on public organizations have offered an important insight: they argued that learning in the public sector should lead both to new approaches internally and to new approaches to their outside environment (see, for example, Vogelsang-Coombs 1997 Vogelsang-Coombs and Miller 1999, Dekker and Hansen 2004).

3. See Haveman (1992) and Audia, Locke, and Smith (2000) for careful discussions of these prospects.

4. The closest he came to this behavior was describing what he would like to do if new federal funds became available.

5. The police chief had remarked in an earlier report that the tribe was gathering more information about the nature of drinking problems on the reservation. Here, we see the application of that information.

6. I selected cases where I was able track down reports for all three agencies for that date. For the most part, these records are maintained by individual departments; each department had some gaps in its record-keeping. I also considered the level of detail in the report and the relative consistency of formats across agencies.

7. All of Walke's figures are in 1997 dollars.

8. Other sources were preponderantly tribal revenues, generated mainly through natural resources extraction, although they also included small amounts from nonprofits, states, and localities.

9. In this arrangement, the DOE would take over responsibility for abandoned mine sites on the reservation and would exchange other, more useable federal lands in replacement.

10. I report the number of behaviors per page. Over the time period studied, departments experimented a great deal with reporting formats. For example, at one moment, the length of the natural resources report quintupled from one year to the next, and then it returned to its prior length in the following year. The agency's scope, mission, and budget were relatively stable across this time window; it seems reasonable to assume that the change in length reflected different writing styles. The longer reports delved into far more detail; the shorter reports gave highlights. To allow for consistent comparisons, I accounted for the length of a division's report.

CHAPTER 5

1. Numerous authors have documented particular interactions between tribes and nearby governments. Two themes emerge from the accumulation of these case studies. First, the literature has indicated that relations between tribal governments and neighboring localities are framed by long-standing racial tensions and stark disparities in economic resources. As a result of these social divisions, tribal-local relations are vulnerable to hostility and poor coordination (see Clow 1991, Goldberg 1999, Paredes 1992, Rosenblatt 1985). At the same time, many authors also have pointed to examples where tribes have successfully negotiated policy coordination with neighbors (Lopach, Brown, and Clow 1998; Peregoy 1999; O'Brien 1989). Some have found that tribal-local relations are marked by more beneficial policies when Native Americans possess more institutional advantages (Berman and Salant 1998, Mason 2000, Taylor 1972). In sum, the existing literature indicates that states and local governments often approach tribal interactions with hostility, but it also indicates that, at least sometimes, tribes can shape these interactions to serve their interests.

2. For most of the tribes in the sample, their population was overwhelmingly concentrated in one county. There are few cases that are exceptions. In the analysis that follows, I ran multiple robustness checks that controlled for the population patterns in multicounty tribes. The key results persisted.

3. Meetings of county commissions, councils, and courts are open to the public.

4. There was disagreement with statements that American Indians are "honest" (24%), "considerate of others" (29%), and "equal in intelligence to the average person" (17%); and agreement with statements that Indians are "envious of others" (27%), "discourteous" (19%), and "have a tendency to be insubordinate" (24%). Peterson polled a random sample of 101 freshmen at a state university. He received 80 responses.

5. On another occasion, South Dakota's governor reputedly remarked that he wouldn't advise tourists to visit Indian reservations because "he couldn't send someone to a place where they'd be panhandled" (Schwab 1997) or where they would have "fear of someone hitting 'em head on by a drinking driver [sic]" (Melmer 1997). The Denver Post contacted the governor's press secretary for comment; he neither confirmed nor denied the report.

In this same time period, there were cases from the criminal justice system that provoked well-publicized charges of differential treatment of Indians. In one instance, an 18-year-old Indian woman who struck and killed a white motorist while driving intoxicated was convicted of manslaughter and sentenced to 14 years in prison. Later, the prosecutor in the case reported that "he examined court records to compare the sentences of as many similar cases as he could find. The longest sentence for a comparable offense was 3 years." (South Dakota Advisory Committee to the United States Commission on Human Rights 2000, 10) Criticisms intensified the following year when, in the same county, a 17-year-old white driver who was driving intoxicated struck and killed an Indian, but the prosecutor dropped charges of vehicular homicide and the driver pled guilty to driving while intoxicated.

6. I use census data from the 1990 and 2000 decennials to construct such a measure. To calculate population between decennials, I assumed a linear change in population. For the sake of comparability across the two censuses—one of which allows respondents to identify more than one race—from 2000 I included as non-Indian everyone who identified more than one race.

7. LexisNexis Academic maintains a database of these cases. I considered whether some cases were far less demanding than others, and as a robustness check I controlled for cases where a given tribe's counsel was clearly not the primary legal team. The results didn't change.

Most of the lawsuits in the sample involve conflicts with state governments. I excluded disputes with the federal government and with corporations for two reasons. First, since the resolution of those cases was more likely to involve very large financial settlements, the dynamics might be quite different. Second, tribes might have a fixed set of resources with respect to state and local interactions of any type. For example, state and local issues might be more common in some policy domains and less common in others.

8. As a robustness check for this and for subsequent analysis, I did separate out analysis of the Northwest and Southwest as well, but the key results remained unchanged.

9. Also, issues should be fairly portable across local legislative bodies, which should allow for savvy venue-shopping.

10. It is reasonable to ask whether this measure was really about differences between more remote and less remote reservations. Some of these incorporated towns, however, were very tiny. Also, I introduced controls for degree of remoteness in case selection, as described in chapter 2.

11. Thus, it appeared that the circumstances and regulations around land had important impacts on regional politics, for both the Upper Plains and the Pacific Northwest. Where land was a more prominent issue—either due to 19th-century federal checkerboarding policies or to 20th-century state regulatory mandates—interactions rose.

12. One could hypothesize that "harder" interactions necessarily entailed more stages of decision-making, and thus by definition harder interactions in the recent past would increase

harder interactions in the near future. I believe that other phenomena drove these results, however. There was only slight variation in the number of stages in decision-making across types of interaction. Also, note that different stages of decision-making could fall into different types of interactions. Indeed, it was not uncommon for areas that led eventually to extensive commitments to start with some small, low-stakes engagement.

13. As a robustness check, I examined whether variables of interest worked differently between the Northwest and Southwest for this and subsequent models; the key results held when the regions are examined separately.

Here and in tables that follow, it became difficult to include all tribe-specific variables when the sample was cut from 12 tribes into subsamples of 8 tribes and 4 tribes, respectively. Thus, some variables from the overall model must fall out of the models with regional breakdowns.

14. Because there were only four cases in this part of the analysis, it was difficult to control for many features of a case all at once. As a robustness check, I respecified the variables to accommodate the measure of racial conflict and cruder measures of tribal traits in a single model; the effects from racial conflict dominated.

15. In contrast, for Northwest tribes, the results don't explain away a regional difference. Interactions over zoning in growth management states had an insignificant, negative effect.

16. Also, as noted above, interactions over zoning in growth management states had a negative, but insignificant, effect.

17. Previous models showed that tribes weren't just substituting away from county interactions when additional venues were present; rather, the level of county interactions appeared to be constant. The results from this model show that they just interacted with counties with greater skill.

Some effects from the overall model faded away when attention turned specifically to the Southwest and Pacific Northwest. Agenda-setting and previous experience were positive but not statistically significant. Urbanization no longer had a significant effect.

18. In the calculation, I included most variables at their means or at the most common value for noncontinuous variables. The predicted outcomes presented here were for issues generating both support and opposition, with the regional effect for the Southwest, and with public safety as the policy area.

19. When exhaustion was higher, the number of interactions averaged 0.85 of the baseline low-exhaustion volume.

20. Success rates fell in the Upper Plains when exhaustion was higher, with an average decline of 22 percentage points. Success rates in the Southwest and Northwest had an average decline of 17 percentage points.

21. Policy areas were public safety, natural resources, business regulation and development, and elections. Policy types were small-scale subsidy or support, endorsements, new tribal representation, large-scale delivery of goods and services, regional initiatives and authorities, and negative externalities. For more details, see section III. Repeat issues were specific items on which there had been earlier interactions.

22. There was other evidence that Northwest and Southwest tribes presented plans when facing uphill battles. Northwest and Southwest tribes were less likely to present detailed plans for interactions in urbanized areas, and I expected that the stakes would be lower and the issues less charged in cities. The only exception to this trend was that tribes were more likely to present plans for easy interactions, and the effects were significant. But overall, it appeared

that Northwest and Southwest tribes presented fewer plans when, presumably, the county was already receptive and didn't need much persuading.

Another pattern stood out in the Southwest and Pacific Northwest. In interactions over zoning in growth management states, detailed or technical plans were more likely. From reading the minutes, it was striking that nearly everyone who came to the table in these debates over the particulars of growth management had their own detailed plan for action.

23. In the Upper Plains, plans also appeared significantly more likely on all natural resource interactions.

24. Given that the analysis focused on cases in the appeals process, this timing was not entirely under the tribe's control, of course.

25. The association extended membership to all counties with any Indian lands, no matter how small. I limited the analysis to the 11 counties that were at least 5% American Indian in Census 2000. Montana as a whole was 9% American Indian.

CHAPTER 6

1. Montana is a large state, with portions in the Rocky Mountains and portions in the Plains. All but one of the state's reservations are located in the Plains portion of the state.

2. The specific search terms that I used were as follows: native, Indian, tribe, tribal, reservation, pueblo, and nation. LexisNexis searches for whether any of these terms appear in the bill synopsis, the bill title, or the bill keywords. LexisNexis uses bill synopses and keywords produced by StateNet. Of course, these terms occasionally identified legislation that had nothing to do with American Indians and tribal governments; I excluded those items from my analysis. I made some adjustments to the sample to account for some unique legislative procedures in New Mexico. In this time frame, when New Mexico legislators wanted to request an earmark in the biennial budget, they introduced a bill describing the requested earmark. My analysis for other states does not include line item appropriations, so I excluded these New Mexico bills for the sake of comparability. I am very grateful to staff in the New Mexico Legislative Council Service for explaining the details of these procedures to me.

3. These categories drew on classifications of intergovernmental interactions from Bednar (2007) and Burns, Evans, Gamm, and McConnaughy (2009).

4. Absent checkerboarding, there were relatively few non-Indians living within reservations.

5. Presumably, there are legislators in all eight states with a degree of American Indian ancestry but who do not regularly describe themselves as American Indian and for whom contemporary tribal allegiances are not meaningful. Since I wanted the tallies to be comparable across states, I sought out comparable sources of information for all the states. This classification was simplest in Arizona (Arizona Blue Book, 1993–2000), New Mexico, Oregon, and Washington, which produced legislator biographies in the 1990s. Also, the New Mexico Legislative Council Service maintained an official directory of American Indian legislators. For Montana, Nebraska, South Dakota, and North Dakota, biographies were not as thorough and state libraries did not keep formal records.

6. Nebraska has a unicameral legislature. In the data analysis, I treated bills passing Nebraska's legislature as passing the first house and passing the second house, to keep the Nebraska sample comparable to the other states.

7. There were 70 state-years observed. Legislatures in Oregon, Montana, and North Dakota meet only in odd-numbered years.

8. While data on donations to state-level candidates are easily available for all these states in the present day, they are not easily obtained for the 1990s for all of these states.

9. I operationalized the measure of support by policy area in the following manner. BIA's policy area breakdowns grouped into six categories: social services (which included housing), education, public safety, community development (which included transportation, economic development, and job training), natural resources, and land management. Since health programs were funded through the Indian Health Services, health legislation was excluded from this analysis.

10. *The Book of the States* tracks these numbers. For Arizona, the data were missing from 1996 through 1999. To approximate the actual values, I substituted the 1994 variables for 1996, the 1995 variables for 1997 and 1999, and the 2000 variables for 1998.

11. Since my findings so far offered have indicated outcomes in the Upper Plains might be different than in other states, in results not shown, I first ran the model for North Dakota, South Dakota, and Nebraska—three Upper Plains states that consider a very small volume of Indian legislation—and then I ran the model for the other states. I found that the forces shaping the fate of bills tended to be relatively consistent across the states.

References

I. ANONYMOUS, ARCHIVAL AND UNPUBLISHED MATERIALS CONSULTED

Bureau of Indian Affairs [Area Office deleted]. 1984–1989. *Law and Order Reports* from Tribes A and C. National Archives and Records Administration.

Bureau of Indian Affairs [Area Office deleted]. 1980–1988. *Indian Self-Determination Contract and Grant Files* from Tribes A and C. National Archives and Records Administration.

Bureau of Indian Affairs [Area Office deleted]. 1980–1989. *Tribal Resolutions* from Tribes A and C. National Archives and Records Administration.

Department of the Interior, Office of the Special Trustee for American Indians. 1993–2000. *American Indian Records Repository*. Lenexa, KS: National Archives and Records Administration.

Minutes and Resolutions from County Boards of Supervisors, County Commissions, and County Courts of the 12 counties in the sample. 1990–2000.

Montana Association of Reservation Counties. 1993–1998. *Minutes*.

Navajo Nation Division of Economic Development. 1993–2000. *Quarterly Reports to the Navajo Nation Council*. Window Rock, AZ: Navajo Nation Division of Economic Development.

Navajo Nation Division of Natural Resources. 1992–2000. *Quarterly Reports to the Navajo Nation Council*. Window Rock, AZ: Navajo Nation Division of Natural Resources.

Navajo Nation Division of Public Safety. 1993–2000. *Quarterly Reports to the Navajo Nation Council*. Window Rock, AZ: Navajo Nation Division of Public Safety.

Navajo Nation, Office of the President. 1997. *The Navajo Nation- Fiscal Year 1998 Budget*. Window Rock, AZ: Navajo Nation Library.

Newsletters for Tribes E, F, G, and H. 1980–2005.

Tribal Council Minutes and Resolutions from Tribes F and J. 1985–2000.

Zah, Peterson Manuscript Collection. 1969–1994. Phoenix, AZ: Labriola American Indian Data Center, Arizona State University.

II. PUBLISHED MATERIALS CONSULTED

Alfred, Taiaiake. 1999. *Peace, Power, Righteousness: An Indigenous Manifesto*. New York: Oxford University Press.

Andrews, Kenneth T. 2001. "Social Movements and Policy Implementation: The Mississippi Civil Rights Movement and the War on Poverty, 1965 to 1971." *American Sociological Review* 66(1):71–95.

Argus Leader (Sioux Falls, South Dakota). 1990. "Slam of Indians Challenged." September 6, 1.

Argyris, Chris, and Donald A. Schön. 1978. *Organizational Learning: A Theory of Action Perspective*. Reading, MA: Addison-Wesley.

Arizona Blue Book. 1993–2000. Phoenix: Arizona Secretary of State.

Arizona Commission on Indian Affairs. 2008. Accessed December 18. http://www.indianaffairs.state.az.us.

Ashley, Jeffrey S., and Secody J. Hubbard. 2004. *Negotiated Sovereignty: Working to Improve Tribal-State Relations*. Westport, CT: Praeger.

Audia, Pino G., Edwin A. Locke, and Ken G. Smith. 2000. "The Paradox of Success: An Archival and Laboratory Study of Strategic Persistence Following Radical Environmental Change." *The Academy of Management Journal* 43(5):837–853.

Bachrach, Peter, and Morton S. Baratz. 1962. "Two Faces of Power." *American Political Science Review* 56(4):947–952.

Barfield, Chet. 2001."Casinos Force Tribes, Counties to Sit Down at the Same Table." *San Diego Union-Tribune*. June 24, B1.

Baumgartner, Frank R., and Bryan D. Jones. 1993. *Agendas and Instability in American Politics*. Chicago: The University of Chicago Press.

Bee, Robert L. 1981. *Crosscurrents along the Colorado: The Impact of Government Policy on the Quechan Indians*. Tuscon: University of Arizona Press.

Benally, Stacey. 2000. "Corrections Facility Seeks to Help Native Youth." *Navajo Times* (Window Rock, Arizona). January 20, A1.

Beyal, Duane A. 2000. "New School for Indian Wells." *Navajo Times* (Window Rock, Arizona). December 14, A1.

Beck, David. 2005. *The Struggle for Self-Determination: History of the Menominee Indians since 1854*. Lincoln: University of Nebraska Press.

Bednar, Jenna. 2007. "Credit Assignment and Federal Encroachment." *Supreme Court Economic Review*. Vol. 15:285–308.

Berkhofer, Robert F., Jr. 1979. *The White Man's Indian*. New York: Vintage Books.

Berman, David R., and Tanis J. Salant. 1998. "Minority Representation, Resistance, and Public Policy: The Navajos and the Counties." *Publius* 28(4):83–104.

Biolsi, Thomas. 1992. *Organizing the Lakota: The Political Economy of the New Deal on the Pine Ridge and Rosebud Reservations*. Tuscon: University of Arizona Press.

Biolsi, Thomas. 2001. *"Deadliest Enemies": Law and the Making of Race Relations On and Off Rosebud Reservation*. Berkeley: University of California Press.

Bobo, Lawrence D., and Mia Tuan. 2006. *Prejudice in Politics: Group Position, Public Opinion, and the Wisconsin Treaty Rights Dispute*. Cambridge, MA: Harvard University Press.

Boehmke, Frederick J., and Richard Witmer. 2002. *Resource Accumulation and Political Lobbying: The Empowerment of Native Americans through Gaming Revenue.* Working Paper. University of Iowa.

Book of the States. 1992–2002. Lexington, KY: Council of State Governments.

Bureau of Indian Affairs, U.S. Department of the Interior. 1992–1999. "Justification of the Budget Estimates." In *Department of the Interior and Related Agencies Appropriations for: Hearing before a Subcommittee of the Committee on Appropriations, House of Representatives.* Washington, D.C.: U.S. Government Printing Office.

Bureau of Indian Affairs, U.S. Department of the Interior. 1999. "Justification of the Budget Estimates." In *Department of the Interior and Related Agencies Appropriations for 2000: Hearing before a Subcommittee of the Committee on Appropriations, House of Representatives, One Hundred Sixth Congress, First Session.* Part 2, pp. 861–1344. Washington, D.C.: U.S. GPO.

Bureau of Indian Affairs, U.S. Department of the Interior. 2000. "Budget Justifications and Annual Performance Plan, Fiscal Year 2001." In *Department of the Interior and Related Agencies Appropriations for 2001: Hearings before a Subcommittee of the Committee on Appropriations, House of Representatives, One Hundred Sixth Congress, Second Session.* Part 2, pp. 723–1322. Washington, D.C.: U.S. Government Printing Office.

Bureau of Indian Affairs, U.S. Department of the Interior. 2010. Accessed November 5. http://www.bia.gov/FAQs/index.htm

Burns, Nancy. 1994. *The Formation of American Local Governments: Private Values in Public Institutions.* New York: Oxford University Press.

Burns, Nancy, Laura Evans, Gerald Gamm, and Corrine McConnaughy. 2010. "Urban Politics in the State Arena." *Studies in American Political Development 23 (April 2009)*:1–22.

Campbell, Andrea Louise. 2003. *How Policies Make Citizens: Senior Political Activism and the American Welfare State.* Princeton, NJ: Princeton University Press.

Carpenter, Daniel C. 2001. *The Forging of Bureaucratic Autonomy: Reputations, Networks, and Policy Innovation in Executive Agencies, 1862–1928.* Princeton, NJ: Princeton University Press.

Castile, George Pierre. 1998. *To Show Heart: Native American Self-Determination and Federal Indian Policy, 1960–1975.* Tuscon: University of Arizona Press.

Center for Responsive Politics. 1990–2000. Accessed December 15, 2005. *Open Secrets.* http://www.opensecrets.org.

Clemens, Elisabeth S. 1997. *The People's Lobby: Organizational Innovation and the Rise of Interest Group Politics in the United States, 1890–1925.* Chicago: The University of Chicago Press.

Clow, Richmond L. 1991. "Taxation and the Preservation of Tribal Political and Geographical Autonomy." *American Indian Research and Culture Journal* 15(2):37–62.

Cohen, Felix S. 1942. *Handbook of Federal Indian Law.* 1st edition. Washington, D.C.: U.S. Government Printing Office.

Cohen, Felix S. 1988. *Handbook of Federal Indian Law.* Reprint edition. Buffalo, NY: William S. Hein & Co.

Cornell, Stephen. 1988. *The Return of the Native: American Indian Political Resurgence.* New York: Oxford University Press.

Cornell, Stephen, and Joseph Kalt. 1992. *What Can Tribes Do? Strategies and Institutions in American Indian Economic Development.* Los Angeles: American Indian Studies Center, UCLA.

Cornell, Stephen, and Joseph Kalt. 1998. "Sovereignty and Nation-Building: The Development Challenge in Indian Country Today." *American Indian Culture and Research Journal* 22(3):187–214.

Corntassel, Jeff J., and Richard C. Witmer. 2008. *Forced Federalism*. Norman: University of Oklahoma Press.

Cortes, Ernesto, Jr. 1993. "Reweaving the Fabric: The Iron Rule and the IAF Strategy for Power and Politics." In *Interwoven Destinies*, ed. Henry G. Cisneros, pp. 295–319. New York: Norton.

Cowger, Thomas W. 1999. *The National Congress of American Indians: The Founding Years*. Lincoln: University of Nebraska Press.

Daft, Richard L., and Karl E. Weick, 1984. "Toward a Model of Organizations as Interpretation Systems." *Academy of Management Review*. 9(2):284–295.

Dekker, Sander, and Dan Hansen. 2004. "Learning under Pressure: The Effects of Politicization on Organizational Learning in Public Bureaucracies." *Journal of Public Administration Research and Theory* 14(2):211–230.

Deloria, Philip Joseph. 2004. *Indians in Unexpected Places*. Lawrence: University of Kansas Press.

Deloria, Vine, Jr. 1969. *Custer Died for Your Sins: An Indian Manifesto*. New York: The Macmillan Company.

Deloria, Vine, Jr. 1970. *We Talk, You Listen: New Tribes, New Turf*. New York: Macmillan.

Deloria, Vine, Jr., and Clifford M. Lytle. 1984. *The Nations Within: The Past and Future of American Indian Sovereignty*. Austin: University of Texas Press.

Deloria, Vine, Jr., and David E. Wilkins. 1999. *Tribes, Treaties, and Constitutional Tribulations*. Austin: University of Texas Press.

Drinnon, Richard. 1987. *Keeper of Concentration Camps: Dillon S. Myer and American Racism*. *Berkeley:* University of California Press.

Dudas, Jeffrey R. 2008. *The Cultivation of Resentment: Treaty Rights and the New Right*. Stanford, CA: Stanford University Press.

Dudziak, Mary L. 2000. *Cold War Civil Rights: Race and the Image of American Democracy*. Princeton, NJ: Princeton University Press.

Duerst-Lahti, Georgia. 1989. "The Government's Role in Building the Women's Movement." *Political Science Quarterly* 104(2):249–268.

Eight Northern Indian Pueblos Council. 2002. Accessed October 31. http://8northern.org.

Elkin, Stephen L. 1987. *City and Regime in the American Republic*. Chicago: University of Chicago Press.

Environmental Protection Agency. 1991a–1994. *Environmental Activities on Indian Reservations: FY 90*. Washington, D.C.: United States Environmental Protection Agency.

Environmental Protection Agency, Radon Division, Office of Radiation Programs. 1991b. *Guidance for the Indian Radon Pilot Projects*. Washington, D.C.: United States Environmental Protection Agency.

Esterling, Kevin M. 2004. *The Political Economy of Expertise: Information and Efficiency in American National Politics*. Ann Arbor: The University of Michigan Press.

Fahey, John. 2001. *Saving the Reservation: Joe Garry and the Battle to Be Indian*. Seattle: University of Washington Press.

Fiols, C. Marlene, and Marjorie A. Lyles. 1985. "Organizational Learning." *Academy of Management Review*: 10(4):803–813.

Fossett, James W. 1984. "The Politics of Dependence: Federal Aid to Big Cities." In *The Changing Politics of Federal Grants*; Lawrence D. Brown, James W. Fossett, Kenneth T. Palmer, pp. 108–163. Washington, D.C: Brookings Institution.

Fowler, Loretta. 1982. *Arapahoe Politics, 1851–1978: Symbols in Crises of Authority*. Lincoln: University of Nebraska Press.

Franzese, Robert J., Jr. 2002. *Macroeconomic Policies of Developed Democracies*. Cambridge: Cambridge University Press.

Ganz, Marshall. 2000. "Resources and Resourcefulness: Strategic Capacity in the Unionization of California Agriculture, 1959–1966." *American Journal of Sociology* 105(4):1003–1062.

Gaventa, John. 1980. *Power and Powerlessness: Quiescence and Rebellion in an Appalachian Valley*. Urbana: University of Illinois Press.

Giles, Cate. 2000. "Canyon Debate." *Navajo Times* (Window Rock, Arizona). October 5, A1.

Goldberg, Carole. 1999. "Public Law 280 and the Problem of 'Lawlessness' in California Indian Country." In *Contemporary Native American Political Issues*, ed. Troy R. Johnson, pp. 197-225. Walnut Creek, CA: AltaMira Press.

Goss, Kristin A. 2006. *Disarmed: The Missing Movement for Gun Control in America*. Princeton, NJ: Princeton University Press.

Gottschalk, Marie. 2006. *The Prison and the Gallows: The Politics of Mass Incarceration* in America. New York: Cambridge University Press.

Groark, Virginia. 2001. "First One Casino, Then Two. Now What?" *New York Times*. September 2, 14CN-1.

Hall, Peter A. 2009. "Historical Institutionalism in Rationalist and Sociological Perspective." In *Explaining Institutional Change: Ambiguity, Agency, and Power*, ed. James Mahoney and Kathleen Thelen, pp. 204–224. New York: Cambridge University Press.

Hall, Richard L. 1996. *Participation in Congress*. New Haven, CT: Yale University Press.

Hansen, Dan. 2002. "Tribes Take Bigger Role in Dam-Related Issues." *The Spokesman-Review* (Spokane, Washington). March 26, A1.

Harmon, Alexandra. 1998. *Indians in the Making: Ethnic Relations and Indian Identities around Puget Sound*. Berkeley: University of California Press.

Harring, Sidney L. 1994. *Crow Dog's Case: American Indian Sovereignty, Tribal Law, and United States Law in the Nineteenth Century*. Cambridge: Press Syndicate of the University of Cambridge.

Harrison, Cynthia Ellen. 1988. *On Account of Sex: The Politics of Women's Issues, 1945–1968*. Berkeley: University of California Press.

Harvard Project on American Indian Economic Development. 2007. *Honoring Nations: A Directory of Honored Programs*. September. http://www.ksg.harvard.edu/hpaied/documents/Dir_web.pdf.

Harvard Project on American Indian Economic Development. 2008. *The State of the Native Nations: Conditions under U.S. Policies of Self-Determination*. New York: Oxford University Press.

Haveman, Heather A. 1992. "Between a Rock and a Hard Place: Organizational Change and Performance under Conditions of Fundamental Environmental Transformation." *Administrative Science Quarterly*. 37(1):48–75.

Heclo, Hugh. 1974. *Modern Social Policies in Britain and Sweden: From Relief to Income Maintenance*. New Haven, CT: Yale University Press.

Henson, E. C., J. Taylor, S. Bean, K. Bishop, S. S. Black, K.W. Grant, M.R. Jorgensen, J. King, A. J. Lee, H. Nelson, and Y. Roubideaux. 2002. *Native American at the New Millennium*. American Indian Research and Grants Assessment Project, the Harvard Project on American Indian Economic Development.

Hirsch, Arnold R. 1983. *Making the Second Ghetto: Race and Housing in Chicago, 1940 to 1960*. Cambridge: Cambridge University Press.

Holm, Tom. 2005. *The Great Confusion in Indian Affairs: Native Americans and Whites in the Progressive Era*. Austin: University of Texas Press.

Horn, Sasheen Hollow. 2000. "Youth Voice Concerns at Behavior Summit." *The Navajo Times* (Window Rock, Arizona). June 15, A1.

Hosmer, Brian C. 1991. "Creating Indian Entrepreneurs: Menominees, Neopit Mills, and Timber Exploitation, 1890–1915." *American Indian Culture and Research Journal.* 15(1):15.

Hoxie, Frederick. 1992. "Crow Leadership Amidst Reservation Oppression." In *State and Reservation: New Perspectives on Federal Indian Policy,* ed. George Pierre Castile and Robert Bee, pp. 38–60 Tuscon: University of Arizona Press.

Hoxie, Frederick. 2001. *Talking Back to Civilization: Indian Voices from the Progressive Era.* Boston: Bedford/St. Martin's.

Hoxie, Frederick, and Tim Bernardis. 2001. "Robert Yellowtail." In *The New Warriors: Native American Leaders since 1900,* ed. R. David Edmunds, pp. 55–77. Lincoln: University of Nebraska Press.

Hyneman, Charles S. 1938. "Tenure and Turnover of Legislative Personnel." *Annals of the American Academy of Political and Social Science* 195:21–31.

Indian Health Service, U.S. Department of Health and Human Services. 2001. *Justification of Estimates for Appropriations Committees, Fiscal Year 2002.* Accessed July 30, 2003. http://www.ihs.gov/AdminMngrResources/Budget/FY_2002_Budget_Justification.asp93_URBAN_HEALTH.doc.

International Association of Chiefs of Police. 2001. *Improving Safety in Indian Country: Recommendations from the IACP 2001 Summit.* http://www.theiacp.org/documents/index.cfm?fuseaction=document&document_id=. Accessed October 30, 2004.

Jackson, Kenneth T. 1985. *Crabgrass Frontier: The Suburbanization of the United States.* New York: Oxford University Press.

Jay, John. 1982. "The Federalist Number 3." In *the Federalist Papers by Alexander Hamilton, James Madison, and John Jay,* ed. Garry Wills, pp. 10–13. New York: Bantam Books.

Jenkins, Craig J. 1983. "Resource Mobilization Theory and the Study of Social Movements." *Annual Review of Sociology* 9:527–553.

Jenkins, Craig J., and Craig M. Eckert. 1986. "Channeling Black Insurgency: Elite Patronage and Professional Social Movement Organizations in the Development of the Black Movement." *American Sociological Review* 51(6):812–829.

Jenkins, Craig J., and Charles Perrow. 1977. "Insurgency of the Powerless: Farm Worker Movements (1946–1972)." *American Sociological Review* 42(2):249–268.

Johnson, Susan, et al. 2002. *Government to Government: Models of Cooperation Between States and Tribes.* Denver: National Conference of State Legislatures. Washington, D.C.: National Congress of American Indians.

Jones, Bryan D. and Frank R. Baumgartner. 2005. *The Politics of Attention: How Government Prioritizes Problems.* Chicago: University of Chicago Press.

Jones, Bryan D., Tracy E. Sulkin, and Heather Larsen. 2003. "Policy Punctuations in American Political Institutions." *American Political Science Review* 97(1):151–169.

Katzenstein, Mary Fainsod. 1998. *Faithful and Fearless: Moving Feminist Protest Inside The Church and Military.* Princeton, NJ: Princeton University Press.

Keck, Thomas Moylan. 2004. *The Most Activist Supreme Court in History: The Road to Modern Judicial Conservatism.* Chicago: University of Chicago Press.

Key, V.O., Jr. 1949. *Southern Politics in State and Nation.* Knoxville: The University of Tennessee Press.

Kim, Daniel H. 1993. "The Link between Individual and Organizational Learning." *Sloan Management Review* 1993(Fall 1993):37–50.

Kingdon, John W. 1984. *Agendas, Alternatives, and Public Policies*. New York: Harper Collins Publishers.

Kretzmann, John P., and John L. McKnight. 1996. "Assets-Based Community Development." *National Civic Review* 85(4):23–29.

Lamb, Charles M. 2005. *Housing Segregation in Suburban American since 1960: Presidential and Judicial Politics*. New York: Cambridge University Press.

Lapre, Michael A., Amit Shankar Mukherjee, and Luk N. Van Wassenhove. 2000. "Behind the Learning Curve: Linking Learning Activities to Waste Reduction." *Management Science*: 46(5):597–611.

Lawrence, Regina G. 2000. *The Politics of Force: Media and the Construction of Police Brutality*. Berkeley: University of California Press.

Lewis, David E. 2007. "Testing Pendleton's Premise: Do Political Appointees Make Worse Bureaucrats?" *Journal of Politics* 69(4):1073–1088 (2007). Dataset available at http://people.vanderbilt.edu/~david.lewis/data.htm.

LexisNexis. 1990–2000. *LexisNexis State Capital Database*.

Lieberman, Robert. 1998. *Shifting the Color Line: Race and the American Welfare State*. Cambridge: Harvard University Press.

Lopach, James L., Margery Hunter Brown, and Richmond L. Clow. 1998. *Tribal Government Today: Politics on Montana Indian Reservations*. Niwot: University Press of Colorado.

McAdam, Doug. 1982. *Political Processes and the Development of the Black Insurgency, 1930–1970*. Chicago: University of Chicago Press.

McAdam, Doug. 1996. "Political Opportunities: Conceptual Origins, Current Problems, Future Directions." In *Comparative Perspectives on Social Movements: Political Opportunities, Mobilizing Structures, and Cultural* Framings, eds. Doug McAdam, John D. McCarthy, and Mayer N. Zald, pp. 23–40. Cambridge, UK: Cambridge University Press.

McCarthy, John D., and Mark Wolfson. 1996. "Resource Mobilization by Local Social Movement Organizations: Agency, Strategy, and Organization in the Movement Against Drinking and Driving." *American Sociological Review* 61(6):1070–1088.

McCarthy, John D., and Mayer N. Zald. 1977. "Resource Mobilization and Social Movements: A Partial Theory." *American Journal of Sociology* (82)6:1212–1241.

McClure, Robert. 2001. "Tribes Reignite Legal Battle over State's Fish Catch." *The Seattle Post-Intelligencer*. January 17, A1.

McConnell, Grant. 1966. *Private Power and American Democracy*. New York: Alfred A. Knopf.

McCool, Daniel. 1985. "Indian Voting." In *American Indian Policy in the Twentieth Century*, ed. Vine Deloria, Jr., pp. 105–134. Norman: University of Oklahoma Press.

McCool, Daniel, Susan M. Olson, and Jennifer L. Robinson. 2007. *Native Vote: American Indians, the Voting Rights Act, and the Right to Vote*. New York: Cambridge University Press.

Madison, James. 2000. "The Federalist Number 10 and Number 51." In *Government in America: People, Politics, and Policy*, ed. George C. Edwards III, Martin P. Wattenberg, and Robert L. Lineberry, pp. 730–735. New York: Longman.

Mahoney, James and Kathleen Thelen. 2009. "A Theory of Gradual Institutional Change." In *Explaining Institutional Change: Ambiguity, Agency, and Power*, ed. James Mahoney and Kathleen Thelen, pp. 1–37. New York: Cambridge University Press.

Manna, Paul. 2006. *School's In: Federalism and the National Education Agenda*. Washington, D.C.: Georgetown University Press.

March, James, and Johan Olsen. 1984. "The New Institutionalism: Organizational Factors in Political Life." *American Political Science Review* 78:734–749.

Mason, Sheryl and Bruce Mason. 1995. *The Directory of American Indian Casinos and Bingo Halls*. Lone Star, TX: The Lone Star Connection.

Mason, W. Dale. 2000. *Indian Gaming: Tribal Sovereignty and American Politics*. Norman: University of Oklahoma Press.

Melmer, David. 1997. "South Dakota Governor: Tourists Not Safe on State's Reservations." *Indian Country Today*. March 31, B4.

Miller, Bruce G. 1993. "The Press, the Boldt Decision, and Indian-White Relations." *American Indian Culture and Research Journal* 17(2): 75–97.

Miller, Lisa Lynn. 2008. *The Perils of Federalism: Race, Poverty, and the Politics of Crime Control*. New York: Oxford University Press.

Minow, Martha. 1990. "Putting Up and Putting Down: Tolerance Reconsidered." In *Comparative Constitutional Federalism: Europe and America*, ed. Mark Tushnet, pp. 77–113. New York: Greenwood Press.

Moe, Terry M. 1980. *The Organization of Interests: Incentives and the Internal Dynamics of Political Interest Groups*. Chicago: University of Chicago Press.

Montana Office of Indian Affairs. 2008. Accessed December 18. http://tribalnations.mt.gov/.

Morris, Aldon D. 1984. *The Origins of the Civil Rights Movement: Black Communities Organizing for Change*. New York: The Free Press.

Mukherjee, Amit Shankar; Michael A. Lapre; and Luk N. van Wossenhove. 1998. "Knowledge Driven Quality Improvement." *Management Science* 44(11):S35–S49.

Nagel, Joane. 1996. *American Indian Ethnic Renewal: Red Power and the Resurgence of Identity and Culture*. New York: Oxford University Press.

National Congress of American Indians. 2004. *Indian Organizations. Accessed October* 30. http://www.ncai.org/main/pages/tribal_directory/indian_org.asp.

National Indian Gaming Commission. 2006. *Gaming Revenues 2001–2006.* http://www.nigc. gov/Portals/0/NIGC%20Uploads/Tribal%20Data/gamingrevenues2006.pdf.

National Indian Gaming Commission. 2009. *Gaming Revenues 2005–2010.* http://www.nigc. gov/LinkClick.aspx?fileticket=1k4B6r6dr-U%3d&tabid=67.

National Indian Gaming Commission. 2010. *Gaming Tribe Report.* Accessed November 5. http://www.nigc.gov/LinkClick.aspx?fileticket=z_cmbWn3JQA%3d&tabid=68.

Navajo Nation, Office of Navajo Government Development. 1998. *Navajo Nation Government*. Window Rock: The Navajo Nation.

Navajo Times, (Window Rock, Arizona). 1999a. "Antelope Point Marina Gets Major Funding Boost." December 16, A1.

Navajo Times, (Window Rock, Arizona). 1999b. "New State Law Will Bring Dine College Millions." May 13, A6.

Navajo Times, (Window Rock, Arizona). 1999c. "Tribes, Towns Teaming Up With Office of Tourism." December 23, A1.

Nebraska Commission on Indian Affairs. http://www.indianaffairs.state.ne.us/. Accessed December 18, 2008.

Neidt, Christopher, and Margaret Weir. 2010. "Property Rights, Taxpayer Rights, and the Multiscalar Attack on and the State: Consequences for Regionalism in the United States." *Regional Studies* 44:2, 153–165.

New Mexico Indian Affairs Department. 2008. Accessed December 18. *http://www.iad.state. nm.us/index.html*.

North, Douglass C. 1990. *Institutions, Institutional Change, and Economic Performance*. Cambridge: Cambridge University Press.

North Dakota Indian Affairs Commission. 2008. http://www.nd.gov/indianaffairs. Accessed December 18.

Northwest Indian Fisheries Commission. 2008. Accessed December 19. http://www.nwifc.wa.gov.

Northwest Indian Fisheries Commission. 1990–2001. *Northwest Indian Fisheries Commission News*. Tumwater, WA: Washington State Library.

Northwest Portland Area Indian Health Board. 2002. *Tribal Profiles*. http://www.npaihb.org/profiles/tribal_profiles/interface.htm. Last modified July 23.

Office of Management and Budget, Executive Office of the President. 2010. *ExpectMore.gov*. http://www.whitehouse.gov/omb/expectmore/index.html. Accessed March 1.

O'Brien, Sharon. 1989. *American Indian Tribal Governments*. Norman: University of Oklahoma Press.

Ogunwole, Stella. 2002. *The American Indian and Alaska Native Population: 2000*. Census 2000 Brief. Washington, D.C.: U.S. Census Bureau.

Oregon Legislative Commission on Indian Services. 2008. Last accessed December 20. http://www.leg.state.or.us/cis/cisinfo.htm.

Paredes, J. Anthony. 1992. "Introduction." In *Indians of the Southeastern United States in the Late 20th Century*, ed. J. Anthony Paredes, pp. 1–7. Tuscaloosa: The University of Alabama Press.

Payne, Charles M. 1995. *I've Got the Light of Freedom: The Organizing Tradition and the Mississippi Freedom Struggle*. Berkeley: University of California Press.

Peregoy, Robert M. 1999. "Nebraska's Landmark Repatriation Law: A Study of Cross-Cultural Conflict and Resolution." In *Contemporary Native American Political Issues*, ed. Troy R. Johnson, pp. 229–274. Walnut Creek, CA: AltaMira Press.

Peterson, Dan. 1987. "A Study of the Relative Contribution of Selected Sociocultural and Personality Variables to the Explanation of Prejudice and Discrimination in South Dakota." PhD diss., Brookings: South Dakota State University.

Peterson, Paul E. 1981. *City Limits*. Chicago: University of Chicago Press.

Phelps, Glenn A. 1991. "Mr. Gerry Goes to Arizona: Electoral Geography and Voting Rights in Navajo County." *American Indian Research and Culture Journal* 15(2):63–92.

Philp, Kenneth. 1999. *Termination Revisited: American Indians on the Trail to Self-Determination, 1933–1953*. Lincoln: University of Nebraska Press.

Pierson, Paul. 2004. *Politics in Time: History, Institutions, and Social Analysis*. Princeton, NJ: Princeton University Press.

Piven, Frances Fox, and Richard A. Cloward. 1977. *Poor People's Movements: Why They Succeed, How They Fail*. New York: Pantheon Books.

Pleasant, Deb. 2009. "Syd Beane: 'You Learn Organizing By Doing Organizing.'" *Twin Cities Daily Planet*. 22 November. http://www.tcdailyplanet.net/news/2009/11/19/mn-voices-syd-beane-you-learn-organizing-doing-organizing.

Polsby, Nelson W. 1968. "The Institutionalization of the U.S. House of Representatives." *American Political Science Review* 62(1):144–168.

Pralle, Sarah Beth. 2006. *Branching Out, Digging In: Environmental Advocacy and Agenda Setting*. Washington, D.C.: Georgetown University Press.

Pratt, Richard H. 1892. "The Advantages of Mingling Indians with Whites." *Official Report of the Nineteenth Annual Conference of Charities and Correction*, pp. 46–59. Reprinted in *Americanizing the American Indians: Writings by the "Friends of the Indian," 1880–1900*. 1973, pp. 260–271. Francis Paul Prucha, editor. Cambridge: Harvard University Press.

Prucha, Francis Paul. 1984. *The Great Father: The United States Government and the American Indians*. 2 vols. Lincoln: University of Nebraska Press.

Rainey, Hal G. 1997. *Understanding and Managing Public Organizations*. Second Edition. San Francisco: Jossey-Bass Publishers.

Reina, Edward. 2002. "Indian Country Law Enforcement Section Seizes Opportunities to Improve Justice in Indian Country." *Police Chief*, special issue on Safety in Indian Country. LXIX(1):25–27.

Rosenblatt, Judith. 1985. *Indians in Minnesota*. Minneapolis: University of Minnesota Press.

Ruby, Robert H., and John A. Brown. 1992. *A Guide to the Indian Tribes of the Pacific Northwest*. Norman: University of Oklahoma Press.

Rusco, Elmer R. 1976. *A Fateful Time: The Background and Legislative History of the Indian Reorganization Act*. Reno: University of Nevada Press.

Sayer, John William. 1997. *Ghost Dancing the Law: The Wounded Knee Trials*. Cambridge, MA: Harvard University Press.

Schattschneider, E. E. 1960. *The Semisovereign People: A Realist's View of Democracy in America*. New York: Holt, Rinehart, and Winston.

Schein, Edgar H. 1987. *Process Consultation, Volume II: Lessons for Managers and Consultants*. Reading, MA: Addison-Wesley.

Schwab, Robert. 1997. "Tribes Offended by Remarks of S.D. Governor." *Denver Post*. March 22, B6.

Schulman, Bruce J. 1991. *From Cotton Belt to Sunbelt: Federal Policy, Economic Development and the Transformation of the South, 1938–1960*. New York: Oxford University Press.

Shebala, Marley. 1999. "House Speaker Urges State-Tribe to Work Together." *Navajo Times* (Window Rock, Arizona). July 29, A1.

Shebala, Marley. 2000. "Window Rock Road to See The Lights." *Navajo Times* (Window Rock, Arizona). March 30, A1.

Sheingate, Adam D. 2000. "Institutions and Interest Group Power: Agricultural Policy in the United States, France, and Japan." *Studies in American Political Development*. 14 (Fall 2000):184–211.

Sheingate, Adam D. 2003. "Political Entrepreneurship, Institutional Change, and American Political Development." *Studies in American Political Development*. 17 (Fall 2003): 185–203.

Skocpol, Theda. 1979. *States and Social Revolutions*. Cambridge: Cambridge University Press.

Skocpol, Theda. 1992. *Protecting Soldiers and Mothers: The Political Origins of Social Policy in the United States*. Cambridge, MA: Belknap Press of Harvard University Press.

Sonenshein, Raphael J. 2004. *The City at Stake: Secession, Reform, and the Battle for Los Angeles*. Princeton, NJ: Princeton University Press.

South Dakota Advisory Committee to the United States Commission on Human Rights. 2000. *Native Americans: An Erosion of Confidence in the Justice System*. March. http://www.usccr.gov/pubs/sac/sd0300/main.htm. Accessed December 1, 2007.

South Dakota Tribal Government Relations Office. 2008. Accessed December 18. http://www.state.sd.us/oia/index.asp.

Spokesman-Review, (Spokane, Washington). 2000. "Flexing Too Much Muscle?" December 25, A1.

Stinchcombe, Arthur L. 1990. *Information and Organizations*. Berkeley: University of California Press.

Stone, Clarence N. 1989. *Regime Politics: Governing Atlanta, 1946–1988*. Lawrence: University Press of Kansas.

Sturtevant, William C., general editor. 1978–2001. *Handbook of North American Indians, Volumes 4, 7–13*. Washington, DC: Smithsonian Institution.

Sugrue, Thomas. 1997. *The Origins of the Urban Crisis: Race and Inequality in Postwar Detroit.* Princeton, NJ: Princeton University Press.

Sweeney, James P. 2001. "Casino Cross Fire." *The San Diego Union-Tribune.* September 9, G1.

Tarrow, Sidney. 1994. *Power in Movement: Social Movements, Collective Action and Politics.* New York: Cambridge University Press.

Taylor, Theodore W. 1972. *The States and Their Indian Citizens.* Washington, DC: U.S. Department of the Interior, Bureau of Indian Affairs.

Thelen, Kathleen Ann. 2004. *How Institutions Evolve: The Political Economy of Skills in Germany, Britain, and the United States.* Cambridge: Cambridge University Press.

Tiller, Veronica E. Velarde. 1996. *American Indian Reservations and Indian Trust Areas.* Washington, DC: U.S. Department of Commerce, Economic Development Administration.

Tiller, Veronica E. Velarde. 2005. *Tiller's Guide to Indian Country.* Albuquerque, NM: BowArrow Publishing Company.

Tsebelis, George. 2002. *Veto Players: How Political Institutions Work.* New York: Russell Sage Foundation.

U.S. Census Bureau. 1992a. *1990 Summary Tape File 1 (STF 1) – 100-Percent Data.* http://factfinder.census.gov/servlet/DatasetMainPageServlet?_program=DEC&_tabId=DEC2&_submenuId=datasets_1&_lang=en&_ts=247767989870. Accessed December 18, 2008.

U.S. Census Bureau. 1996, 2000, 2001. *Statistical Abstract of the United States.* http://www.census.gov/prod/www/statistical-abstract-us.html.

United States Census Bureau. 2002. *Census 2000 Summary File 4.* http://factfinder.census.gov/servlet/DatasetMainPageServlet?_program=DEC&_lang=en&_ts=. Accessed December 18, 2008.

U.S. Census Bureau. 2008. *Local Governments and Public School Systems by Type and State: 2007.* http://www.census.gov/govs/cog/GovOrgTab03ss.html. Accessed December 18, 2008.

United States Commission on Civil Rights. 2003. *A Quiet Crisis: Federal Funding and Unmet Need in Indian Country.* Washington, DC: U.S. Commission on Civil Rights.

Valandra, Paul. 1992. *Consider the Century: Native American Perspectives on the Past 100 Years.* Videorecording. Volume 3.

Verba, Sidney, Kay Lehman Schlozman, and Henry E. Brady. 1995. *Voice and Equality: Civic Voluntarism in American Politics.* Cambridge, MA: Harvard University Press.

Vogelsang-Coombs, Vera. 1997. "Governance Education: Helping City Councils Learn." *Public Administration Review* 57(6):490–500.

Vogelsang-Coombs, Vera and Melissa Miller. 1999. "Developing the Governance Capacity of Local Elected Officials." *Public Administration Review* 59(3):199–217.

Walke, Roger. 2000. "Indian-Related Federal Spending Trends, FY 1975-FY 2001." In *Fiscal Year 2000 Budget, Hearing before the Committee on Indian Affairs, United States Senate,* pp. 281–333. Washington, D.C.: Government Printing Office.

Walker, Jack L. 1983. "The Origins and Maintenance of Interest Groups in America." *American Political Science Review* 77(2):390–406.

Walker, James R. 1982. *Lakota Society.* Raymond J. DeMallie, ed. Lincoln: University of Nebraska Press.

Warren, Mark R. 2001. *Dry Bones Rattling: Community Building to Revitalize American Democracy.* Princeton, NJ: Princeton University Press.

Walsh, James P. 1995. "Managerial and Organizational Cognition: Notes from a Trip Down Memory Lane." *Organization Science* 6(3):280–321.

Washington Governor's Office of Indian Affairs. 2008. Accessed December 18. http://www.goia.wa.gov.

Weir, Margaret, Ann Schola Orloff, and Theda Skocpol. 1988. "Introduction: Understanding American Social Politics," and "Epilogue: The Future of Social Policy in the United States: Political Constraints and Possibilities." In *The Politics of Social Policy in the United States*, ed. Margaret Weir, Ann Schola Orloff, and Theda Skocpol, pp. 3–27; pp. 421–445. Princeton, NJ: Princeton University Press.

Wilkins, David E. 1996. "Indian Treat Rights: Sacred Entitlements or 'Temporary Privileges?'" *American Indian Culture and Research Journal* 20(2):87–129.

Wilkins, David E. 1998. "Tribal-State Affairs: American States as 'Disclaiming' Sovereigns." *Publius* 28(4):55–81.

Wilkins, David E. 2002. *American Indian Politics and the American Political System*. Lanham, MD Rowman and Littlefield Publishers, Inc.

Wilkins, David E. 2009. *Documents of Native American Political Development: 1500s to 1933*. New York: Oxford University Press.

Wilkins, David E., and K. Tsianina Lomawaima. 2001. *Uneven Ground: American Indian Sovereignty and Federal Law*. Norman: University of Oklahoma Press.

Wilkinson, Charles, and The American Indian Resources Institute. 2004. *Indian Tribes as Sovereign Governments: A Sourcebook on Federal-Tribal History, Law and Policy*. Second Edition. Oakland, CA: American Indian Lawyer Training Program, Inc.

Wilkinson, Charles. 2005. *Blood Struggle: The Rise of Modern Indian Nations*. New York: W.W. Norton & Company.

Wissler, Clark. 1912. Societies and Ceremonial Associations in the Oglala Division of the Teton-Dakota. *Anthropological Papers* 11(1):1–99.

Williamson, Oliver E. 1981. "The Economics of Organization: The Transaction Costs Approach." *American Journal of Sociology* 87(3):548–577.

Wood, Robert. 1958. *Suburbia: Its People and Their Politics*. Boston: Houghton Mifflin.

Wray, Jacilee, ed. 2002. *Native Peoples of the Olympic Peninsula: Who We Are*. Norman: University of Oklahoma Press.

Zald, Mayer N. and John D. McCarthy. 1979. "Introduction" and "Epilogue: An Agenda for Research." In *The Dynamics of Social Movements: Resource Mobilization, Social Control, and Tactics*, eds. Mayer N. Zald and John D. McCarthy, pp. 1–5; pp. 238–245. Cambridge, MA: Winthrop Publishers.

Index

Administration for Native Americans (ANA), 38, 63
agriculture, 70–71, 89, 94, 118
Agriculture, United States Department of (USDA), 119
Alfred, Taiaiake, 20, 43
American Indian Movement (AIM), 36
American Indian Records Repository (AIRR), 52
anticipating. *See* expertise-centered behavior
Arapaho Indians, 30–31
Arizona. *See also* Navajo Nation
 data collection, 221 n. 5, 222 n. 10
 history, 30
 Indian relations, 172–175, 187, 199
 legislation, 168–171, 179–180, 182–183, 184, 186, 187–193, 196–197
 public safety, 214 n. 10
assimilation, 17–20

Baumgartner, Frank, 10, 13
Biolsi, Thomas

evolution of tribal governments, 20, 28–29, 43, 163, 213 n. 6
 tribal governments today, 126, 130
Bobo, Lawrence
 fishing controversies, 126, 130
 media coverage, 129, 212 n. 8, 213 n. 5
 racial attitudes, 21–22
Brown, Margery Hunter, 44, 126, 164, 213 n. 7, 218 n. 1
Bureau of Indian Affairs (BIA). *See also* Consolidated Tribal Government Program, Indian Child Welfare Act, Self Determination and Education Assistance Act, Self-Government Compacts
 aid to tribes with ranching programs, 68, 89
 aid to tribes with substance abuse programs, 78–80
 area offices' relations with tribes, 65–66, 70–71, 91–94
 budget, 37–39, 45–46, 86, 93, 216 n. 20
 general aid to Navajo Nation, 121
 general aid to Tribe F, 65–66, 110–111

Bureau of Indian Affairs (BIA) (*continued*)
  history, 28–32, 34–35
  multiagency coordination, 64, 72–74
  records 52
  relations with Congress 84, 90–91, 229 n. 33
  role on land issues 70, 91–92
  self determination grants, 34, 42, 58,
    60–63, 64, 103–108, 181, 191–197 201–210
Bureau of Land Management (BLM), 82,
    84, 91
Bureau of Reclamation, 88, 118–119
business. *See* economic development
buttressing political opportunities, 7–8, 55,
    78–93

Carlisle Indian Industrial School, 209–210
Carpenter, Daniel, 16, 35
casinos. *See* gaming
Castile, George Pierre, 33–36, 213 n. 2
Census, United States Bureau of
  2000 census, 4, 24–25, 138, 172, 221 n. 25
  1990 census, 25, 162, 172
  census of governments, 23
checkerboarding, 130–132, 135, 164, 171,
    175–178. *See also* land
  history of, 41
Cherokee Nation v. Georgia, 26
Cheyenne Indians, 29, 31
Cheyenne River Sioux, 31, 169, 209, 217
children. *See* youth
Clemens, Elisabeth, 12, 16, 44
Clinton, Bill, 70, 84–85
Clow, Richmond, 44, 126, 164, 213 n. 7,
    218 n. 1
Cohen, Felix, 25–28, 33, 126–127
Collier, John, 30–31, 35
Colorado, 119, 213
commissions on Indian affairs in states, 169,
    173
Congress, 209
  appropriations committees, 81, 87, 93,
  funding for tribal ranching programs, 68
  as general check on federal agencies 83
  interactions with Bureau of Indian
    Affairs, 81, 89–95
  legal powers over Indian affairs, 25–27,
    32, 126
  regulations around child abuse, 78
  support to Navajo Nation, 75–78, 93

Consolidated Tribal Government
    Program, 42, 45, 181
Constitution, United States, 26, 27, 126, 131
consultants, private, 32, 65, 102–103,
    109–112, 124
cooptation, 17–18, 98–99, 161
Cornell, Stephen
  American Indian political activism 28, 30,
    32, 213 n. 2, 213 n. 3
  design of tribal governments 20, 42–43,
    163
Corps of Engineers, United States Army, 94,
    119
creatures of the state. *See* Dillon's Rule
crime. *See* public safety
Crow Nation, 29–30

Dakota Territory, 31
Daschle, Tom, 94
Deer, Ada, 93
Defense, United States Department of, 69, 70
Deloria, Vine, Jr., 21, 27, 31–33, 209, 212 n. 8,
    213 n. 5
demonstration projects. *See* pilot programs
devolution. *See* federalism
diagnosing. *See* expertise-centered behavior
Dillon's Rule, 23, 213 n. 18

"easy" issues, 134, 144, 150–152, 155–166
economic development, 37–39, 42–46, 50–53,
    207. *See also* gaming
  and expertise-centered behavior, 99, 102,
    109, 116–117, 121
  and federal relations, 56, 60–61, 63, 65–66,
    80, 83, 84–85, 95–96
  and tribal-county relations, 127–128,
    134–161, 165
  and tribal-state relations, 169, 171, 198,
    201–205
Economic Development, Navajo Nation
    Division of (DED), 50, 116–118, 120–123
Education, Navajo Nation Department of, 59,
    75–78
education, 4, 33–34, 37–39, 105, 169, 222 n.9
elections, 175–178
  redistricting and, 161
  campaign contributions and, 181–185, 199
Endangered Species Act, 87
Energy, United States Department of, 119, 218

environment. *See* natural resources
Environmental Protection Agency,
    United States (EPA), 52, 57, 64, 72, 87,
    89, 90, 94
expansion of powers, 89–90, 97
    funding, 75–77
    multiagency interactions, 64, 72–74,
        90–91, 97
    records, 53
evolution of institutions. *See* institutional
    change
exhaustion, 126, 132–134, 137–138, 140–153,
    156–157, 169–172, 220 n. 20
expertise, 5–7, 10–13, 15–18, 21, 42–44,
    201–204, 206
    and federal relations, 54–55, 60–87, 96
    and tribal-county relations, 125–127,
        129–130, 132, 135, 150–151, 153, 158,
        171–172
    and tribal-state relations, 167–168, 181,
        194, 195, 199–200
expertise-centered behavior, 98–124, 130,
    166, 195

Federal Listening Conference, 85, 95, 215
federalism, 8–15, 21, 23, 33, 36, 126, 133, 203,
    205
Federalist Papers, 5
fishing and fisheries, 87–93, 130, 171. *See also*
    National Marine Fisheries Service,
    Northwest Indian Fisheries Commission.
Forest Service, United States, 81, 84
Frank, Billy, Jr., 87. *See also* Northwest
    Indian Fisheries Commission
frequency of interactions. See volume of
    interactions

gaming. *See also* Indian Gaming
    Regulatory Act
    and county relations, 131–132
    and economic development, 44, 46
    and expertise, 99–108
    and sovereignty, 206–208
    tribal-state relations over, 3, 126, 169,
        171–174, 181–185, 187, 188–199
Ganz, Marshall, 12, 217
General Allotment Act, 28, 41
Gila River Indian Community, 69
Gorton, Slade, 96

government institutionalization, 42–46,
    49–52, 213n.8
    and federal relations, 53, 56, 60, 65–66,
        81, 82
    and expertise-centered behavior, 99,
        102–103, 107–108, 112–116
    and tribal-county relations, 125–126,
        129–130, 139–161, 165
government-to-government relations, 206
    with federal government, 33, 84–86, 171
    with states, 174–178
Grand Ronde Agency, 31

Hale, Albert, 93
"hard" issues, 134, 140–143, 148–149,
    156–160
Harvard Project on American Indian
    Economic Development, 4, 41, 43, 45,
    163, 173
Head Start, 59, 76
health 66, 86, 170. *See also* substance abuse,
    Indian Health Services
Heclo, Hugh, 16
historic preservation, 169
Honoring Nations award, 45, 163
Hopi Tribe, 119
Housing and Urban Development,
    United States Department of (HUD), 38,
    63, 72, 81
Hoxie, Frederick, 29–30
hunting, 82, 162
Hyneman, Charles, 200

incremental change. *See* institutional change
Indian Child Welfare Act (ICWA), 34
Indian Gaming Regulatory Act (IGRA), 36
Indian Health Service, United States
    (IHS). *See also* health
    budget, 38–39
    service population 25
    services, 59, 71–73, 80, 86, 89–90, 94
Indian Reorganization Act (IRA), 30–31, 34
Indian Self-Determination and Education
    Assistance Act, 34
Indian-white conflict. *See also*
    checkerboarding, exhaustion
    history of, 28, 30, 37
    in county relations, 126, 134, 136–137, 139,
        140–154, 163–165, 202

Indian-white conflict (*continued*)
  in state relations, 167–168, 175–179,
    219 n. 5
  measurement, 130–134, 171, 220 n. 14
  racial attitudes, 21–22, 130–131, 218 n. 1
  Industrial Areas Foundation, 22
  initiating. *See* expertise-centered behavior
  institutional change, 6–16, 58–60, 88–90,
    93–96, 201–205, 223 n.9, 212 n. 9-n. 17. *See*
    also buttressing political opportunities,
    expertise, expertise-centered behavior,
    marginalization
  history of, 24–37, 53
  in tribal-county relations, 160, 165–166
institutional niches, 5–9, 18–20, 22, 35–36, 37,
  54–55, 74, 88, 93–96, 102, 109, 201–206.
  See also buttressing political opportunity,
  expertise, and institutional change.
Interior, United States Department
  of, 30–35, 38–39, 52, 95. *See also* Bureau
  of Indian Affairs, Bureau of Reclamation,
  National Park Service
International Association of Chiefs of
  Police, 52, 57, 70
Intertribal organizations, 81, 105, 109–111,
  159, 213 n. 7. *See also* International
  Association of Chiefs of Police, National
  Congress of American Indian, Northwest
  Indian Fisheries Commission,
  as indicator of government
    institutionalization, 45–46, 103
  records of, 47–49, 51
  role of, 40, 57

Jay, John, 27, 210
Johnson v. McIntosh, 26
Jones, Bryan, 10, 13
Justice, United States Department of, 57, 90,
  95, 119, 214 n. 10. *See also* Office of Tribal
  Justice

Kalt, Joseph, 20, 41, 43, 163
Katzenstein, Mary Fainsod, 18
Key, V.O., 171
Kootenai Tribe, 91

Lakota Indians, 28–29, 43, 170
  Pine Ridge reservation of, 28
  Rosebud Sioux tribe of, 28, 178

land
  allotment of, 28, 30–31, 41 (*See also*
    checkerboarding)
  acquisition of, 69–70
  claims on, 156–158, 162, 170
  Indian Land Consolidation Act, 91–92
  management of, 84
  removal from, 27
  zoning of, 156–157, 161
lawsuits. *See* legal context
Leech Lake Reservation, 89
legal context, 109–110, 173–177, 219 n. 7.
    See also sovereignty
  history of, 31–32
  in tribal-county relations, 127, 132–135,
    140–141, 143, 149–153, 157–165
Lewis, David, 35, 213 n. 4
LexisNexis, 168, 173, 219 n. 7
Lone Wolf v. Hitchcock, 27
Lopach, James, 44, 126, 164, 213 n. 7, 218 n. 1
"losers" in politics, theories of, 9–14, 203
Lower Elwha Klallam Tribe, 88, 214 n9,
  2116 n21
lump-sum assistance, 7, 55, 58–74
Lytle, Clifford, 31, 33

McCarthy, John 17, 212 n. 15, 212 n. 17
McCool, Daniel, 127, 133, 173, 181, 182
Makah Tribe, 72, 214 n. 9, 216 n. 21
marginalization, theories of, 4–6, 9–14,
  16–22, 44, 126, 165–166, 202, 203, 206,
  211 n. 6, 212 n. 9, 212 n. 10, 212 n. 12,
  212 n. 16
Marshall, John, 26
Muckleshoot Indian Tribe, 69, 213 n. 9,
  216 n. 21
Menominee, 30
Montana
  Bureau of Indian Affairs officials in, 72
  data collection 179, 221 n. 25, 221 n.1,
    221 n . 5, 222 n. 7
  Indian relations 165, 172–174, 176, 178
  state legislation 168, 170, 172, 180, 186
  tribal-county relations, 163–165

National Congress of American Indians
  (NCAI)
  federal relations, 69–70, 84–86, 216 n. 19
  history, 32

records on, 49, 57
state relations, 126
National Marine Fisheries Service, 87
National Park Service, 88, 121, 214 n. 10
natural resources, 4, 39, 42–49, 69, 72, 80,
    220 n.21, 221 n. 23, 222 n. 9. *See also*
    Environmental Protection Agency,
    fishing and fisheries, Forest Service,
    hunting, National Park Service
  and expertise-centered behavior, 105,
    111–112
  and tribal-county relations, 126–127, 131,
    138, 147, 149, 158–159
  and tribal-state relations, 169, 185,
Natural Resources, Navajo Nation Division
    of, 50, 116–119, 121–123
Navajo Nation, 3. *See also* Economic
    Development, Navajo Nation Division
    of; Education, Navajo Nation
    Department of; Hale, Albert; Natural
    Resources, Navajo Nation Division of;
    Public Safety, Navajo Nation Division of;
    Zah, Peterson
  and expertise, 102
  and military base closures, 69–70
  budgets, 117
  county relations, 159, 160, 162
  features of, 49
  federal relations, 78–79, 93, 217 n. 33
  history of, 33
Nebraska
  data collection in, 179, 221 n. 5, 221 n. 6,
    222 n. 10
  Indian relations, 172–174, 177–179
  public safety 214 n. 10
  state legislation, 168–169, 180, 182–183,
    184, 186, 188–189, 191, 192–195
negative externalities, 22, 134, 144–149,
    220 n. 21
New Mexico. *See also* Navajo Nation
  data collection in, 168, 221 n. 2, 221 n. 5
  history, 31
  Indian relations in, 119, 172–175
  public safety, 214 n. 10
  state legislation, 170, 177–180, 182–184,
    186, 188–189, 192–197, 199
newspapers, tribal
  archives, 48, 213 n. 5
  format, 49, 112–113

use in data analysis, 50–53, 56–57, 63,
    81, 109
newspapers, non-Indian, 128–129, 131
Nixon, Richard, 33–34
Northwest, Pacific, 37, 41, 44, 53, 56, 67, 81,
    95–97, 213 n. 6–n. 7. *See also* Northwest
    Indian Fisheries Commission, Oregon,
    Tribe D, Tribe E, Tribe F, Tribe G,
    Washington
  tribal-county relations in, 130–132,
    134–137, 139, 140–158, 166, 219 n. 8,
    219 n. 11, 220 n. 13–n. 22
  tribal-state relations in, 168, 171
Northwest Indian Fisheries Commission, 41,
    51, 57, 86–88, 90
North Dakota
  history, 31
  Indian relations, 172–174, 176
  state legislation, 168–169, 178–180, 182–186,
    188–189, 191, 192–193, 196–197, 199
number of interactions. *See* volume of
    interactions

Office of Congressional and Legislative
    Affairs (OCLA), Bureau of Indian
    Affairs, 90–91
Office of Management and Budget (OMB)/
    Bureau of Budget, 33, 86, 213
Office of Tribal Justice, United States
    Department of Justice, 90
Oklahoma, 31, 213, 214
Olson, Susan, 127, 133, 173, 175–176
Omnibus Antiquated Laws Act, 91
Oregon
  data collection, 221 n. 5, 222 n. 7
  history, 31
  Indian relations, 172–174, 177
  state legislation, 168–171, 179–180,
    182–184, 186, 188–189, 192–193, 196–197
  tribe-county relations, 135
organizational learning, theories of, 98–101,
    108–109. *See also* expertise

Pacific Northwest. *See* Northwest, Pacific
partnering. *See* expertise-centered behavior
Philp, Kenneth, 32–33
pilot programs, 6, 55, 59, 67–68, 89
physical infrastructure, 19, 58, 61–62, 64,
    66–69, 77, 79

Pierson, Paul, 8, 10, 14

police. *See* public safety

Polsby, Nelson, 43

Pratt, Richard C., 209

Prucha, Francis Paul, 31, 33–35, 213 n. 2

Public Law 280, 33

public safety, 53, 116–120, 123, 170. *See also* International Association of Chiefs of Police, substance abuse.

  analysis of, 147, 149, 157

  building inspections and, 160, 168, 170

  cooperation regarding, 161

  expertise and, 103–108

  fire hydrants and, 61

  and Indian-white conflict, 131

  jurisdiction over, 126

  juvenile crime prevention, 159

  training for, 66

  tribal-county interactions about, 138, 146–149, 156–157

Public Safety, Navajo Nation Division of (DPS), 50, 116–123

Pueblo Indians, 31, 40

racial conflict. *See* Indian-white conflict

research design

  anonymous cases, 46–48

  case selection, 42–44, 56–57, 101–102, 132–135, 218 n 6

  case studies, methods of, 101–102

  coding of expertise-centered behavior, 103–104, 217 n.1–n 2

  coding of institutional niches, 58, 60

  coding on tribes' relations with counties, 135–137, 141, 153, 221 n 21

  coding on tribes' relations with states, 168–171, 181–184, 186–187, 221 n 5, 222 n 7

  dates selected, 42, 109, 182, 218 n 7 n 8

  regions selected, 37–38

  sources of data, 49–54, 56, 111–112, 117, 127–130, 180–184, 186, 191, 221 n 24, 231 n 10

  statistical methods used in,

Robinson, Jennifer, 127, 133, 173, 175, 176

Roosevelt, Franklin, 30–31

San Carlos Apache Tribe, 69

San Manuel Band of Mission Indians, 69

Self Determination Program. *See* Bureau of Indian Affairs

Self Government Compacts, 42, 181, 185–187, 191–195

Shoshone Wind River Tribe, 69

Sisseton Agency, 31

social movements, theories of, 11–12, 16–18, 224 n. 11, 224 n. 15–17, 217 n 2

Soil Conservation Service, United States Department of Agriculture, 119

South Dakota. *See also* Tom Daschle

  Bureau of Indian Affairs in, 75

  data collection in, 221 n 5, 222 n 9

  history, 31

  Indian relations, 172–174, 176–177, 219 n 5

  state legislation, 163–166, 178–180, 184–190, 192–194, 196–198, 199

Southwest, 37–38, 40, 99. *See also* Arizona, Colorado, International Association of Chiefs of Police, Navajo Nation, New Mexico, Tribe A, Tribe B, Tribe C, Utah

  tribal-county relations in, 129–130, 133–138, 141–152, 169, 219 n 5, 220 n 13

Southwest Tribal Leaders, 78, 79, 215 n 5

sovereignty, 20–23, 25–27, 31–32, 35–38, 207–208, 211. *See also* checkerboarding, government-to-government relations, legal context

  and tribal-county relations, 125, 131, 132

  and tribal-state relations, 171–172, 175

Spokane Tribe, 72

substance abuse, 62, 78–80

  driving while intoxicated (DWI), 103–105, 165, 219 n 5

success in interactions

  between tribes and counties, 3–4, 129–137, 145–155, 158–165

  between tribes and states, 3–4, 167–169, 179–188

Supreme Court, United States. See Constitution, United States; Marshall, John

Suquamish Tribe, 89, 213 n 9, 216 n 21

Stinchcombe, Arthur, 16, 43, 211 n 5

technical assistance, 6, 16, 19, 34, 54, 55, 58, 59, 62, 78, 80, 87, 96, 103, 105, 109, 118, 121, 163, 208

termination, 31–33

Thelen, Kathleen, 9, 11
training. *See* technical assistance
transportation, 170
Tribal Priority Allocation, 181
Tribe A, 46
    federal grants to, 50, 56, 60–63, 102–108,
        214
Tribe B, 46
Tribe C, 46
    federal grants to, 50, 56, 60–63, 102–108,
        214
Tribe D, 46
Tribe E, 46, 50, 56, 63–65, 82
Tribe F, 46
    expertise in, 102, 108–119
    federal relations, 62, 65–66, 83–84
    records of, 50, 56, 214 n 4
Tribe G, 46
    federal relations, 62, 65–66, 81–82
    records of 50, 56, 214 n 4
Tribe H, 46
    federal relations, 66–69, 76, 77
    records of 50, 56, 214 n 5
Tribe J, 46
    federal relations, 66–69, 76, 78
    records of 50, 56, 214 n 5
Tribe K, 46
Tribe L, 46
Truman, Harry, 33
Tuan, Mia
    on fishing controversies, 126, 130
    on media coverage, 129, 212 n 9, 213 n 5
    on racial attitudes, 21–22

Umatilla Reservation, Confederate Tribes of
    the, 77
Union Agency, 31
Upper Plains, 37–38, 42, 49, 221 n 1. *See also*
    Montana, Nebraska, North Dakota,
    South Dakota, Tribe H, Tribe J, Tribe K,
    Tribe L
    history of, 29, 164–165, 213 n 6
    Indian-white conflict, 130–131, 163–165
    tribal-county relations in, 134–137,
        139, 140–160, 166, 220 n 20,
        221 n 222 n 11
    tribal-federal relations in, 90

Utah, 47
    law enforcement in, 213–214 n 10
    reservation land in, 213 n 1

venues, 9, 13, 133, 136, 153–154, 199–200,
    212 n 9, 219 n 9, 220 n 17
volume of interactions
    between tribes and counties, 132–147,
        153–154, 157–158
    between tribes and states, 180–187,
        199–200
Voting Rights Act, 133

Walke, Roger, 36, 39, 116–117, 218 n 7
Walker, Jack, 17
War on Poverty, 33
Washington, state of. *See also* Slade Gorton
    data collection on, 179, 221 n 5
    Indian relations in, 172–174, 177–178
    state legislation 168, 170, 182, 184,
        187–190, 193, 194–197, 199–200
    tribal-county relations in, 135
waste management, 72–74, 169–170
    and landfills, 64–65, 163
    and water, 168
Wilkins, David
    federal Indian policy today, 36
    history of tribal governments, 27, 31, 41,
        213 n 6
    structure of tribal governments, 21, 126, 173
Wisconsin, 30
    law enforcement in, 213–214 n 10
    reservation land in, 213 n 1
Worcester v. Georgia, 26
Wyoming, 30, 40, 213 n 5

Yakama Indian Nation, 90
youth. *See also* Indian Child Welfare Act
    child support and, 170
    crime prevention and, 159, 161
    reporting abuse of, 77–78
    substance abuse programs and, 79–80
Yuma, 30

Zah, Peterson, 49, 50, 56, 59
Zald, Mayer, 17
zoning. *See* land